Praise for *Disciples of White Jesus*

"Readers should not be fooled by Angela Denker's storytelling ease and graceful prose into thinking this is simply another anodyne book about child-rearing. Her arguments about the sources and the persistence of racism, misogyny, and what she calls 'brutish masculinity' are powerful and, sadly, all too relevant. More important, she offers a way out—the examples of godly men who are working to subvert this toxic culture. In the author's words, 'Only the stories can save us.'"

—**Randall Balmer**, author of *Saving Faith: How American Christianity Can Reclaim Its Prophetic Voice*

"Angela Denker's deft storytelling critically examines the crisis of masculinity that white Christian boys and young men face today. With journalistic skill and heartfelt love for the church, she highlights the problem and offers a powerful, Jesus-centered way forward."

—**Pastor Caleb E. Campbell**, author of *Disarming Leviathan: Loving Your Christian Nationalist Neighbor*

"This is a beautiful book, haunting and hopeful. As Angela Denker takes us on a journey across the nation, she helps us learn more about our society, our churches, and our young men. It's a gift that we get to tag along. This is a book I needed as a Christian, a man, and the father of an adolescent boy."

—**Brian Kaylor**, president of Word&Way and coauthor of *Baptizing America*

"Angela Denker's *Disciples of White Jesus* is a much-needed interjection into one of the most vexing and troubling components of modern America—white Christian masculinity. Denker has a journalist's touch, a theologian's eyes, and a pastor's heart. She brings us into the sites, the currents, and the media where young white Christian men are taught to be masculine and analyzes them with unflinching honesty and truth-telling. Denker's analysis of masculinity leads to examinations of race, love, and other touchstones of modern identity. The result is a book that will be a salvo for many parents, pastors, and anyone else worried about the fate of young Christian men in America—and the people around them. This book explains the mechanisms of toxic

American masculinity and provides hope for developing a different model. I can't recommend it enough."
—**Bradley Onishi**, author of *Preparing for War: The Extremist History of White Christian Nationalism—and What Comes Next* and cohost of the *Straight White American Jesus* podcast

"In this profoundly humane and personal book, Angela Denker recognizes that the 'crisis of masculinity' is not worse for white Christian boys, but *is* different. Our nation's history of patriarchy, white supremacy, and Christian nationalism makes it so. And those differences are producing a dangerous cocktail of internalized victimization, anger, and violence. With powerful stories of radicalization and redemption, Denker not only diagnoses the problem; with a pastor's heart, she shows us the way out."
—**Samuel L. Perry**, coauthor of *The Flag and the Cross* and *Taking America Back for God*

"As an expert on influencers and the mom of a boy, I know how desperately we all need this book. Angela Denker lays out clearly the insidious dangers facing white boys and young men in America, but she didn't leave me in despair. Instead, *Disciples of White Jesus* gave me hope of a better future for us all, for white boys and men, and for those of us who love them."
—**Jo Piazza**, bestselling author and host of the *Under the Influence* podcast

"In a moment of chaos and ever-present danger, Angela Denker has emerged as a vital and necessary voice. Her explorations into religious extremism and the mounting heresies of authoritarianism are invaluable. With *Disciples of White Jesus*, we see another volume in that work, but also something new and even more impressive and pressing. For anyone wanting to understand what we are facing, and what we must ultimately face, I cannot recommend Denker or this masterpiece any more highly."
—**Jared Yates Sexton**, author of *The Man They Wanted Me to Be* and *American Rule*

"This frank, bold book unflinchingly examines ways white boys and men are becoming radicalized within some forms of American Christian faith. Denker shows how Christian nationalist theology warps sons into celebrating dominance and grows them into men who revel in violence that lashes out widely—and often destroys the boys themselves in the process. This tale is told in the compassionate voice of a mother and pastor, who wraps it all in the piercing reporting of a veteran journalist. This book dissects the mythology of 'White Jesus,' revealing its falsehoods, but also showing how some men have tried to recover, reclaim their faith, and walk in ways far more aligned with a figure known for radical love, not the pale-skinned and bellicose strongman evoked by swearing pastors and used to justify atrocities."
—**Sarah Stankorb**, author of *Disobedient Women*

"Angela Denker has seized the bull by the horns with *Disciples of White Jesus*, a searing and personal look into the thorny entanglement of race, religion, and politics in America. Read this book if you want to be challenged to think differently—indeed, *Christianly*!—about white masculinity."
—**Matthew D. Taylor**, author of *The Violent Take It by Force: The Christian Movement That Is Threatening Our Democracy*

"This is a book about identity—its loss, its malformation, and the struggle to forge new ones. With the tenderness of a mother and the insight of a scholar, Denker pulls us off the path of easy outrage and leads us to look more closely at the inner lives of white boys and men. For those of us who seek a healthier church, community, and nation, *Disciples of White Jesus* is timely and essential reading."
—**Jemar Tisby**, PhD, *New York Times* bestselling author of *The Color of Compromise* and The Spirit of Justice; professor of history at Simmons College of Kentucky

DISCIPLES OF WHITE JESUS

ANGELA DENKER

DISCIPLES OF WHITE JESUS

THE RADICALIZATION OF

American Boyhood

Broadleaf Books
Minneapolis

DISCIPLES OF WHITE JESUS
The Radicalization of American Boyhood

Copyright © 2025 Angela Denker. Published by Broadleaf Books. All rights reserved. Except for brief quotations in critical articles or reviews, no part of this book may be reproduced in any manner without prior written permission from the publisher. Email copyright@broadleafbooks.com or write to Permissions, Broadleaf Books, PO Box 1209, Minneapolis, MN 55440-1209.

29 28 27 26 25 24   1 2 3 4 5 6 7 8 9

Library of Congress Cataloging-in-Publication Data

Names: Denker, Angela, author.
Title: Disciples of white Jesus : the radicalization of American boyhood / Angela Denker.
Description: Minneapolis : Broadleaf Books, [2025] | Includes bibliographical references.
Identifiers: LCCN 2024020356 (print) | LCCN 2024020357 (ebook) | ISBN 9798889830757 (print) | ISBN 9798889830764 (ebook)
Subjects: LCSH: Conservatism--Religious aspects--Christianity. | Right and left (Political science)--United States. | Violence--Religious aspects--Christianity. | Boys--United States. | White people--Race identity--United States.
Classification: LCC BR526 .D464 2025 (print) | LCC BR526 (ebook) | DDC 303.6088/2773--dc23/eng/20240805
LC record available at https://lccn.loc.gov/2024020356
LC ebook record available at https://lccn.loc.gov/2024020357

Cover image: © 2024 Shutterstock; Residential two story wood sided home/3379066 by Anne Kitzman; © 2024 Shutterstock; Boy silhouette/2324270243 by Osvaldo Chavez
Cover design: Faceout Studio

Print ISBN: 979-8-8898-3075-7
eBook ISBN: 979-8-8898-3076-4

Printed in India

To Jacob and Joshua

My love for you is deeper than the deepest well.
When I grew worried or afraid or frustrated
in telling these stories of boys and men, I drew
water from my well of love for you, and my
words became truer and more meaningful.

Contents

Introduction ... ix

1. The Violence of White Christian Masculinity ... 1
2. White Christian Men
   Archetype and Reality ... 29
3. Created in ~~His~~ God's Image? ... 43
4. WWJB
   Who Would Jesus Be? ... 57
5. Oppressors and Victims ... 79
6. Schoolboys ... 101
7. To Fear and Love God So That?
   Confirming White Boys in the Faith ... 121
8. Innocuous White Supremacists and Midwestern Small Towns ... 147
9. Wild West, Wild Men, and De-radicalization ... 163

   Conclusion ... 195

Acknowledgments ... 201
Notes ... 205

Introduction

Researchers, authors, journalists, parents, teachers, faith leaders, scientists, doctors—so many are writing right now and trying to understand what's going on with boys and men. Even while American women continue to face an onslaught of government control and loss of bodily autonomy when it comes to reproductive health care, and Christian groups continue to target the rights of LGBTQ Americans, it's clear that we all, on all spectrums of the political divide, feel that something unsavory is happening among men and boys in America. For our purposes, I'm focusing this study in particular on *white Christian* men and boys. This is for a couple of reasons, one of which is professional: leadership positions in American government and industry are still overwhelmingly occupied by white Christian men, and also my education and expertise in writing about right-wing Christianity and politics mean I'm well placed to research and examine this particular population. The second reason is more personal. The majority of my immediate family is made up of white Christian men and boys. I'm an older sister to a white Christian brother. My dad is a white Christian man. I serve in a Christian denomination that is the whitest in America, in a pastorate still made up of a majority of white men. And I happened to start my journalism career as a pro hockey beat writer, which is as good an introduction as any to the world of white masculinity, though with a Canadian flair.

Of course, I couldn't write about boyhood without thinking about my own sons. While I wrote about and researched boys and young men, I was living through that golden moment in time with my sons, while they were looking and acting more like young men, on the cusp of becoming teenagers. But when they looked deep into my eyes and smiled those wide, grateful grins, I could still see them as toddlers, wide-eyed, outstretched arms, taking those first wobbly steps, knowing that I would catch them when they fell, all sharp elbows and knees.

The dream of motherhood, or parenthood, or the dream of anyone who loves and cares for young kids, is that you'll always be there—right? To catch them, when they fall. You soon learn that you won't be, like the time last summer when my youngest son came home crying in the neighbor's bike carrier, with a swollen and throbbing ankle. Or when my oldest son got elbowed in the cheek during a basketball game, just below the eye, and immediately it swelled out a few inches, and they rushed around frantically to find ice at the concession stand while I stood there next to him, helplessly. He held back his tears, but the eye was black and blue and greenish for weeks.

I remember sitting around a brown, wooden table in a nondescript hotel lobby in Iowa with a bunch of fellow moms from my son's basketball team. I had watched their sons play basketball with skill well beyond their years, had watched them be tough and dedicated and launch into the air, their elbows aloft with perfect form on yet another three-pointer. Many of these parents were athletes themselves, sculpted and fit, and some had played professionally. These were the boys for whom it seemed the world was at their fingertips. But as we moms talked, I noticed that what we all had in common was the terrible sense of fragility wrapped up in our young boys' futures, and the gentleness and kindness and vulnerability that lived just beneath the surface of their vaunted athletic prowess.

We talked about night-lights, and nighttime meditations, and reading books or watching family TV shows together, strategies we'd all employed around that time to help our tween boys calm down when they were feeling anxious or restless, unable to fall asleep at night. We talked about our hopes and our fears for our lovable and sensitive boys. I sensed that all of us—alike—wanted most for our boys to love and to be loved. We wanted them to be strong but kind. To somehow wear a suit of armor but also easily take it off. I noticed, too, that we were all grasping for any kind of guide, as parents and caregivers who loved these kids, to help them make it through somewhat unscathed. The process of becoming men was no longer a clear and straightforward one, if it ever really was. We didn't want to break them of their sensitivity and vulnerability, even if the world still sometimes did. I had this feeling, as

I watched my boys grow up, like I did when I first went to the lake and saw the minnows swimming around my pale legs in the murky water. It seemed like it would be so easy to cup my hands and grab one of them, hold it aloft in the shimmering sunlight close to my chest. But every time I tried, the water and the tiny fish just slipped right through, out of my hands, and I couldn't hold on.

Boys will not be little boys forever. This desire to hold them close, to keep them safe and kind and vulnerable and sensitive is ultimately as futile as the hope of grabbing minnows out of slimy lake water with bare, tiny, unskilled hands. I understand the desire, though: oh, how I understand the desire. At its root is not only love but also fear and recognition. I would be lying if I said that in my research and personal experiences I did not see within the American boys I know and love at the same time a terrible capacity for hatred, fear, and violence. Mass shooters and neo-Nazis and white supremacists have mothers and fathers and teachers and coaches too. Many of them ran around on the soccer field as little boys, coming together en masse at halftime to snack on cut-up juicy oranges and pour red Gatorade down their throats, eyes dancing and mouths chattering, in the golden years of American boyhood.

I think of the Church, of little boys with high voices wearing white choir robes and singing, "Away in a Manger." I think of my own boys holding shepherds' crooks, wearing ancient green and maroon costumes, at the Christmas pageant; I see holy water pouring over their heads in baptism like a fountain, and I imagine them in just a few years as teenagers, professing their faith in front of the church. If only all these things were solid inoculations against that terrible threat of hatred, violence, and despair—directed both outward and inward for so many American boys and men.

I think, too, of Jesus. Of how when I told people I was writing about boys and men and religion and radicalization, invariably, from New York City to the rural Midwest to Phoenix to South Carolina, they'd look at me with a little twinkle in their eye, and they'd ask: "Are you going to talk about White Jesus?"

As an ordained pastor with a master's degree in divinity from a Christian seminary, talking about Jesus is kind of one of my specialties. But these folks weren't asking me for a sermon, or for an explanation of a Bible verse, or even for a prayer. They wanted me to distinguish between the theological and the historical, brown-skinned, Middle Eastern, and Jewish Jesus, and the Jesus who is a creation of white American Christianity, a progenitor of the Christian industrial complex that brought us megachurches and celebrity preachers and *New York Times* bestsellers and the prosperity gospel and Donald Trump. White Jesus is to Jesus Christ as Instagram momfluencers and babies are to actual mothers and children. One is a brand meant to sell and control and influence and manipulate and create division and hierarchy. The other is complicated, humble, incarnate, vulnerable, persecuted, redeemed.

There is a movement afoot in America that says in order to protect and "save" young boys and men, they must become disciples of the movement of White Jesus. Unlike Jesus Christ, White Jesus is on a violent quest for naked power and influence and wealth. White Jesus deals in absolutes, and those who are among the "chosen" are absolutely convinced of their own sanctification and worthiness, and the damnation of all those who disagree. White Jesus is boorish and controlling, positioning himself at the head of the family and the government, at the top of the hierarchy, ignoring the truth that the Trinity of God taught by Orthodox Christianity is necessarily reciprocal and relational, requiring three coequal parts of God, traditionally known as Father, Son, and Holy Spirit.

You can make the argument that much of what is wrong in America and in the world has come at the hands of wealthy and powerful white men. You can start to see them as the walking dead, marching forward incessantly to trample upon the rights and freedom of the vulnerable, especially women, people of color, and poor people. But I don't know—that straightforward future story of zombified, irredeemable, angry, violent white men and boys doesn't quite work for me. There has to be another possible future on the horizon for white men and boys. I see my baby boys in my arms. I see mothers and fathers, grandparents, coaches and teachers, and instructors and religious leaders—so many of us striving to hold on to the idea that, at root, boys and men can and will love and be loved. Like baby Jesus.

White Jesus comes upon boys and men in their living rooms, on their iPads, and in blaring font and catchy music, he says: "Follow me." He leads them toward empty self-aggrandizement, toward anger and violence and grievance. But that was never really where they wanted to go, or who they wanted to be; it led only to destruction: their own and of those around them. So much tragedy and death and despair. There has to be another way. That's the warning and the hope at the heart of this book, and as you can see, it lies deep in my own mother soul.

CHAPTER 1

The Violence of White Christian Masculinity

For a white mom like me, traveling to Charleston, South Carolina, was usually about forgetting, about getting away from it all and enjoying a few kid-free days of sunny bliss. This Southern coastal paradise, on a seventy-degree November afternoon when the Spanish moss hung heavy in the palmetto trees next to an ornate black iron gate surrounding the courtyard of a college made for Southern belles, was the perfect destination for a moms weekend away. We could wear pink pastel dresses—maybe even Lilly Pulitzer—and sip mojitos with perfectly mottled mint leaves on the top of a hotel balcony overlooking the posh shops of King Street and the Baroque-era mansions South of Broad.

A few bites of cracker smeared with pimento cheese dip, a couple of day drinks in, you could forget about the kids and the husbands back home, about the credit card bills and missing assignments and marriages stagnating in the face of after-school activities and shallow, desperate upward mobility. You could forget about the worry that your womb was the topic of political discourse and control, forget about the chance that your life might hang in the balance of a doomed pregnancy. You could forget about all the ways institutions and government and religion had let you and your family down, forget about your worry that the ADHD medication wasn't working, that your kids seemed to have inherited your anxiety, that you couldn't afford therapy anymore plus Botox, and you wanted to say you were happy with everything as it was, but how could you be, really?

Charleston offered an opportunity for white moms like me to forget. Drink, shop, walk, forget. Forget we did. Forget I had, many times before, elsewhere but also here, years ago, taking the tourist boat to Fort Sumter without thinking about the enslaved people of Charleston desperate for freedom, about free Black people forbidden from associating with enslaved Black people for fear they'd teach them to read and write and inspire them to freedom. Forget that this stately city had been home to hatred and death and the monied privilege that makes such violence invisible, hidden behind ivy-covered fences and tall, crisply painted doors with heavy locks and security cameras.

It would have been easy to come here and forget. Instead, maybe for the sake of my own little boys, I had come to Charleston to try and remember.

That beautiful, balmy weekend in Charleston, homecoming weekend at the Citadel (and more on that later), I found myself at St. Matthew's Lutheran Church on Saturday morning, on world-famous King Street, known for partying and shopping and hordes of blonde white women like me wearing pastels and sipping fruity cocktails in the afternoon sun.

The Reverend Dr. Eric Childers, pastor here since 2016, walked me into the ornately preserved sanctuary, all white walls and swooping Gothic arches and gleaming mahogany pews. He told me this building was finished in 1872, designed by architect John Henry Devereux, who was also the architect of Mother Emanuel AME Church, just a few blocks away.

I was learning that in Charleston, like in all of human history, our stories overlap and intertwine in ways we might later rather deny. Childers, who has a degree in higher education from the University of Virginia in addition to his ordination as a pastor in the Evangelical Lutheran Church in America, imagined he'd spend his career in academia. Instead, he found himself called to this venerable and historic congregation, one with a proud history here on King Street. For generations, St. Matthew's has been known as an affluent congregation, but Childers says it didn't start out that way, instead begun by working-class German immigrants.

The costs and challenges of maintaining the building weigh heavy on the congregation's budget, and Childers said that with the threat of climate change and inclement weather, he'd just found out recently that the church's insurance company had cancelled on them. He found himself balancing maintenance projects and weekly worship services and sermons and, beginning his tenure around the same time as the election of President Donald Trump, navigating the choppy waters of a politically purple congregation, with worshipers ranging from very liberal to very conservative.

An avid reader and studier of culture and human behavior, Childers told me he was "obsessed" with trying to understand why so many devoted American Christians had dedicated themselves so completely to the causes of right-wing politics and Trumpism. He gestured to books all over his office that he'd read, trying to figure it out. His brow knit itself together. Affable and gregarious by nature, father of two teenagers, the eldest a boy, Childers didn't like to be so baffled. He didn't want to ignore the problems of division and anger and hate; he wanted to address them. But try as he might, he couldn't figure out a solution.

Just across the street from St. Matthew's, on the way to Mother Emanuel, was Marion Square, where protesters gathered to call for the removal of the John C. Calhoun statue. It was finally removed from the square in 2020. During that same time period, Childers was guiding his church through the COVID-19 pandemic, through mask-wearing and event cancellations and even the hiring of a new part-time minister, the Reverend A. J. Houseman, who is a lesbian and married to a woman.

In 2019, the archivist at St. Matthew's was going through some old papers and found that the church had formerly owned an enslaved person during the Civil War. Childers said initially some of the church leadership wanted to cover it up, but instead they implemented a plan: going public about what they'd found and committing themselves to a series of church events and trainings on anti-racism, many led by Dr. Bernard E. Powers Jr., founding director of the College of Charleston's Center for the Study of Slavery. Childers said his messages to the church at the time were founded in words of confession and forgiveness. He said he'd learned that he couldn't call for reconciliation when there had never been conciliation in the first place. You had to build trust and build relationships before you could start to mend them. You had to confront the past truths and confess before healing could begin.

St. Matthew's was still a wealthy, white congregation in 2023. Maybe it always would be. Maybe it was smaller than it once had been. But when I joined their church again that evening for a Mardi Gras dinner, I saw that their joy and sense of themselves had been made richer by the process they'd gone through together of acknowledgment and grief and confession.

John, Ryan, and Travis[1] were all teenagers helping to serve food and collect plates at the St. Matthew's Mardi Gras dinner that night. They told me about growing up in the stratified culture of Charleston, where they said the school system could be "awful," and their parents called it a "second job" trying to make sure their kids got into the right high school. While these boys were proud of South Carolina for removing the Confederate symbol from its state flag, saying it was time to "move on," that there was "no denying" the legacy of slavery as the reason for the Civil War, and that "history" or "family" was no defensible reason for the ongoing veneration of the Confederacy in Charleston—they also had a clear sense that the city's most undesirable schools were almost always the schools that were predominately Black.

Like all white boys their age growing up in America in 2023, John, Ryan, and Travis were navigating lots of social changes, sorting through them to the best of their abilities, at turns embracing the tolerance and acceptance that Gen Z is known for, and at other turns frustrated or confused by the lack of clarity given to them by adults in their lives, especially when it came to things like an increasing number of students in their school identifying as transgender or non-binary, but then changing their minds. Like teenagers throughout history, these boys had the sense that their parents were often trying to foist their own experiences as teens onto their children, even though history had shifted in the meantime. They found themselves trying to understand social change on social media too and said that they felt the increased pressure of appearances in a world where everyone was constantly taking and sharing pictures of themselves.

As younger teens, they'd lived through COVID-19 and the racial reawakening and upheaval that shook Charleston after the murder of George Floyd by the Minneapolis (Minn.) police in May 2020. In many ways they came across as well-adjusted and tolerant, hopeful for the future, willing to share their emotions and feelings. But there were parts of them that were guarded too and uncertain about what it means to be a white teenage boy in America.

"We have to be on our toes a little bit because you don't want to be cancelled," Ryan said. "That has serious effects. You could not go to college. You could not get opportunities."

Even for these boys, who attended some of Charleston's best high schools, there was a sense of anxiety about the future, a seeping in of a message for white men in America that as other people got more access to opportunities, it might mean something less for them. They didn't understand why Black business owners got special designations on social media, or, if they understood it, in some sense it seemed vaguely threatening.

The truth is that anxiety about the future and one's place in the world is a normal part of growing up. It's just that in America, too often we haven't allowed white boys to experience those normal anxieties and insecurities. We've taught them to push those feelings down, cover them up with machismo and bravado and projected strength. So many white American men never let themselves feel those feelings of insecurity or inadequacy. Or if they did, those feelings came to seem overwhelming and insurmountable. Better to normalize those feelings. Yes, the world can treat any of us unjustly or unfairly. And I can understand why some white boys see it as unfair that they have to carry "baggage" because of what other white boys have done. But it happens to everyone. I want to tell those boys: You're going to be OK. Being vulnerable is an entry to connection and empathy with others, a necessary precursor to building and maintaining healthy and intimate relationships.

Racism and violence persist in America often because white Americans convince ourselves we have a certain distance from such ugliness. We talk about slavery and racial violence, and even segregation and the civil rights movement, as though they were part of a forgotten, distant past. We speak of purveyors of racist hatred and violence as though they were of another species, with omnipresent white sheets and long beards and burning crosses and tiki torches and swastikas, and we assure ourselves that because we have never uttered the "n-word" aloud that we have no such culpability or complicity in such matters.

We imagine that we are further evolved than we are, like in 2008 when Barack Obama became America's first Black president, leading many to proclaim that racism was dead. We point to Black celebrities and millionaires and billionaires; we casually mention our Black friends and relatives.

"I'm not racist."

As though "being racist" were the worst thing that you could be, so we try to place it in another category altogether, out of sight, out of mind. Never realizing that worse than "being racist" would be being beaten, arrested, even killed—because of racist violence.

"I don't see color."

As the children's church song goes, "Jesus loves the little children of the world."

Unaddressed, shunted into dark alleyways and covertly shared jokes and whispered slurs, racism spreads like a pathogen, a potent virus, one whose symptoms are rendered invisible by the very ways that racial prejudice is structured into American society.

Too often, white Christian boys in America are taught about race in a way that overemphasizes shame and deemphasizes truth-telling and justice-seeking. They are given mixed messages about race and racism. They have a sense that something very bad has happened in this country, and maybe they are somehow connected to the badness, but to mention it would make it worse.

Our perceived distance from a racist past is an illusion. Hope and pain, violence and peace, dwell right next to one another. One is not possible without acknowledging the other.

Mother Emanuel and the Power of the Black Church

A year before Childers came to Charleston to pastor St. Matthew's, back when John, Ryan, and Travis were just elementary school boys growing up in Charleston, another young, white, Lutheran boy from South Carolina would shake the city out of its gentility, comfort, and complacency. He came to another church in Charleston not to go to worship or to serve Mardi Gras dinner but instead, in his words, to start a race war.

Dylann Storm Roof, a twenty-one-year-old from Columbia, drove into downtown Charleston on a Wednesday, the day when most churches host Bible studies, youth groups, and Christian education classes. He went past St. Matthew's to, instead, walk up to the basement door at Mother Emanuel African Methodist Episcopal Church, less than a ten-minute walk from St. Matthew's, past Marion Square, on Calhoun Street. When he got there, Pastor Clementa C. Pinckney welcomed Roof in to their Bible study group, where he listened for an hour, reading from his Bible, until the closing prayer, when Roof set down his Bible and pulled out a handgun, shooting and killing nine of the Black Bible study participants with whom he had just joined in prayer.

God, have mercy.

I had been told that it might be possible for me to join a group tour at Mother Emanuel that Saturday morning, so after leaving St. Matthew's, I hurried past Marion Square down Calhoun Street to stand in front of another proud nineteenth-century church building, this one painted bright white on the outside, with a silver cross and pointy black steeple. A brown metal plaque bordered with gold was placed in front, on the outside of the front stairwell for all to see:

In Remembrance of Emanuel 9

Rev. Clementa C. Pinckney (41)
Sharonda Coleman-Singleton (45)
Cynthia Marie Graham Hurd (54)
Susie Jackson (87)
Ethel Lee Lance (70)
DePayne Middleton-Doctor (49)
Tywanza Sanders (26)
Daniel Simmons (74)
Myra Thompson (59)
"LOVE IS STRONGER THAN HATE"

Around the corner, behind the stairwell, I saw a doorway with a buzzer. The front sanctuary door had been locked. I felt conspicuous coming here as a white person, remembering that they had welcomed Roof as a fellow white stranger, and he had returned their Christian hospitality with hatred, violence, and death. I didn't deserve for them to trust me in return. I rang the buzzer anyway, nervously.

Brother Lee Bennett, Mother Emanuel's historian, answered the door wearing a red half-zip polo sweater. He looked confused, clearing his throat and telling me that the next tour wasn't starting for an hour or two—a group from Queens University in Charlotte, North Carolina.

Bennett, who said he'd been a member at Mother Emanuel since 1957, wanted to help me, though. We talked for a few minutes, in that same basement space where Roof had attended Bible study in 2015, and we made the connection that Mother Emanuel's current pastor, the Reverend Eric S. C. Manning, had indeed talked to both of us about each other, and about my wanting to join a tour. Bennett told me that he thought I might have time before the next tour to walk up Calhoun Street toward Gadsden's Wharf—where the Cooper River entered the Atlantic Ocean and where up to 40 percent of all enslaved persons disembarked onto American soil; where, just south of the ferry to Fort Sumter, South Carolina seceded from the Union to ignite the Civil War and fight to maintain the institution of slavery; and where the city had constructed the International African American Museum, which opened in June 2023.

I walked as fast as I could to get to the museum, but it was like my feet were trudging past the wreckage of American history, held down in the muck and sins of the past. I noticed that while King Street and much of downtown Charleston were filled with white tourists, in this area of the city, white people were a minority, including at the museum. Here, again, I was graciously allowed to enter with two tour groups and what seemed to be a few extended families of Black Americans.

The museum elegantly traced the pride and carnage of being Black in America, from slavery and civil rights to Obama and Black Lives Matter. There were quiet rooms where people could go and shut the door, and I couldn't imagine how triggering it would feel for a Black American to walk through this space, reliving some of the pain and torture their ancestors experienced as enslaved people. There was much to celebrate here, too, though: music and art and so many pastors and churches who had fostered the strength, resilience, and endurance of African Americans.

Before I left, I squeezed myself in between tables of a group of older Black people, who looked to be in their 60s, 70s, and 80s. Behind them was a portrait of Jesus, with dark brown skin and black braids. A woman watched me taking photos of Black Jesus, and she asked if I wanted a picture. So that's the only photo I have of myself that day, standing awkwardly, straight-faced, blond hair, black tank top, tan pants, next to Black Jesus, whom I could feel watching me.

It was time to return to Mother Emanuel. I hurriedly rushed out of the museum, down the stone steps, away from the wharf, stepping quickly along the sidewalk at Gadsdenboro Park, named for South Carolina Revolutionary War patriot Christopher Gadsden, who owned enough enslaved African Americans to decree that "my negroes" be divided equally with the rest of his estate into nineteen shares.

This was Charleston, and America, really. On one block, a fist raised for Black freedom and equality, and a painting of Black Jesus, who judged between the righteous and the unrighteous. On the next block, a five-acre park dedicated to a slaveholder, whose name also graced the yellow flag, popular today with right-wing movements, depicting a coiled-up snake and the menacing words: "Don't Tread on Me."

In the park, I passed by several white men who appeared to be unhoused doing their best to sleep on park benches in the November afternoon sun.

I rushed down the last three blocks of Calhoun Street, seeing in front of me that the tour group from Queens University had finished their lunch in the basement at Mother Emanuel and had gathered on the front steps for their tour. I took what I hoped was an inconspicuous place in the back, explaining to the students that I'd been given permission to join their group. They welcomed me. Their tour group, like Queens University itself, was racially diverse, made up of Black students, white students, Latinx students, Asian students, and a number of international students. One of the group's leaders had grown up here in Charleston, and he and Brother Bennett shared notes about their neighborhoods, which weren't far from where we sat that afternoon, ushered in together into Mother Emanuel's historic sanctuary.

Bennett told the group that they'd have to bear with him: he was recovering from a respiratory illness that had weakened his voice, and he didn't hear well in one ear. But clearly this work at Mother Emanuel was, for Bennett, a ministry, a calling, one that mattered deeply to him, and so he soldiered on. Soldiering, after all, came naturally to Bennett. Bennett was a retired military veteran who had spent twenty-six years in the 82nd Airborne Division of the US Army. He bristled a bit when asked about the presence of the American flag behind the altar at Mother Emanuel—a flag that many white congregations had decided to remove from their altars in a protest against right-wing Christian nationalism, which used the flag and the cross as symbols together to support American power and strength, sometimes over and above the gospel of Jesus. Bennett said it was different at Mother Emanuel. Here, in a sanctuary first constructed just seven years after the end of the Civil War, the American flag still meant a protest against a South Carolina history that had prized the Confederacy over the Union, where the Confederate flag was brought back out again in the 1960s as a protest against civil rights and integration of schools, where for a Black church to bravely call itself American was not a paean to entrenched white power, as it was for so many majority-white congregations who fly the flag, but instead a protest against entrenched white power, which had fought to keep African Americans enslaved.

As in so many places here in Charleston, and across America, history hung in the air, like the wet humidity and the damp Spanish moss in the trees all over the city. Past, present, and future ran into each other, and Bennett told us about all of it. He said Mother Emanuel, like St. Matthew's, its white counterpart a few blocks away, was awash in restoration work and repairs. They were fixing the ceiling and redoing floors that had broken and warped. But it would be OK, Bennett said, because it took them more than one hundred years even to get restrooms in the church.

He told our group about how the African Methodist Episcopal Church had started, back at the end of the eighteenth century, around the same time the white American founders had determined that enslaved people would count as three-fifths of a person in the determination of states' Congressional representation. He told us about church founders Richard Allen and Absalom Jones, free Black men who walked into their Methodist Episcopal Church in Philadelphia in 1787 and were told they could no longer pray in the pews where they ordinarily sat for church.

Church leadership had opted to segregate the church without informing Jones and Allen, and Bennett said that the story was that they'd been forcibly removed from their pew in the middle of their prayers. Nine years later, these two men and others founded the Free African Society, and in 1792, the first African Methodist Episcopal Church began, followed by a second two years later, with the denomination officially forming at a meeting in Philadelphia in 1816.

Mother Emanuel is the oldest African Methodist Episcopal congregation in the South, formed by disgruntled Black members of what was then an all-white Methodist church called Bethel. Led by Morris Brown, Black members of Bethel left in protest when the church determined to build a carriage house over the top of the church's Black burial ground. They founded a new church, then called Hampstead Church, and one of the founders was the lottery-winner and future leader of the 1822 rebellion against Charleston slaveholders, Denmark Vesey, who was executed with other revolt organizers on July 2, 1822. That same summer, a crowd of angry and fearful whites burned down the original church building. The congregation that would become Mother Emanuel met in secret for the next five decades, finally rebuilding the church in 1872.

These builders of the church where I sat that day, in the original pews, were men and women who had known great strife and trauma. Many had been born into slavery, had been separated from their mothers and fathers, sisters and brothers, spouses, and children. They had watched as Vesey, their friend and fellow church member, had his coffin paraded around the city while white people sat on top of it and cheered. In the midst of the white celebration, they watched an enslaved child fall from a wagon and die. And to make matters worse, when the white law enforcement officials tried to hang Vesey and the other revolt leaders, the gallows didn't work, and the Black men—husbands, fathers, brothers, friends, church leaders—were shot in the back of the head. Of the 130 people arrested in the rebellion, Bennett told us, fifty-seven were executed. African Americans in the city, free or enslaved, lived in constant fear, and they worshipped Jesus only in secret. Free Black people, Bennett said, were seen as the greatest threat, and so, from 1834 to 1865, South Carolina made it against the law to teach Black people to read and write.

Just fourteen years after Mother Emanuel's first church building was constructed, it was destroyed in the earthquake that hit Charleston in 1886. The new building, as history crisscrossed over itself again, was designed by Devereux—the architect who'd designed white, Lutheran St. Matthew's—a former captain in the Confederate Army.

Bennett told us we were sitting in the original pews, our feet touching the original floors, both from 1891. The gas lighting and stained-glass windows were still originals. So was the communion rail. The organ had persevered since 1908, though they'd finally refurbished it in recent years. At a capacity of more than 1,200 people, Mother Emanuel was the largest Black church in the city of Charleston. Booker T. Washington graced its pulpit in 1909, followed by a visit from Dr. Martin Luther King Jr., in 1962, at the height of the civil rights movement. Coretta Scott King, his widow, returned to Mother Emanuel in 1969 for the first, and last, major labor action put on by the Southern Christian Leadership Conference after Dr. King's assassination the year before.

This had long been a place of Black pride and Black power, a place where America was revered as a country that had fought against slavery and tyranny alike, a place where Jesus came "to let the oppressed go free."[2]

In the eyes of many white Americans, then, Mother Emanuel also represented a sort of threat: because Black power necessitated a defense of white power, or else white men might no longer find themselves atop their self-constructed and imagined hierarchy. Rich Southerners had long known this game: that to keep their access to undiminished wealth and power, they had to keep poor white Southerners from uniting their cause for economic and social justice with Black Southerners. Their best tools for keeping the two groups apart were racism, hatred, fear, and violence. Of inciting this, of course, they'd always wash their hands.

As I write this, I realize I'm getting closer to the person and the story of the Charleston shooter, Dylann Roof, whose story violently intersects with Mother Emanuel's story and also collides, unavoidably, with my own. I realize how scared I am to even write about Roof, to acknowledge how his story and his violent actions are bound up unavoidably with the lives and future of the young, white Christian men and boys in your life and mine. Bennett's hoarse voice keeps creeping closer and closer to June 17, 2015.

He tells us what happened that Wednesday night, that Roof walked up to the church door and asked for the pastor. They welcomed him in, and Roof sat right next to Rev. Clementa C. Pinckney, who used to spend a lot of time in Roof's hometown of Columbia, in the State House right across the street from the church where Roof went to worship, because Pinckney was also a South Carolina state representative; in fact he was the youngest Black man ever elected to the South Carolina General Assembly, at the age of twenty-three.

Like the pastor who would be called to Roof's family's side after the shooting, Pinckney had also studied at the Lutheran Theological Southern Seminary. He and Roof had spent their lives in overlapping circles, contrary to the racist lie of mutually exclusive lives. But if Roof and Pinckney recognized each other, neither one said so. Roof had come to the church on a mission to kill Black people, and he was determined to carry it out no matter what, though Roof later reportedly told investigators that he almost didn't go through with it, because the church members had been so nice to him, in the hour they studied the Bible together and prayed, before he opened fire.[3]

Roof shot Pinckney first, in the head. Firing indiscriminately, angrily, out of control, like a man possessed, he killed eight more people. Five survived, enduring, living, forever scarred. Bennett said, his voice full of pride and beyond reproach, that Mother Emanuel never missed a single worship service, never missed a single Bible study after the 2015 shooting, even though for many people the eight years since the shooting "is more like eight days." Many church members still didn't set foot in the space where the shooting occurred. The trauma went on. Some conversations were just starting to be had, Bennett said, even though national media made much of the fact that victims' families had offered forgiveness for Roof just a month after the shooting.[4]

Bennett bristles a bit when asked if church members had asked to bring guns to church to protect themselves after the shooting, as had occurred in other faith communities, many of them predominately white, after other churches experienced mass shootings in their midst.

"We did *not* change who we are," Bennett said, defiantly. "He wanted to start a race war. We don't have metal detectors. The doors of the church are open."

As far as weapons in the sanctuary?

"That has not happened. That will not happen."

Confronting the Shooter in the Church

I think back then to how eager so many white Christians were to share the inspiring story of the Charleston church members' forgiveness. I think about how often I had heard the victims' names ring out in my mind, as I replayed that video of then-President Barack Obama singing "Amazing Grace," and the whole congregation swaying and singing, and how badly I wanted that story to be my story.

But my story is much closer to Dylann Roof's. Remember the lessons of Charleston, and of American history, how it all intertwines, and how the past, as Faulkner wrote, is "never dead. It's not even past."[5]

Roof's and my stories collide because we were both baptized into the same church body, the Evangelical Lutheran Church in America, where I have been ordained as a minister for more than ten years. While the ELCA is part of the so-called "mainline," a more politically progressive group of traditional Protestant denominations including the Episcopal Church and the Presbyterian Church (USA), among others, the ELCA is also America's whitest denomination.

I knew that Roof had been brought up, at least partially, in an ELCA congregation, though people were also quick to point out that his attendance had been spotty, especially in his later years. His parents, who divorced when he was a baby, weren't regular churchgoers, and the family's Lutheran roots were on his dad's side—a man who was better known for getting Roof the money for his first gun and permit for his twenty-first birthday.[6]

Before coming to South Carolina in November 2023, what I mostly knew about Roof's church roots were what I'd seen in the Pulitzer Prize–winning article in *GQ* about Roof, written by Rachel Kaadzi Ghansah. In that article, Ghansah attended church at St. Paul's in Columbia, and spoke briefly to the Reverend Tony Metze, who came across as a tragic mix of defensive and defeated, sad, broken, and also maybe insensitive or ignorant to the role of racism in his midst. Her article about Roof's roots was, rightly, a tragedy and an indictment of white American racism in general, about how the majority's inability to confront racism had emboldened a minority in our midst to carry out acts of violent hatred, again and again and again.

Metze and I had mutual friends on social media, and our lives intersected the way that lives often do in smaller and sometimes insular religious communities in America, despite the distance between my home in Minneapolis and his ongoing pastoral work in South Carolina. Other white Lutheran pastors in South Carolina told me that they didn't know Metze well, but that he was known to be more conservative, politically. Other South Carolina pastors told me that Roof's connection to our denomination had been underplayed. They said he'd gone to church camp, and that one of his cousins was an ELCA pastor.

Maybe it's for these reasons that I knew immediately when I took up the task of writing about young, white Christian men in America that I would have to confront the story of Dylann Roof. I would have to look in the eye of the racist hatred and violence that drove him, to see where it intersected with the stories of young, white Christian boys and men in America—to try and understand what had happened, and how we could tell the truth about it. Because I knew that part of what ails young, white Christian men and boys is the stifling silence of shame, fear, and unwillingness to tell the truth.

Part of that truth is that Roof's story is not singular. While it's unique in its connections to my own church and faith background, young white men continue to commit mass murder against Black people in America, leaving behind statements of racist hatred and fear. In August 2023, a white man walked into a Dollar General in Jacksonville, Florida and killed three African Americans, then himself. Before that, in May 2022, an eighteen-year-old white man killed ten Black people at a grocery store in Buffalo, New York. He had written a 180-page manifesto about the need for racial purity before driving more than six hours to a place he'd researched in hopes of finding the most Black people gathered in one space to murder.[7] When a white New Zealand man killed fifty-one people at two different mosques in Christchurch in 2019, he cited Roof's massacre in Charleston as an inspiration.

And Roof's racist hatred did not arise out of vapor, ex nihilo. While there's no evidence his family was involved in white supremacist activities, and Roof was known to have friends who were Black, Roof was radicalized online, and he was an active reader of and visitor to sites like the Council of Conservative Citizens, which denied responsibility for his actions and claimed to "responsibly report on Black on white crime."[8] Roof mentioned the Council as part of his "awakening" in an unsigned, 2,444-word manifesto on his website, lastrhodesian.com, which also included photos of himself taken with a self-timer at slavery-related sites across South Carolina, and a mention of Seattle-based white supremacist organization Northwest Front.[9]

While there's a rightful caution against writing too much about mass murderers, for fear of the same contagion effect cited by the New Zealand shooter about Roof, I wonder sometimes if white Christians have used that caution as an excuse to avoid confronting the ways in which our own society and institutions have been home to boys and young men like Roof. There is a desire on the part of well-meaning white Christians to put people like Roof into some kind of alternative box, to avoid any way in which his life and actions might intersect with our own. I fear that our hesitancy to confront his story has been perilous for young, white Christian men and boys. Maybe by speaking about what happened with Roof we could head off this hatred and violence in other young white men and boys in our midst. Maybe they can learn to recognize it in one another and say something or do something. Closing our eyes and wishing it would go away, or pretending that the racism right in front of us is far outside our midst, has not worked thus far.

Still, everything within my body rebelled against me as I forced myself to make the drive to Columbia the day after I toured Mother Emanuel, retracing Roof's steps in reverse. I knew that St. Paul's Lutheran Church would feel familiar to me, and maybe I didn't want it to feel familiar. I was longing for that comfortable sense of distance that white people often employ to keep ourselves from having to confront the consequences of racism in our own lives, our own histories.

"My ancestors didn't own slaves."

"They were too poor."

"They hadn't come from Europe yet."

It is so much more convenient to locate the problem outside ourselves, to point to those who are increasingly radical and loud and other. I knew I would not be able to do that anymore when I came to St. Paul's.

There was something else too. I'd come to South Carolina with the intention to remember, not to forget, and I had promised to come with my entire self. Unlike years ago, when I'd come here on assignment as a sports beat reporter in my early 20s, this time I'd come to Columbia, South Carolina, not only as a journalist or as a white woman but also as a mother of two white sons. To watch your children grow up and to release them into the world every single day, in an era of school shootings and cyberbullying and revenge porn and nudes, is an exercise in abject terror. Even more terrifying, as a mom of white sons, is to imagine that your child is not a victim of such violence and bullying but the perpetrator. I wanted to distance myself, not just from Dylann Roof but also from the idea that I could have been his mother. No, not possible. Make it go away.

Most of the white people I'd spoken to in Charleston told me that, in so many words, they were more moderate and maybe more evolved than the rest of the state. They told me that the kind of blatant racism and prejudice that many Northerners still associated with the South, like Confederate flags and racial slurs, were still prominent in the state's more rural areas, and I'd likely see more of it when I came toward Columbia. I was surprised, though, throughout the course of my drive, that I saw far fewer Trump signs or anti-abortion billboards or even Confederate flags than I was used to seeing on my drives throughout the Upper Midwest, including parts of rural Minnesota, Iowa, and northern Missouri. Instead, I mostly saw signs of accident injury lawyers and advertisements for pain clinics, two common sights in poorer communities across America, regardless of race.

Located less than a mile from both the State House and the University of South Carolina, like St. Matthew's and Mother Emanuel, Roof's home congregation of St. Paul's was also a historic church, according to its bulletin "ministering on the corner of Bull and Landing Streets since 1886."

It is not easy for churches to endure for nearly 150 years, especially in a climate where the religious "nones" are growing faster than any other faith group in America. Most people just don't go to church anymore on Sunday mornings, and the story was the same at St. Paul's, where Metze and Nola Freeman, the Director of Youth and Family Ministry at the church, were hosting a lunch after worship that morning to try and convince a few more families to sign up for acolyte duties, a tougher position to fill week in and week out.

St. Paul's was much like I expected, and also not. I entered there prepared to be met with the trappings of conservative white Christian nationalism, defensiveness, suspicion. I was prepared for Metze to say he wouldn't talk to me, not at all. Instead, I met Freeman during the service, and I felt my heart open a bit, as the choir sang a haunting and exquisite opening chorale in the loft. Freeman is the one who later invited me to stay for acolyte lunch, and then Metze agreed to meet me in his office after lunch for a longer conversation. I had lucked out: he had no afternoon plans, his wife was out of town, and I think we shared a sense of trust as two fellow ELCA Lutheran pastors doing the best we could in these post-COVID-19 church years with declining attendance and nonstop political tensions in the pews. Metze would tell me later that despite his reputation as a "conservative," the church's director of music and organist, Henry Fulmer, was openly gay, as were other members and church musicians.

"They ask him, hey, how's your partner?" Metze said. "Nobody has a problem with that."

But Metze, who has served as pastor of St. Paul's since 2007, when Roof was thirteen, acknowledged that, in many ways, he felt he was holding the church's politically divided congregation together. He wasn't sure what the future would hold for St. Paul's, after he left. Metze had steadfastly stayed under the fold of the purportedly "liberal" ELCA, even when his two sons became ordained as pastors in a breakaway Lutheran denomination that did not support gay marriage or openly gay pastors.

"I really wish you wouldn't do this," Metze said he told his sons, which surprised me, given that I had perceived Metze to be more aligned politically with the conservative breakaway sects. Ultimately, though, he was a dad and a pastor who loved both his sons and his church.

"I wish my sons were here," Metze said, of the ELCA, remembering clergy events where he felt lonely.

The Sunday I attended St. Paul's was All Saints Sunday in the church year, and so we opened the service by singing *For All the Saints*, and after the kids headed off to the Sunday school program with Freeman, that morning's acolyte approached the altar to light candles as part of the *Rite of Remembrance*.

Metze read the names of those who had died from St. Paul's in the past year, and I was surprised to read the third name listed in the bulletin insert: Benn Roof, Dylann's dad. Metze told me after the service that Benn had died in a four-wheeler accident earlier that year.

"Benn always lived on the edge," Metze said.

The Roof family was still a tangential part of St. Paul's, eight years after the Mother Emanuel massacre. Dylann had been sentenced to death and was on death row in Indiana. His grandfather had died in 2022. His uncle attended rarely, and very infrequently they'd see Dylann's mom and sister.

Metze told me about how he'd pulled a hood over his head and carried trash bags to the dumpster walking out of church in the months following the Mother Emanuel massacre, because the Roof family had asked him not to talk to reporters, and also because he didn't know what to say. He had previously been called in to support other young boys and men in the congregation who had gotten into trouble for much more minor reasons, but in those situations, Metze had always had a sense of what went wrong, or how to fix it, or what words to offer to struggling parents. He recounted a time when one young man had gotten into trouble in the military, and Metze realized that his father had been totally absent from his life, unable to remember spending even fifteen minutes one-on-one with his son. Metze valued relationships, connection, the role of a father.

"Benn did spend time with Dylann, though, he did," Metze said.

Tracing the roots of Dylann's radicalization wasn't so simple. Here was a faith background that bordered on theologically liberal, a pastor who told me that one of his core beliefs was in an "inclusive" gospel. Here was a family who, despite divorce and some financial instability, spent time together, grandparents who were involved and active congregation members, a teenager who struggled in school, and with substance abuse, but never before seemed outwardly violent.

There were Christian groups for whom white supremacy was an overt founding myth, American denominations like the Southern Baptist Convention who were founded in support of slavery. St. Paul's story was not that; its past and present included a racism that was more subtle, structural, like my own and like most white Americans' past and present. I noticed that the pillows around the communion rail at St. Paul's featured a white, blond Jesus, and the stained-glass windows, which had come directly from Germany, depicted European-looking biblical figures. But the same can be said for the majority of white churches across America.

It seems for Dylann that the problem was not an actively white supremacist identity but instead the lack of a positive rooted identity for himself. He struggled in school; struggled with friends. Anywhere he went, he was on the outside. He fit a profile of a teenaged boy I kept hearing about in my interviews with parents, pastors, and teen boys themselves: a kid who was always on the outside, who didn't have a sport or a hobby or a talent. He found his identity instead, ultimately, in hatred of others, and, as seems to be the case in stories like these, that identity of hatred festered and grew in social circles where people may have mentioned racism or prejudice but didn't confront it in our own midst, preferring to avoid uncomfortable topics or introspection.

After the service, during which Metze preached a sermon about the inarguable inclusivity of heaven, and its lack of divisions, Metze and Freeman invited me to join them and other church members for a traditional Southern lunch of slow-cooked green beans, shaved beef, scalloped potatoes, fruit jello, and sweet tea. I looked around the Fellowship Hall, somewhat similar to the basement space with the same name at Mother Emanuel, and noticed to my surprise that St. Paul's had been one of the first ELCA congregations to employ an ordained woman pastor. Her portrait hung near another pastor who was pictured in his military uniform. I share this detail to remind you, and to remind myself, that the most important work in raising our boys, these young, white Christian men—and combating the forces of their radicalization—takes place in spaces that hold within them competing truths about their history, bringing to mind the complicated truth about white American Christianity itself: that it has incubated both racial justice and racial hatred; that it has advocated for freedom and equality and concern for the poor, while at the same time embracing policies and people who would limit freedom and equality, and exacerbate the suffering of the poor.

Even as he sits on death row, his latest appeal being denied after Roof fired his lawyers and refused to entertain arguments of his own mental incapacity, Roof seems beyond contrition and rehabilitation. He is uninterested in repenting or repudiating his own racist ideas. He seems instead to cling to them, to the identity that they created for him. His story remains a tragedy, and that's probably the way it has to be.

More fruitful, more hopeful, perhaps—or at least more instructive as we consider the work of fighting the radicalization of young, white Christian men and boys—is Metze's story. After lunch, he and I sat in his church office, talking for hours before I would head back into Charleston that afternoon. We shared a suspicion and a distrust of the institutional church, and he carried a bit of a chip on his shoulder that I recognized in myself, well-worn for those of us who grew up with a legacy of working-class families in a clergy church hierarchy sometimes rife with elitism and private school privilege.

Metze told me that he tried to raise his kids with the example of an egalitarian marriage, in which he said he vacuumed and cleaned the house, just as his father had. But Metze was still deeply ingrained with a traditional teaching of masculinity all the same.

"Emotions . . . I've not done well with that, to be honest," he said. "If there's an Achilles heel for me, it's that."

Metze said he had always had a hard time expressing emotion, "sorting them" he called it. "This job doesn't help," he added.

He told me that he was stunned recently when he broke down into uncontrollable sobbing at the burial of a friend and church member earlier that year.

Metze hadn't publicly shared his grief or emotion after the Mother Emanuel massacre. He told me about trying to figure it out in his head, rationally sorting through the whole thing, retracing what he knew of Dylann and the Roof family. Some people in the community figured the Klan had to be involved, their shadow still lurking to the point that no one I spoke to wanted me to say they'd mentioned the Klan aloud. Metze said the South Carolina ELCA bishop mentioned the shooting every time he made a public address, noting that Roof had come from the synod. Every time people at St. Paul's heard it, Metze said, the sense of shame grew more and more unbearable. He felt it, too, and he didn't know quite what to do with it.

I wrote earlier that shame is silencing and suffocating, which is why it's such a powerful weapon in perpetuating hatred and violence. It was not the Black church or Mother Emanuel who wanted to shame the people of St. Paul's. They knew well that shame would only end up in racism and hatred going deeper underground, where it would be more powerful and violent and deadly. As Bennett reminded me, Mother Emanuel knew who they were—as a people and a church. They would not give Roof the race war he wanted. They knew, correctly, that this was a white Christian problem: avoidable only when white Christians at-large would move past shame, or the desire to blame "other" white Christians for the problems of racism, hatred, and violence—and instead confess of our own participation in the systems that fed racism and shame, admitting the ways that shame and racism harmed us, too.

As our conversation drew to an end, Metze told me that there was a story he'd never shared before, and he wanted me to hear it.

"I met Clementa Pinckney," he said.

Because of his work as a state representative, Pinckney spent a fair amount of time in Columbia at the State House, where he had gotten to know another one of St. Paul's church members, who also worked there. It was February of 2015, and Ash Wednesday was coming up on the eighteenth of that month, the date when Christians gather to receive ashes on their foreheads to signify the beginning of the season of Lent, when Christians remember Jesus's death on the Cross, often spending additional time in lament and contemplation, sometimes "giving up" indulgences like chocolate or alcohol, or engaging in other kinds of fasting, in a desire to seek repentance and complete acts of penance.

Metze said that the church member from St. Paul's who worked at the State House was talking to Pinckney about the traditional practice of making ashes for Ash Wednesday, sometimes done by burning palm branches from the previous Easter season. She told Pinckney that Metze would be "making ashes" that week, and Pinckney was welcome to join.

So that February, just four months before Roof would commit mass murder at Mother Emanuel, the two pastors, Metze and Pinckney, gathered at St. Paul's, home congregation to the Roof family, to make ashes, in preparation for their church members to come forward, receive the sign of the cross in ashes on their foreheads, and hear these weighty words that signified the beginning of the Lenten season: "Remember that you are dust, and to dust you shall return."

As Metze remembered it, he and Pinckney got along well, making plans to get together again in the future.

"He was a good man," Metze said, with a thickness in the back of his throat. "He was a good man."

"We said, we've gotta get together again," Metze continued, his voice cracking, his eyes watering as emotion threatened to overcome him. "And then four months later he was shot dead in his church by my, basically, parishioner."

In that moment I saw clearly before me the weight of grief and shame and how it lay upon Metze, how much he wished he could have done . . . something? anything? . . . to stop what Dylann did.

"They think this wasn't personal," Metze said, his voice catching again. "It was personal."

I didn't get the sense that Metze was looking for sympathy or compassion in sharing this story with me, nor that he was looking to be relieved from his or his church's culpability in the forming of a racist mass murderer. Instead, I saw at long last an acknowledgment, so desperately needed in white Christian circles, of how inextricably connected we are to both hatred and love, to violence and peace, to life and death.

Dylann Roof had found and rooted his identity in hatred and violence. There is profit to be made, online, in white supremacist forums and groups, and in right-wing movements that teeter close to the edge of racist language, couching it as "anti-immigration" or "pro-Christian." Many more young white men and boys besides Dylann had found identity there, are finding identity there.

Most pernicious of the lies about white Christian masculinity is the one that weakness is something to be avoided at all costs, that showing vulnerability and emotion is a recipe for disaster, a potential upheaval in a society that has placed white Christian men at the top of a teetering house of cards. To worship a crucified and resurrected Jesus instead is to know, as Mother Emanuel long has known, that the greatest strength is found in accepting weakness and vulnerability.

The forgiveness offered to Roof by members of Mother Emanuel was a showing, therefore, not of weakness but of strength. He had robbed them of their beloved ones, but they would not—could not—allow him to make them as hateful, angry, and alone as he was. In their vulnerability and grief, God had made them strong.

As I sat at St. Paul's across the table from a wounded, broken, grieving Metze, I wished more white American Christians could have seen this side of him, could have heard his personal story of loss and regret and shame. In sharing it, he freed himself. Forgave himself? Entrusted God to do the hard work of justice, punishment, redemption, and resurrection.

This example, this clear portrayal of what racist hatred does to white men themselves, is unequivocally more of what young, white Christian men need desperately to see: that the change, like the violence initially, could only come from within the heart of white Christianity itself.

The Courage White People Need

I walked out of Metze's Columbia church office that day shaken but renewed in my purpose, chastened by my own initial desire to separate myself from him, to not allow our shared stories of complicity and shame to open ourselves to God's work of repentance and healing, even in the midst of ignominious sin, hatred, and violence.

Our conversation and the work ahead reminded me of a talk I'd had a few weeks earlier with another ELCA church leader, Metropolitan Chicago Synod bishop, the Reverend Yehiel Curry, a Black man who had first entered ministry as a volunteer with a program that focused on training and support of young Black men.

Curry had joined Safe in My Brother's Arms (SIMBA) and attended his first camp in 1999, back when he was still working as a Chicago social worker. He later became a teacher in the Chicago Public Schools and continued to bring students and staff with him to SIMBA camps. Curry's own life had been irreparably tainted by violence: when he was just two years old, Curry's father, Charles Curry Jr., was shot and killed right outside the apartment building where the family lived.

The seventh of eleven children and the third of four boys, Curry said he was fortunate to have the support of other family members, including some "unique uncles," someone he calls a stepfather, and a smattering of elementary school teachers to help him find his way in the world. Principally, he relied upon his older sisters, though, and his mother, Regina.

As a Black boy growing up on the South Side of Chicago, Curry faced challenges different from those of the young white boys and men that are our primary focus in this book. Like all Black men and boys in America, I imagine he shouldered the additional burden of being seen as uniquely violent and threatening, menacing. He faced additional scrutiny from the police and risked being stereotyped as violent, dangerous, or criminal—in places like stores, schools, and even churches.

Curry has spent most of his career in ministry working to refute and combat that stereotype of Black men, and he currently does so as one of sixty-five synodical bishops in the whitest denomination in America. He went from pastoring predominately Black Shekinah Chapel Lutheran Church, on the Far South Side of Chicago, to heading up one of the ELCA's most prominent synods, home to the institution's churchwide headquarters.

Like many Black people working in leadership positions in predominately white Christian organizations and churches, Curry has often felt the unspoken expectation that it is his job to help white Christians fight racism or know what to say in tragic incidents involving racist hatred, like the Mother Emanuel massacre, or the 2020 murder by Minneapolis police of George Floyd.

Curry said that knowing how to respond as bishop in the midst of his own trauma and grief after George Floyd's murder marked one of the most difficult experiences of his life.

"I got a lot of emails and text messages asking me to say something," Curry said. "Most of those asking when I was going to say something were from my white counterparts."

"I ended up sending my statement out really late. It was traumatic for me because I saw myself on the ground. Every time I was detained . . . sirens flashed on the mirror . . . in an instant, my life could be gone."

"I wasn't sure how to speak not only to my synod but also to those from the larger church. I wasn't even sure how to speak to my own children. There were things that were so hard to say. I didn't know what to say and how to say it, and I was feeling this pressure and obligation, to use my written words to talk about something that was extremely painful, but also feeling like—there will be another George Floyd."

I remember reading Curry's powerful statement after George Floyd's death, and I remember feeling so grateful that he was a leader in my church. Like finally someone was saying something real, not overly scripted or careful or pedantic or detached. But I heard now how much it had taken from Curry to write that statement, to speak in that moment. And I heard his lament, that this still wouldn't be the moment for white Christians where we were really ready to tackle this head-on, where we would take on the problem ourselves, vulnerably, openly, willingly, emotionally.

I thought about how often white Christians turn to Black leaders in times of crisis, hoping that, somehow, they'll have the right words to solve racism for us, or at least salve our wounds. Talking to Curry, I saw how we had been selfish, and how his mission was vitally different from the one so many white Christians had foisted upon him.

When Curry was working with young, Black men in Chicago, he'd never had the luxury to avoid the legacy and stereotype of violence that had shadowed them all their lives, their unavoidable interactions with law enforcement, the fraught encounters they had with white women, who were usually oblivious.

But in the midst of an environment haunted by death, loss, poverty, and injustice, Curry saw the needs of the young men and boys he worked with clearly, in the same way he remembered himself as a young boy on the South Side of Chicago, growing up without his dad.

So often the response of dominant white culture and white Christianity to a perceived crisis among young white men has been to introduce more bravado, more rigid masculinity: youth group football night, Men on a Mission, war, fighting, sports, football, wrestling, MEAT. That is not what young, white Christian men and boys need, as I saw clearly when I talked to grieving and broken and emotional Tony Metze in Columbia, South Carolina.

Instead, Curry walked into spaces filled with tough and hardened boys and young men who had often been assumed to only respond to more toughness, hardness, and hard knocks. With him, he brought not Fight Club but instead something utterly more powerful and immovable: his mother, Regina.

"Most of my major lessons came from my mother. About it being OK to cry. I could show affection to my siblings," Curry said. "There was nothing wrong with me when I had these uncontrollable emotions and feelings that others might see as a minor incident. My mom knew there were bigger questions to ask me."

Curry sighed, looking back on his decades of ministry to the Black church and the white church.

"We box in men, and—anything that comes outside of that box, we tell them it's wrong. They've gotta be tough and they've gotta be mean and they've gotta have muscles. It's this whole paradigm of what it means to be a man in a box. My mom was very instrumental in how to be a man outside of that box," Curry said.

I thought about all the boys, parents, teachers, pastors, who had told me about the teenage boys they knew who found themselves outside of the box. How in their loneliness they created identities elsewhere, identities often rooted in escapism or depression or hatred. I imagined taking the anger and shame and regret we all felt in our inability to reach these lost, young boys and men—and instead of turning that anger inward and locking ourselves in a spiral of shame, or turning it outward toward people we considered to be unlike ourselves, what if we took all that rage and used it to smash the box?

CHAPTER 2

White Christian Men
Archetype and Reality

When I arrived at the Citadel, the Military College of South Carolina, in late autumn 2023, I don't think I'd ever seen an American fortress quite like this one. The buildings were impossibly white, shimmering in the late-afternoon sunlight on homecoming weekend, while alumni and their wives (the alumni were still overwhelmingly white and male at this point) milled around the lawn, pointing out landmarks and reminiscing about weapons and cannons and drill and yelling and pranks and camaraderie.

Most of those who had returned today were older now: they looked to be baby boomers in their 60s, 70s, and 80s, with gray hair, walking slower than they once had in early-morning required jaunts around the campus. Some had canes and thick glasses.

Some of them must have been around when Charles Foster, then seventeen years old, became the first Black cadet to enter the campus, in 1966.[1] The school had asked the media not to publicize his entry, but still, white cadets would often shout racial epithets at Foster when he walked from class to class across the grassy, picturesque quad flanked by military symbols and statues.[2] Once a group of cadets charged at him wearing white sheets and evoking the Klan. Somehow, Foster endured, and he graduated four years later.[3]

I reckon most of these men, in their Citadel hats and trousers, were also long gone by 1994, when Shannon Faulkner became the first woman to enter the Citadel cadet corps. Faulkner had first entered two years earlier, when she was only allowed to attend classes as a civilian student, exiting campus by the time retreat was played each day.[4] She couldn't enter the barracks or wear the cadet uniform.[5] It was only after a lawsuit, based on the Citadel's status as a school receiving public funding, that Faulkner officially matriculated with her class in August 1995. Much to her male classmates' overall delight, she dropped out at the end of Hell Week, citing psychological and emotional abuse and physical exhaustion.[6] Twenty-nine other cadets dropped out at the end of that week, but Faulkner's departure was the only one that ignited on-campus celebrations.[7]

Five years later, future South Carolina congresswoman Nancy Mace challenged Faulkner's allegations about the climate for women at the Citadel, becoming the first female cadet corps graduate in 1999.

A lot has changed at the Citadel since many of these men attended. But change happens slowly at the Citadel, and at places like it all over America. Its buildings are a stalwart monument to constancy and tradition, rather than to progress. Thus, according to the most recent statistics, the Citadel's undergraduate student body in the 2022–23 school year was 88 percent male and 77 percent white,[8] which is slightly more than the white population of Charleston, at 72 percent,[9] and slightly more than the white population of South Carolina, at 69 percent.[10] Charleston County, meanwhile, is 52 percent female.

I came to Charleston and to the Citadel in particular because here was a place uniquely suited to identify and demonstrate a particular kind of white male American identity, an identity rooted in history and tradition and militarism and, yes, to some extent the Confederacy and white supremacy.

In 1842, South Carolina was home to more enslaved people than any other place in the United States. One hundred years before that, two-thirds of the colony's population was Black. Like in apartheid South Africa, or in feudal Europe, the oppressed far outnumbered their oppressors. The Citadel was born out of this race-based fear, tracing its origins to an arsenal constructed in response to Denmark Vesey's rebellion against white slaveowners in 1822.[11]

The posh reputation of Charleston, made famous by Bravo's reality TV show *Southern Charm*, was enabled only by the entrenchment of a closely guarded white male supremacy, and the wealth that went along with it, on the backs of Black people's labor, and "prettied-up" by white Southern belles who often attended the College of Charleston, still reputed to turn away prospective freshman who aren't feminine enough, or so I was told by a number of longtime Charleston residents.

To visit the Citadel today is to experience so much beauty alongside so much ugliness—a history marred by violence and civil war, the acrimonious end of a state flag that glorified the Confederacy, the tearing down of the statue of notorious slavery defender John C. Calhoun, whose name still graces the boulevard that's home to Mother Emanuel African Methodist Episcopal Church, the home of Clementa C. Pinckney and Brother Lee Bennett, whom we met in the last chapter.

I came here because in order to understand white Christian boys in America, in order to understand what's happening today to the white boys and young men in our lives, many of whom we love dearly, we have to understand the roots of the identity they've inherited, what it means and has meant to be a white Christian man in America. You can see much of that right here, as the cannons fire and the buglers play taps as the sun sets, casting a hazy orangey glow over the military parade.

I hadn't planned on watching the parades that Friday November night in Charleston. I had only the day before learned that I would gain access to the Citadel, to have a chance to interview one of its cadets. I knew a bit about the vaunted military college, but I didn't know that the cadets' time was so closely guarded that my only chance to gain access was to talk with the cadet on campus, and for him to have special permission to do so from one of the campus's sanctioned outside denominational ministers, who had worn his collar for official effect.

I came in as a whirlwind, all sweat and frenzy, gliding my rented Nissan Altima into the only available parking spot off the quad, something the campus pastor called "a miracle." I was instantly humbled when I learned that Connor[12] was talking with me at the risk of getting in trouble for missing the drill and parade. He had an openness to share with me that maybe I hadn't expected from a cadet at the Citadel. But there we were, in the campus Chick-fil-A where I later learned that freshman (known as "knobs" at the Citadel) weren't ever allowed to set foot, and so I had better take my chance to learn all I could.

If you close your eyes and imagine a stereotypical portrait of a Citadel cadet, a Southern young man at a military college, I bet you'd summon up something like Connor in your mind. He had sandy blond hair, long enough to blow up in the Atlantic breeze, but short enough to suit his omnipresent military uniform, with his last name imprinted on the pocket. Connor came to the Citadel from the small town of Irmo, population just under 12,000, located about a fifteen-minute drive from the state capital of Columbia, and about a two-hour drive west of Charleston. Irmo, ironically, is also where Dylann Roof, a Columbia native, briefly worked for a pest control company in the years around when he became radicalized as a white supremacist.

Irmo is both much less wealthy and much more diverse than the Citadel. Its population, as of the 2020 Census, was more than 30 percent Black, with a median income for males of about $41,000, and about $30,000 for females.

Still, Connor found ample Citadel connections in Irmo, and he saw it as a way out and also a way to harness his wandering brain. He said he'd been diagnosed with attention-deficit disorder as a young kid, like 13 percent of American boys aged three to seventeen.[13,14] Structure was necessary for him.

"Without structure," Connor said, "I have very little incentive to get things done. I do very good when I'm physically active. The Citadel does a very good job of keeping you physically active."

That's likely an understatement. Connor told me about a highly regimented life, one that led him to consider, at times, leaving the school during his "knob" year, when he was subjected to lots of yelling, commands, and occasional humiliation, which he tended to refer to euphemistically as "catching grief." He told me about the highly complex and detailed system of punishments, also called "demerits." These could lead to consequences like confinement, or basically an hour of detention, or tours, consisting of a monotonous hour of walking back and forth across the quad holding a rifle. More demerits and punishments—incurred, for instance, for an alcohol violation—could lead to a battalion transfer, meaning the cadet would have to pack up all of their belongings and move to a new battalion, likely being screamed at and mocked most of the way.

Early on in our conversation, I kept wondering why Connor, a good student and well-spoken, would want to subject himself to such a college experience. I told him the Citadel sounded like a fraternity, except with all of the hazing and none of the parties. But I learned as we kept talking that it was a little bit more complicated than that. It seemed, if you could survive the hazing, that there *were* parties to be had at the Citadel, if only you followed the unwritten rules and codes of conduct, like drinking only off-campus, and making sure not to get your girlfriend pregnant, in a state where abortion was officially outlawed beginning at six weeks, before many women even know they're pregnant, in 2023.

Following unwritten rules at the Citadel seems complicated, especially if you're a woman or a person of color. Connor went out of his way to reiterate and point out to me all of the battalion leaders and prominent cadets who were women and/or people of color. He was proud of the progressive changes the Citadel had made, and his girlfriend was also a Citadel cadet. Still, he admitted that sometimes the white male students had talked about the lower physical standards for women, based on biology, and he acknowledged that he was frustrated by the outside world's perception of the Citadel as a racist place.

Just that past January 2023, *Post and Courier* reporter Hillary Flynn had written an article with this headline: "Citadel Cadets, Faculty Say There's Pervasive Racism at the School." The article begins in this way: "A Citadel cadet on cleaning duty was going through the school's closets when he discovered a snowman statue. Its face was painted black, and a chain was drawn around its neck. Six cadets, all White, had signed their names on its bottom."[15]

The cadet who found the statue was Jeremy Walker, someone Connor had mentioned to me as a mentor of his and a leader at the school. Walker, who is Black, is a company commander at the Citadel. He told the *Post and Courier* that he had been the only person of color at the meeting to determine the six cadets' punishment, and while he'd advocated for a harsher sentence, at a school known for intense discipline, the offending cadets received only community service and a requirement to attend a diversity training workshop. In the *Post and Courier's* ten-month long investigation, it found, among other things, the following:

- After a Black female cadet was named a company commander in spring 2021, a recording circulated of a classmate calling her the n-word.

- During the 2021–22 school year, a cadet took a picture of a portrait of The Citadel's first two Black graduates getting displayed in the school's library. He posted the picture to social media. "They're hanging these (n-words). This is my school," the caption read.
- In fall 2020, several Black cadets witnessed a White classmate sing "Dixie" in front of a group during a holiday gathering.
- In January 2020, a Black cadet emailed a professor about issues he had concerning the tone of a class discussion about the welfare state. The professor linked it to higher divorce rates and poverty in Black communities. In the email, the cadet wrote that one of his classmates said, "I think that the welfare state should be compared to why you shouldn't feed wild animals; they'll just keep coming back for more."
- In 2018, a Black cadet reported that an assistant football coach twice referred to him using the word monkey. He used terms similar to "you play like a lost monkey" and "you run around the field like a lost monkey."[16]

All of these aforementioned incidents cited by the *Post and Courier* had taken place since 2018, without any of the participants being expelled or fired. The rest of the article details an ignominious history of racist and violent activity at the Citadel directed especially against Black cadets, and a culture of administrative impunity when it comes to punishing those incidents or even acknowledging their racist origins. Walker and the other Black cadets mentioned in the story, like fellow company commander Alicia Roberts, represent some of the school's proudest success stories of recent years. But what did they have to endure to survive in that environment?

That's why I wanted my study of young, white Christian men and boys in America to begin right here. For generations, white Americans have striven to defend and protect institutions, like the Citadel, obviously complicit in racism and misogyny, even as those same institutions might take small, halting steps toward equity and racial justice. The white myth of the Citadel, however, is much weaker and more dangerous than those stately, white, castle-like walls that encircle the picturesque campus, set in the heart of one of white America's most popular cities for tourism.

We have long known that the myth of white Christian masculinity, rooted in hatred and violence and privilege and white supremacy, has done irreparable damage to women and to people of color and religious minorities in America. But we can't move forward in this study until we understand why this same myth is also harming the young white men and boys it claims to exalt.

The Performance of Strength and the Presence of Weakness

The Citadel is not a Christian institution, but the tradition of white masculine identity it has long upheld owes much to white conservative American Christianity, particularly as it is preached in the South. Connor, who left his public high school to be homeschooled his junior and senior years, went three times a week to a resource center that was Christian-based, an increasingly common practice in America, where homeschoolers are often taught from online curriculum rooted in right-wing Christian ideology.[17] At the Citadel, Connor attends chapel three times a week in the mornings from 8:00 to 8:45 a.m., and when he was growing up, one of the primary examples he had of what it means to be a man was his pastor, former South Carolina Senate candidate Det Bowers.

Bowers, who sports the close-cropped white hair, broad smile, and lively gray-blue eyes made famous by many a Southern political and/or pastoral scion, made his fortune as a lawyer for timber companies before pastoring Christ Church of the Carolinas, where Connor attended with his family growing up. The church has since been renamed and is now part of the conservative Presbyterian Church in America. It "pretty much fell apart when [Bowers] left," Connor told me. His eyes still light up when Connor talks about listening to Bowers preach: "No one else preaches like that," Connor said. "He's very well-spoken. A strong man."

Bowers left the pulpit in 2012, two years before he would challenge Sen. Lindsey Graham (R-SC) in the Republican Senate primary, when Connor was just ten years old. Bowers ran as a Christian conservative, to the right, especially on social issues, of Graham, a longtime bachelor. Early in his campaign, *Politico* suggested that Bowers could force Graham into a runoff, holding him to less than 50 percent of the vote in the Republican primary.[18] Bowers had raised more than $800,000 by April 2014, and *Red State* conservative website founder Erick Erickson called him Graham's strongest challenger.[19] But that same *Politico* article unearthed a sermon from Bowers, likely preached in either 2005 or 2011, that blamed women for divorces even in cases where their husbands cheated on them.[20]

"And yet, I find that in about 95 percent of broken marriages, though the husband's the one that ran out on his wife, the wife loves her children more than she does her husband," Bowers said in an audio recording obtained by *Politico*. "That is an abominable idolatry."

Bowers added, his voice rising: "Do you hear me ladies? It is an abominable idolatry to love your children more than you love your husband, and it will ruin your marriage. And yet you blame it on him because he ran off with some other woman! He did run off with some other woman, and you packed his bags. All of his emotional bags, you packed for him. Is that true in every case? No, but it's true in the vast preponderance of them."[21]

As I sat there with Connor, at the Chick-fil-A on the Citadel campus, I found it hard to believe that this soft-spoken, even gentle, and friendly young man would have been seduced by such harsh and facile rhetoric. Imagine the consequences of a woman subjected to this sort of marital counseling, in a case where her husband was abusing her and/or the children? Such a "sermon" is much more well-suited to a defense of a patriarchal society than it is a faithful representation of the Gospel of Jesus, who said this of those who would harm children: "If any of you put a stumbling block before one of these little ones who believe in me, it would be better for you if a great millstone were fastened around your neck and you were drowned in the depth of the sea. Woe to the world because of stumbling blocks! Occasions for stumbling are bound to come, but woe to the one by whom the stumbling block comes!"[22]

One of Connor's Presbyterian campus pastors at the Citadel told me he thinks that today Connor would likely be able to point out some of the more troubling aspects of Bowers's theology. But he also knows that pastors like Bowers are attractive to many of the white, Christian teenage boys who come to places like the Citadel. As a pastor and political candidate, Bowers presented himself as totally self-assured, successful, and certain above all else. For boys growing up in an ever-shifting world, with a twenty-four-hour news cycle, evolving understandings of gender and sexuality and race, and in the midst of a global pandemic, you can see how someone offering certainty might seem compelling, like a life raft in the midst of a swirling sea.

But too often, what conservative Christianity offers to these young white men and boys is only an external source of strength to cling onto, when what they really need is to cultivate something solid and strong within themselves. It is that internal place, a place where the Holy Spirit, too, might dwell, to which these boys must go when tragedy and struggle strike close to home, and a simple presentation or appearance of strength is not enough to help them endure.

Connor had become an expert in physical strength and endurance by his second year at the Citadel, and he had honed his sense of discipline and responsibility. He was doing well. Making it. He was even dating a female cadet, and he had close friendships and relationships with many of the campus's most prominent leaders. He was also developing a closer relationship with the campus Presbyterian pastor and her spouse, the two of whom offered a much different vision of Christianity than Bowers did.

"The system that [the Citadel] uses definitely works," Connor said. "It's difficult for me personally. I'm a soft-spoken guy. I don't raise my voice all that much. I don't fit into the mold of the tough-as-nails, yelling-all-the-time, hard-cut kind of guy. Not everybody is going to fit that stereotype. I respond when people say they're disappointed in me."

Connor said his dad was "a yeller," and as a young teenager, he too struggled with his temper.

"I saw that my temper was affecting other people," he said. So he changed.

And what's interesting—and affirming about the Citadel's future—is that Connor has found a place for himself there, even as he says that maybe he learned more about how to communicate from his mom and two younger sisters, who shaped his emotional core. Connor says the platoon leader he looks up to most is "the soft-spoken, gentle type," though "he's very capable of raising his voice."

I asked Connor about how the Citadel's rough and tumble disciplinary reputation handled a generation, Gen Z, known for its emphasis on mental health and for talking openly about anxiety and depression. Connor, like most boys of his generation, was comfortable talking about mental health. He immediately thought of a fellow cadet who'd been struggling with depression, and racked up hundreds of confinements, demerits, and punishments in general. The student ended up leaving the Citadel for a while, and Connor said he was able to get most of his punishments "wiped," as well as getting counseling and therapy. He said the school encourages kids to go to mental health counseling and therapy, but "the problem with any medical thing here is finding the time to do it." The cadets' days begin at 5:30 a.m., and there's not much free time allotted, thus the reason for us meeting in the afternoon on a Friday at Chick-fil-A, and only in the presence of a sanctioned campus pastor, who told me it was only recently that the Citadel had made space in its schedule for cadets to participate in religious activities.

Connor shared widely with me about life at the Citadel in 2023, touching topics like birth control, drinking, drugs, and LGBTQ cadets. He seemed so full of life and promise and hope, with a contagious joy for life. He was so excited for me to see the cadets on parade in just a few minutes. But just before the interview ended, as we talked about mental health, drugs, violence, suicide, and navigating life as a young white man in America, Connor took a deep breath and told me that even though he seemed to have things figured out, "It's still stressful for me."

He'd recently gone back home to Irmo the weekend before, where his friend and former football teammate had died from a fentanyl overdose. We'd been talking about how we all knew those young white boys and men who didn't really find their niche, and they started slipping through the cracks and finding unhealthy places in which to root their identities, whether it was white supremacist websites and groups, or drugs and alcohol, or both.

Connor's friend had stayed back in Irmo while the rest of his high school football teammates went off to college, and "his accountability with us left," Connor said.[23] The friends' parents had gone out of the country, and he overdosed alone.

"Our coaches knew that he was struggling, and they tried to check in with him," Connor said. "His parents had recently kicked him out of the house . . . when you're our age, you think you'll never die. This was a serious wake-up call."

Connor's friend's story is an all-too-common one among distressed and isolated young white boys and men. The violent outbursts they're accustomed to hearing from men in their lives, combined with the societal pressure to stifle all emotion, often ends in one of two ways: with violence directed outward, in mass shootings or domestic violence; or inward, ending in suicides and overdoses and accidents. We'll cover these statistics and national trends in greater detail in chapter five, including the ways that American leaders have discussed both the problems and needs of young white boys and men, to help them prevent violence against others or themselves, at a time when nearly all mass shooters are men,[24] more than half of them white,[25] and 70 percent of suicides involve white, middle-aged men,[26] while two-thirds of mass shootings can be linked to domestic violence.[27]

Connor said he didn't feel like he was wound up tight at the Citadel, going through the motions and responsibilities of each day, hanging out with friends and his girlfriend, making it through to get that coveted Citadel ring—which he hoped would be his ticket to fruitful postgraduation employment. But when he came home that past weekend, and he confronted the death of his friend, Connor felt it all bubble up.

"I sat there, and I cried. I must have cried for an hour and a half," he said, shaking his head. "I never thought crying makes you weak, even though I know a lot of people think that. But it was definitely kind of difficult to break down. I had to break a stigma I didn't even know I had."

As I heard Connor talk, I thought of the white boys and men I've known and loved in my own life: my husband, my brother, my dad, my grandpas, my father-in-law and brothers-in-law, friends and professional athletes and fellow pastors and journalists. Nearly all of them were ashamed to cry, and rarely ever did. I saw again in Connor that duality that is a hallmark of this generation of young, white American Christian boys and men: the young boy who sat in rapt attention to listen to Det Bowers denigrate women, was this same nineteen-year-old baring his soul before me today, admitting that he felt OK to express his emotions, because his mom and sisters had helped him do so. In that, I saw hope—and progress. Maybe Connor could realize that what had seemed to him before like weakness—i.e., expressing emotion and love for a friend—was actually strength, something that enabled him to form bonds with those he loved, and carry himself through tough times and heartbreaking loss. Maybe he could even connect that expression of grief with a Savior who had wept at the death of his friend.[28]

But we were still at the Citadel, and this is still America. As I shoved in a few last waffle fries and pushed in my black metal chair, I noticed something unique about the backs of the chairs at this particular Chick-fil-A. Their metal backs formed the distinct pattern of a rifle on each one. We were surrounded by guns.

I mentioned it to Connor, and he said, yes, rifles were "everywhere" at the Citadel, including in their rooms, even when cadets were struggling with depression. But he and the campus pastor exchanged a quick, knowing glance.

"They're toys," the pastor said, quietly.

"They don't have firing pins," Connor clarified. "Possession of any live ammo or paraphernalia on campus is an expellable offense. It's punishable by law. You'll get arrested."

"There's no way to make those rifles shoot," he continued. "It's so strict that even looking up the word 'firing pin,' gets you in big trouble."

Then we walked outside, toward the sun-dappled quad, as the orange sun sank over glorious, historic, tortured, secessionist, ritzy, tragic, sinful, beautiful Charleston. Connor pointed out all his friends, all the platoon leaders and notable people on campus, making sure I knew that many of them were not white men. We stood underneath magnolia trees, Spanish moss flapping in the breeze, our hands on our hearts, and we listened to the "Star-Spangled Banner."

I thought about all the rules at the Citadel, the ones that were written, which were maybe easy enough to follow if you didn't count physical and mental exhaustion, and the ones that were unwritten, which were much harder to follow when no one told you what they were. I noted that our society is most often most perniciously structured by unwritten rules, that things like sexism and racism and homophobia and stifling gender roles can be defended and upheld best by unwritten rules, which can't be litigated against or prosecuted as hate crimes. It's unwritten rules that have structured this false sense of white Christian male supremacy in America, created a particular type of man who can scream but not weep, who can hit but not knit, who is easily threatened but too insecure to admit he is wrong.

Unwritten rules are being rewritten in America right now, especially when it comes to gender roles and religion. That's a good thing. And still you see how young, white Christian men and boys get lost sometimes in the miasma. They understand in their souls, and they've been taught by various mentors in their lives, that this idea of masculinity as strong and unyielding and harsh, lording yourself over everyone else, is not all it's cracked up to be. They long to replace it with something more complicated and understanding, something that allows them to nurture and be nurtured, in the same way they longed to be held as tiny little babies. But in this transition period, from one kind of masculinity into another, healthier form, many young white boys and men are being lost. Somewhere along the line, they never got that permission to feel, to nurture, and to be nurtured. And so they seek acceptance and strength often in ever-increasingly stereotypical masculine forms and outlets, like incel forums online, or street gangs of neo-Nazis, or white supremacist groups, or Trump rallies, Evangelical megachurches, and Turning Point USA conferences. They grow angrier and angrier. They turn to drugs and alcohol, and hate. They choose to lash out, to hurt, to kill, and they are enabled to do so by an American governmental system held captive to the destructive and seductive power of the gun, by politicians who exploit the idea of white masculine superiority in order to win votes and fundraising dollars.

And sometimes, like in 2015, just three miles away from the Citadel, down Rutledge Avenue to Calhoun Street in Charleston, at one of the nation's most historic and long-standing Black churches, unlike the toy rifles at the Citadel, the assault rifles these young, white Christian men carry, into battles they've made in their minds, are all too capable of firing. Even if we wish it weren't true of the boys and men we know and love—or you are yourself—it's clear that young white men in America are capable of terrible violence.

Chapter 3

Created in ~~His~~ God's Image?

So God created humankind in his image,
in the image of God he created them;
male and female he created them.
—Genesis 1:27

For now we see in a mirror, dimly, but then we will see face to face.
—1 Corinthians 13:12

Many white American Christians are pretty sure they know what God looks like. Most of us won't really say it explicitly, of course: that would invite critique and the possibility that one of our most closely held but unexamined truths could be exposed as false. But most of us heard growing up that we were created in God's image. On first read, maybe you'd think that means we're taught that we look like God. But "no one has ever seen God,"[1] so when you learn that you're created in God's image—as most young, white Christian boys and men have learned—then it makes sense that you think, "God must look like me."

The Genesis verse above is taken from the first chapter of the first creation story in the book of Genesis, where God takes six days to create the world, and on the seventh day, God rests. Did you know there were two separate creation stories in the Bible? Written by two different faith groups, at two different times?

Genesis 2 is the second creation story, likely chronologically written and told orally prior to the Genesis 1 creation story. Genesis 2 is the more fabulistic, involving Adam and Eve as the first created humans, a serpent, and a tree of life. While most Sunday school kids (and adults in general) can tell you that the Bible teaches that the world was created in six days and God rested on the seventh, it is the Genesis 2 creation story that seems to carry more moralistic weight when it comes to our conceptions of who God is.

That's important for our understanding of what's happening among young, white Christian boys and men—because the Genesis 2 creation story is at the heart of many of the gendered identifications of God, and, further, most of the understanding of God's masculinity as a model for boys and young men to follow. It starts with Adam.

Of course, in biblical Hebrew, "Adam" is not so much a name as it is a signifier of humanity. The Hebrew word אָדָם ('ādām) is the same word the Bible uses for "human" in both creation stories. It is not used as a proper name—i.e., Adam—until Gen 4:25. Until then, the word אָדָם ('ādām) is clearly a gender-neutral term, meant to refer to either men or women, much as older versions of English formerly used the term "men" to refer to mixed-gender groups, or "mankind" to refer to humankind.

Perhaps the fact that the Bible uses "Adam" to refer to all mankind is a signal that the Bible can tend to confer a higher form of humanity on men than it does women. But is that intrinsically what the Bible does? Or is that modern readers reading our own gender norms and preferences and hierarchies into the Bible? The stakes for our answer to that question are high when it comes to how young, white Christian men and boys understand themselves. After all, they have been created in the image of God. If that God is thought to be an angry, violent man—then boys and young men will comport themselves in order to fit that image. Our answer to that question also has high stakes when it comes to politics and social order. As Kaitlyn Schiess writes in her book on politics and the Bible, referencing another part of Genesis often used to create social hierarchies: "Just as the curse of Ham fit neatly into Southern culture and racist ideology, other Bible verses fit into a theology that sharply divided spiritual freedom for all Christians and the kind of political liberty that was reserved for white men."[2]

The late twentieth century was rife with white, male Christian leaders who wanted to capitalize (and make money) off of the idea that men, in the image of a manly God, were *created* to be angry, violent, and *in control*. Pastors and writers like Mark Driscoll and John Piper wrote lengthy chapters and books devoted to the Apostle Paul's supposed affirmation of male headship (which we'll cover in the next chapter), and to the entire movement of complementarianism, or the idea that men and women are prescribed different and distinct roles, with men always in positions of headship and women in positions of support. Complementarians, therefore, do not allow women to preach or serve as lead pastors, to teach men, or to serve on elders boards or church councils.

Piper is one of the foremost proponents of complementarianism and of a specifically masculine view of God. In his 1986 book, *Desiring God*, he begins his chapter on marriage by citing "The Old Testament Context," writing that "[a]ccording to Genesis 2, God created Adam first and put him in the garden alone. Then the Lord said, 'It is not good that the man should be alone; I will make him a helper fit for him.'"[3] Here Piper cites verse 18 of Genesis 2 as though it is definitively speaking of male and female roles. But as I mentioned above, the word אָדָם ('ādām) is used interchangeably to refer to human beings in the creation story. Genesis 2:18 is about the human's need for connection and partnership, not for a subordinate woman, for neither is the word helper עֵזֶר (ay'-zer) here referring to Eve directly. Instead, God initially creates animals to be partners to the first human, and it's not until verse 22 that God takes a rib from the first human to create the second, opposite human—or אִשָּׁה (ishshah) (woman).

As I read through these passages again in the original biblical Hebrew, I am struck by their desire for beauty and symmetry. Isn't it tragic that we have taken a story about love, connection, reciprocity, and perfectly created goodness in the image of God—and used that same story to support subjugation, abuse, hierarchy, and even violent war?

Indeed, Piper goes on in this section to use the creation story in Genesis 2 to rail against homosexuality, a concept that would have been utterly foreign to the biblical writers of Genesis, even linking in a later version of his book to his website, *Desiring God*, and a document where he explains why homosexuality is a sin—again, not irrelevant to understanding how young, white Christian men and boys are socialized in the church to define themselves primarily by their own sexuality, virility, and prominence—dating all the way back to the creation story.[4]

Piper concludes about women: "In other words, in the beginning God took woman out of man as bone of his bone and flesh of his flesh, and then God presented her back to the man to discover in living fellowship what it means to be one flesh."[5]

As a woman and a mother reading these words, I can't help but feel the paltriness of the complementarian version of my own creation story. And thinking back to the birth of my own sons, and the visceral experience I had of carrying them within my own womb, my own gift as a vessel of God's very creation, I find it ironic that Piper is so determined to make women secondary in creation's story—when it is women (as mothers) who are in fact essential to the ongoing work of God's creation, much more so than men, and that is the way God designed it to be.

One of Piper's most prolific acolytes and adherents, who got his start partially by blogging on Piper's *Desiring God* site, was Seattle pastor Mark Driscoll, who would popularize a masculine Christianity specifically aimed at young (white) Christian men. While Driscoll would later leave his megachurch Mars Hill after scandals around plagiarism in his books and financial misconduct, as well as inappropriate treatment of colleagues and church members, his legacy lives on in American Christianity. Driscoll brought increasingly uncouth language and frank talk about sex, specifically, that women should be constantly available sexually to their husbands and refrain from working outside the home, to mainstream American Christian dialogue. Along with many Evangelical megachurch pastors of the early 2000s and 2010s, Driscoll helped to popularize the "smoking-hot wife" ideal in his sermons and persuaded young men and boys that to follow Jesus meant being a warrior, not a meek peacemaker who would turn the other cheek.

Driscoll, too, leaned on Genesis 2 to support his belief in complementarianism and extreme male headship. In his book, *Real Marriage*, Driscoll references Genesis 2 to explain why men have authority over their wives:

1. God called the race "man" (Gen. 1:26) and "mankind" (Gen. 5:2).

2. By naming Eve, Adam was exercising authority over her as God commanded (Gen. 2:23).
3. Although the woman sinned first, God came calling for the man (Gen. 3:8–9) and held him responsible because he failed to lovingly lead and protect his family from Satan and sin . . .[6]

Whoa. Let's look at those claims a bit more carefully. As we've previously noted, the use of the word אָדָם ('āḏām) to refer to the first created human does not seem designed to give us some big lesson about gender inequality or male headship. It's just an antiquated convention in the same way that we don't usually say "mankind" anymore. Just because Nat King Cole sang, "Peace on the earth, good will to men," in the Christmas hymn, "It Came Upon a Midnight Clear," does not mean Nat King Cole wanted to make a statement about *only good will to men*! It just means that people used to use masculine plural pronouns to refer to all of humankind. The same is true of the Bible and of the biblical Hebrew used within it.

Secondly, Driscoll's claim that Adam is "exercising authority over [Eve] as God commanded" is breathless in its audacity (but unsurprising if you've ever heard Driscoll preach, I suppose). Nowhere does God "command" the first human to "exercise authority" over the second. When I named my children, I did not think of it as "exercising authority over them." Instead, throughout the Bible, naming is a spiritual and loving act of mutuality. God was not exercising authority over Jacob when he was renamed "Israel";[7] instead, God was making a connection and a promise to recognize a new relationship with Jacob and with Jacob's family. The same is true when Abram became Abraham, or Sarai became Sarah. Or when Saul became Paul. Nowhere else in the Bible is naming seen as an act of exercising authority and dominance. In fact, in Luke 2, Jesus himself is given a name in a naming ceremony at the same time as his circumcision, according to Jewish tradition. Names throughout the Bible have great meaning. The act of naming another is an act of love and connection, prioritizing relationship and not control.

I will not dwell at length on Driscoll's third claim; I will only note that white male pastors of his ilk love to emphasize that Eve, the woman, sinned first. They will make this claim alongside claims that women are fundamentally sneaky and constantly trying to dupe unthinking, doltish men into sin. This line of thinking is a key element of purity culture, which requires women to carefully monitor their appearance, clothing, and actions in order not to "lead men into sexual sin." Thus, you begin to see the double-bind women face in this reading of the Bible: both immensely powerful and, at the same time, denied any authority or mutuality in relationships with men.

But if this kind of teaching about creational gender roles disempowers, confuses, and even abuses women—what does it do to young men and boys? Told again and again that they are the dominant sex, created to rule over and have dominion over not just women but the earth, the land, its animals, and all things on earth—it's often a rude awakening for young, white Christian men when they enter the world and find that most created things are not interested in being ruled over by them. At the same time, these young men and boys have not been given the tools (which can be found in the creation story, too!) for building mutual relationships that are bound together not by control, authority or obligation but instead by love and respect.

Absent those tools, young, white Christian men and boys instead often cast about for role models who fit the image of God they've been taught about: a strong and violent masculine man who rules over everything in his presence. Many young, white Christian men and boys saw that image in Donald Trump, who spared no words talking about his own proclivity to grab women "by the pussy" and take whatever he wanted from them. Trump's boorish comments may not have been what Piper, the proper theologian, had in mind, but they follow naturally from a theological model that privileges a gender hierarchy above all else and creates an image of God as power-hungry and dominating, particularly when it comes to women.

You can also see echoes of this failed creational theology in the "incel" movement, where young (often white, often Christian) men band together on the internet to lament their status as "involuntarily celibate." You can see why it may have come as a shock to these young men when women did not simply make themselves available sexually to them, because that kind of constant availability, absent any kind of emotional connection or intimacy, is exactly what pastors and authors like Driscoll prescribe. Tragically, two years after Driscoll published *Real Marriage*, a twenty-two-year-old shooter killed six people and injured fourteen others by gunshot, stabbing, and by ramming his vehicle into them near the campus of the University of California, Santa Barbara. The shooter, Elliot Rodger, was a part of the incel community, and had uploaded a video to YouTube that stated he was declaring "war on women" and emailing a manifesto to his therapist—which "detail[ed] his hatred for women and white supremacist beliefs that intertwined to fuel a sense of entitlement and rage."[8] Since the Isla Vista shooting, incel communities have continued to grow. The Southern Poverty Law Center documented one popular online forum with a growth of 4,000 new members in 2022 alone.[9] Additionally, the SPLC notes that more than one hundred people have been killed or injured in the name of incel ideology since the Isla Vista shootings, and that "the Isla Vista shooter's violence continues to be celebrated, and he is glorified by this community as a saint and a hero."[10]

In *Jesus and John Wayne*, Kristin Kobes Du Mez documents the troubling spread of militant masculine Christianity across American power structures in the church and government. Du Mez shows how the ideology was pushed forward by writers and policymakers throughout American history, including women like writer Elisabeth Elliot, who likewise used creation theology to claim that "God created male and female as complementary opposites," and that "the very notion of hierarchy came from the Bible," and equality was "not a Christian ideal."[11] And while many of the Christian leaders in Du Mez's book made money and garnered power from their support of this image of God, thousands more young, white Christian men and boys found themselves adrift when this image of God did not comport with their own images staring back at them in the mirror. They had been told that this was who they were created to be, but the world did not reflect the same godly image back at them.

Incel communities and online forums that stoke their senses of rage and resentment are one option for young boys and men who find themselves at odds with their own identities and how they match the image of God they've been taught in their churches and by Christian culture at large. White supremacist groups or far-right political movements offer another option. But none of those groups seem likely to offer lasting relationships, especially for men who are looking for life-long marriages and partnerships to women, or perhaps looking to be parents raising children together. There is a "still more excellent way," as Paul writes in 1 Corinthians 12:31. Maybe the way to help with young, white Christian men and boys' troubled self-images is to change the way they see the image of God.

It's instructive to look back at some of the initial writing, ideas, and books aimed at young men from the '90s and early aughts. When I was in high school and college, all the girls my age were encouraged to give our brothers and boyfriends one book, John Eldredge's *Wild at Heart*, published in 2001. According to Religion News Service, as of 2016, the book had sold more than four million copies.[12] *Wild at Heart* depicts men as one-dimensional warriors whose highest desires are a "battle to fight," "an adventure to live," and "a beauty to rescue."[13] Women are thereby reduced to damsels in distress, valued primarily for their physical beauty and with little agency of their own. Interestingly, Eldredge had served as a Christian counselor at Focus on the Family, not exactly the kind of ninja-warrior, manly background now prioritized by many right-wing leaders who would speak to young, white Christian men and boys. And to present-day readers, Eldredge's language sounds relatively tame. Early in the book, he even warns: "Now, let me make one thing clear: I am not advocating a sort of 'macho man' image."[14] Shortly after that, he writes: "Now, none of this is to diminish the fact that a woman bears God's image as well . . . there is also something wild in the heart of a woman . . ."[15] But this softer language belies a traditionalist view on gender as fundamental, and masculinity and femininity as diametrically opposed to one another. Even as Eldredge writes of God's desire to be loved, of God's humility and vulnerability, the book ends up serving as a lynchpin of the kind of literature that will continue to target young, white Christian men and boys—assuming that to reach or target them, rhetoric must appeal to traditional masculinity as an element of the image of God.

In Driscoll's *Who Do You Think You Are?* he grounds the question of identity again in Genesis 1:27, in our understanding of the image of God: "The world's fundamental problem is that we don't understand who we truly are—children of God made in [God's] image—and instead define ourselves by any number of things other than Jesus. Only by knowing our false identity apart from Christ in relation to our *true* identity in him can we rightly deal with and overcome the issues in our lives."[16]

The problem for Driscoll is that he, and other Christian leaders of the present day, go on to ground and depict the image of God incorrectly, reflecting instead a self-adulating and false idea of glorified, violent, and militant masculinity. The God of the Bible is quite different.

Theologians and sexual abuse survivors Grace Ji-Sun Kim and Susan M. Shaw write about this God in their 2024 book *Surviving God*. While they lament the use of rape throughout the Bible to subjugate women and justify the hierarchical authority of heterosexual men, Kim and Shaw also explain how "neither story of creation in Genesis 1 or 2 assumes or mandates women's subordination."[17]

"In fact, these stories depict a rather egalitarian relationship in the Garden of Eden," Kim and Shaw write. "Only through the Fall does patriarchal dominance become a feature of human relationships; God does not issue male dominance as a punishment. Rather, dominance begins because the actions of the story rupture trust and rupture the egalitarian relationship between the woman and man that God had intended."[18]

Similarly, in her groundbreaking book *The Making of Biblical Womanhood*, Baptist historian Beth Allison Barr refutes the theory that the creation story prescribes the subjugation of women and the upholding of complementarianism in the church and society. Instead, she says, Christian patriarchy is not the image of God but instead the image of patriarchal society, betraying a command that Christians are not to be "of this world,"[19] but instead to offer a vision of a more equal, more benevolent, more loving world, a "foretaste of the feast to come."[20]

"What if patriarchy isn't divinely ordained but is a result of human sin?" Barr writes. "What if instead of being divinely created, patriarchy slithered into creation only after the fall? What if the reason that the fruit of patriarchy is so corrupt, even within the Christian church, is because patriarchy has always been a corrupted system? Instead of assuming that patriarchy is instituted by God, we must ask whether patriarchy is a product of human hands."[21]

Young, white Christian boys and men have been sold an image of God, the Creator, that is wholly false and rooted not in heaven but on earth, in the hands of desperate and insecure Christian male leaders who are grasping at power, influence, and wealth. Our boys need to understand who they were created to be, and in whose image they were created. They need permission to live fully into that image, imperfectly and humbly and in concert with all other human beings, who also reflect the masculine and feminine and ultimately gender-neutral image of God.

The Reverend Heather Roth Johnson, fifty-one, pastor of family ministry at a large urban church in the Midwest, grew up in a deeply gendered and traditional culture in the American South, where she once attended balls as a debutante in her native Charlotte, North Carolina. She says she's a "graduate of white gloves and party manners," and she attended cotillion, where "you learn how men should behave toward women." When Roth Johnson wanted to take physics in her senior year of high school, she was told, "oh no, that's for boys."

But Roth Johnson also had a mom who, she said, would "push for whatever we wanted," and was "quite a feminist herself," even if she constantly reminded her daughters to "sit with their legs crossed!" Roth Johnson's mother insisted to the school that her daughter, along with two other female students, be able to take physics. Together, the three of them won the highest score on the end-of-year physics project.

Roth Johnson took that mix of traditionalism and spunk with her into a career as a missionary, and later, an ordained minister. While she frequently attended youth group at evangelist Jim Bakker's PTL Club in Charlotte, she ended up attending a relatively liberal Lutheran liberal arts college in Minnesota, and later served as a missionary in Madagascar for eight years, during which time both of her sons were born. While in Madagascar, she learned from the local Christian leaders how to teach the Bible and theology through stories, rather than the rote memorization of many American churches. Now, in addition to her role as pastor to a particular congregation, she also runs a ministry and blog called *Storyboarding Church*, focusing on providing resources to other Christian leaders and teachers who want to teach children through story. She still draws inspiration from the first playgroup she taught in Madagascar, where kids spoke a variety of languages, and they had to learn through art and plays and simple words. She noticed in these groups that while girls would often draw nouns to talk about God, boys would draw verbs, and focus on God's actions.

The difficulty for Roth Johnson often came when she attempted to use mainstream and popular Christian curriculum for children. She noticed how heavily the curriculums leaned into gender stereotypes for boys and girls, for biblical characters, and for God. Women were often dismissed as sinful or somehow sexually promiscuous. So Roth Johnson purposefully refers to Rahab, who saved the Israelite scouts by hiding them in her home but is often referred to as a "prostitute," as *Ms.* Rahab. She challenges conventional stories about women in the Bible, wondering if perhaps the reason the woman at the well went to draw water at noon was not because she was a pariah or ashamed due to sexual sin but, "maybe she just wanted some alone time."

Roth Johnson also pushes back against assumptions of male biblical characters as specifically prone to violence, reminding kids that David was reluctant to fight Goliath, and he wore no armor. But she says her most important work, post-pandemic, is helping kids feel comfortable at church again, and getting back to the basics of the stories of the Bible. A positive piece of that, she notices, is that kids are carrying less baggage of purity culture and gendered assumptions about God and Bible stories. Instead, Roth Johnson says, it's the adults who often call or email to complain when she preaches and uses feminine pronouns for God, for example. One of the prime ways she does this is when teaching on creation and noting that, in Genesis 1 and 2, God's Spirit is described with the Hebrew word רוּחַ (rûaḥ), which is feminine. For Roth Johnson, just as Jesus is clearly masculine as the second part of the Trinity, the Son, this means the Spirit is clearly feminine, as the third part of the Trinity.

When Roth Johnson used feminine language for the Holy Spirit at her previous congregation, in an outer ring Midwestern suburb, she received emails saying she was "of the devil."

"[The masculine language for God] is formative for some people, and scary for others," Roth Johnson says. "For some people, you are changing their worldview of how they see God."

Like many Christians who have come to use a mix of gendered pronouns for God, Roth Johnson came to this change slowly herself, after deep study of the Bible and prayer. She also notes that when she taught kids in Madagascar, there was much less emphasis on gender. She says Malagasy was much more neutral.

While Roth Johnson sees her calling from God as one to teach *all* kids through story, to open their minds to a more inclusive, affirming, and feminine God—Roth Johnson was also called as a mom to two of her own white Christian boys, who are now young white men. She says she sees in them the same mix of tenderness and activity and desire to learn and be loved that she sees in so many of the kids she teaches, including the young boys. While she highly emphasized to her boys the importance of respectful touch and controlling their hands, Roth Johnson also gave them permission to understand God's image for themselves, an image that was forever touched by their early years in Madagascar and their ongoing years in the Midwest with a mom who was also a pastor, flouting the conventional wisdom and social strictures of much of American Christianity.

The afternoon I stopped in at church to talk with Roth Johnson was an unseasonably warm one, in early fall in the Upper Midwest. She had always struck me as energetic and irrepressibly optimistic, telling Bible stories to kids, always with entertaining props and occasionally funny facial expressions. But as we talked about her role in offering a new image of God to kids in America, maybe especially to young, white Christian boys, I saw in Roth Johnson's eyes a new acknowledgement of her purpose.

"I guess I never realized it before," she said. "But I'm working to change it. I'm making a difference."

Maybe Roth Johnson's gentler image of God will never reach the four-million-plus readers who read *Wild at Heart*, or the countless Christian parents who grew up irreparably shaped by a masculine, militant, and violent image of God. But her story makes me hopeful, because so many young boys and men are learning, from teachers like Roth Johnson and Du Mez and Barr and Schiess, that God is perhaps more patient, loving, motherly, and forgiving than their parents were taught God was.

As I think about the myriad little boys sitting at Roth Johnson's feet as she tells stories of *Ms.* Rahab, I'm reminded of how Jared Yates Sexton talks about a gentler masculinity in his book *The Man They Wanted Me to Be*. Raised in rural Linton, Indiana, Sexton's parents were estranged most of his life, and his hard-drinking dad exemplified the toxic, violent masculinity that is a hallmark of the American religion of White Jesus. It wasn't until the end of his dad's life that Sexton realized his dad's purported machismo was mostly an act, a cover for an emotional and sensitive, ashamed man who wasn't so different from his emotional and sensitive son.

Sexton writes about a story from Dr. Cordelia Fine's *Delusions of Gender*, how male infants cried more than their female counterparts: "All those babies who haven't been subjected to socialization, to unreasonable societal expectations. All those little boys born more fragile and more vulnerable than the girls around them."[22]

When I read this passage in Sexton's book, I had to stop reading for a moment, so viscerally was I brought back into those early days of motherhood with my two sons, both of whom had tummy troubles, reflux, and colic that led to long, seemingly endless crying jags. They were both male babies, born big and strong, with extremely healthy, even insatiable, appetites for milk right from the beginning. They were also inarguably emotional and sensitive, deeply vulnerable, intrinsically interested in connection and communication—far off from the masculine stereotype or ideal of the strong, silent man. Maybe that's why in my preaching—and probably in my mothering, too—the most powerful story of Jesus I try to pass on to my churches (and to my boys) is the story where Jesus, too, wept, at the death of his friend, Lazarus.[23] In this moment of vulnerability, relationship, friendship, and connection, Jesus is at his most deeply human and most powerfully divine. He is also a model for men and boys.

I think about Roth Johnson cradling her crying little boys in a faded blanket in Madagascar. I think about the wails and moans of my own little boys, and how strong and peaceful I felt once I had comforted them and they finally drifted peacefully off to sleep in my arms, nestled into my embrace, at ease and enveloped and at rest, in deep relationship and in deep need. In these vulnerable little boys, who no longer needed to be strong at every moment, I saw a clearer image of God.

Chapter 4

WWJB
Who Would Jesus Be?

In October 2023, I was teaching a course on Christian nationalism for a group of Midwestern church leaders and politicians, and I came face-to-face with square-jawed Jesus.

Leading up to that evening's class, I received multiple messages from students asking me if I'd seen the meme making the rounds on the internet that week: a fake court sketch of former President Donald Trump in a New York City courtroom, on trial for financial fraud, seated next to a white-robed Jesus with long, flowing, blondish-brown hair—looking suspiciously similar to Mel Gibson, an ironic choice given the latter's alleged history of anti-Semitism.[1]

The sketch was originally shared on Trump's Truth Social network by internet personality Dom Lucre, but it probably wouldn't have gained so much traction had it not been "re-truthed" by Trump himself, with Lucre's eyebrow-raising caption: "This is the most accurate court sketch of all time. Because nobody could have made it this far alone."

In the sketch, Trump is rendered in full color, while Jesus is more sepia toned, making it tough to ascertain for certain what he is intended to look like. But his appearance is definitely more European than Middle Eastern, complete with well-groomed facial hair, a furrowed brow, and light-colored hair.

The students in my course were anxious to talk about this meme because they could sense it held within it a powerful purveyance toward Christian nationalism: the idea that Jesus directly supports and sanctions right-wing American political figures, specifically Trump. For young, white Christian men and boys however, depictions of Jesus might hold an even more subtle power, a particular identity around which to shape and presage their own identities.

Jesus is, of course, the most accessible and human member of the Trinity: he is God Incarnate, God with us. As Egyptian church father Athanasius once put it around 300 years after Jesus's birth: "For the Son of God became man so that we might become God."[2]

The temptation to "become God" is at the heart of the aims of Christian nationalism, a subset of the theology of glory, in which human beings assume that following God will bring us closer to deification ourselves. St. Athanasius's conception of the incarnation had less to do with godly power and more to do with godly relationship with Jesus: the idea that in Jesus human beings could receive forgiveness and resurrection and closer relationship to God than ever before.

Incarnational theology aside, who Jesus actually *is*, and the ways that Jesus is identified and rendered in both popular culture and in the church, has a massive impact on young, white Christian boys and men. As any attentive observer might notice, the most popular (and usually correct) answer to any pastor's children's sermon or any Sunday school teacher's interlocution is: JESUS!

When I was a teenager in the 1990s, WWJD bracelets were popular among certain sets of Youth Group kids. But while our parents and youth pastors focused on teaching us what Jesus might do (namely: not engage in premarital sex or come out as gay), we likely neglected the more important question: Who Would Jesus *Be?* There were plenty of others willing to answer that question, however, and their influence on young, white Christian boys and men throughout the end of the twentieth century and the beginning of the twenty-first is clear to see.

Introducing Angry Jesus

While most artistic and stained-glass depictions of Jesus show pastoral and peaceful scenes, a certain set of Christian leaders, pastors, and right-wing politicians were much more interested in showing a different side of Jesus throughout the second half of the twentieth century: the angry side. They said they were interested in this side of Jesus because they'd noticed that Jesus had been popularly depicted too much as a weakling or as overly emotional, and they wanted to bring back men and boys, with all their militant masculinity, into the church. No one has better documented this spread of "angry Jesus" than historian Du Mez in her aptly titled *Jesus and John Wayne*.

For example, Du Mez wrote of Jerry Falwell's use of military metaphors to explain Christianity in the early 1980s, around the time Ronald Reagan would put Christian conservatism at the heart of the Republican Party. Central to Falwell's claims about Christianity's essential violence and power-hungry nature was his depiction of Jesus: "Falwell couldn't stomach 'effeminate' depictions of Christ as a delicate man with 'long hair' and 'flowing robes.' Jesus 'was a man with muscles . . . Christ was a he-man!'"[3]

The Bible is rife with stories about Jesus's asceticism and nonviolence, such as the many instances when he would leave the crowds and the city to go away by himself to pray, when he rejected the devil's offers of worldly power (Matthew 4:1–11), and when he commanded Peter to "Put your sword back in its place; for all who take the sword will perish by the sword."[4] Christian and political leaders wishing to emphasize a more militant Jesus therefore had only a few Bible passages to emphasize, and you'll notice they again and again reference only two main ones: (1) Matthew 21:12–13, when Jesus overturns the tables of the money changers in the temple; and (2) the book of Revelation's depictions of Christ's return at the end of the world.

It's telling that references to an angry and militant Jesus have such thin scriptural backing, bringing to mind Trump's shameful June 1, 2020, photo op at Washington, DC's St. John's Episcopal Church, during the height of protests and riots following George Floyd's murder by Minneapolis police just days before. Following law enforcement's use of tear gas and other riot control tactics against mostly peaceful racial justice protesters, Trump arranged a walk-up to the church, holding up a Bible next to the church's sign (of note: the church did not approve this presidential photo op). Observers noted that Trump was holding the Bible upside down, and when he was asked if it was his Bible, he famously responded: "It's *a* Bible."[5]

When poring back over the intense effort to remake Jesus in the image of a short-tempered, violent, power-hungry, white man—one could ask the same question, remembering the aforementioned meme of Jesus in the court room next to Donald Trump.

Is that Jesus?

It's *a* Jesus.

Because the scene of Jesus overturning tables in the temple from Matthew 21:12–13 is such a popular one among Christian leaders eager to influence young white boys and men, let's revisit that section of the Bible in detail. After all, it's one of the few places where Jesus is actively raging and destructive. First, what is the context?

Importantly, Matthew 21 marks the beginning of the Christian Holy Week, starting on the day popularly known as Palm Sunday, when Jesus makes his triumphal entry into the city of Jerusalem. But unlike wealthy American Christian leaders and politicians with their private jets and black luxury sedans, Jesus entered Jerusalem on a lowly donkey (or maybe a colt: the Bible isn't quite clear), with his path before him marked not by a red carpet but by the humble tops and tunics of the poor people of the city, who lay down their cloaks before him. It was the city's poor and neglected who welcomed Jesus to Jerusalem, in a reversal of the typical triumphant entry of Roman rulers, who came in on chariots to military fanfare. To Jesus, they shouted, "Hosanna, blessed is the one who comes in the name of the Lord," and their open resistance to calling Caesar, the military Roman leader, "Lord" was a threat to the established political order of the time, as well as a threat to the religious establishment, who later partnered with the Roman government to arrange for Jesus's capital punishment: crucifixion.

Jesus is entering the city as a preparation not for his victory but instead for his defeat, a punishment he willingly enters into for the sake of God's justice, power, and grace. And unlike the popular Christian influencers, who closely monitor their social media followers and spend church money on consultants who promise to help them sell books and amass influence, Jesus was still an unknown to many in Jerusalem. Matthew writes, "When he entered Jerusalem, the whole city was in turmoil, asking, 'Who is this?' The crowds were saying, 'This is the prophet Jesus from Nazareth in Galilee.'"[6]

It is this decisively anti-militant and power-stripped setup that leads into the famous and oft-quoted scene of Jesus at the temple, where he enters into the heart of religious grift and overturns *the tables of the money changers*. Jesus tells them:

> It is written "My house shall be called a house of prayer";
> but you are making it a den of robbers.[7]

Isn't it surprising that the prosperity gospel preachers don't often directly quote this passage when reminiscing about Jesus's propensity to masculine anger in this very scene!

In fact, as I reread the scene closely again, I can't help but think of my many visits to Evangelical Christian conferences, and the marketplace tables that are set up there, selling all sorts of Christian goods and services, including numerous books and videos and "swag" from the very same male pastors who cite this scene as definitive of *who Jesus is*. The hypocrisy is sort of stunning when you pause and think about it for a moment. But that's what happens when we really dive into the Bible, when people really get a chance to read for themselves who Jesus is. For all of their claims to be "Bible-based" in a fallen, secular world, most of the influential male pastors trying to influence young, white Christian men and boys spend a lot more time convincing people to read their own books than they do convincing people to actually read the Bible itself.

What's also instructive about this scene of Jesus in Matthew 21 is how quickly Jesus moves from destructive tyrant to comforting healer. He does not, as many pastors and authors might suggest, simply overturn the tables and storm angrily out of the temple, unwilling to engage with "ordinary" people. Jesus's anger was not empty and performative, all "sound and fury, signifying nothing."[8] Instead, immediately following just two verses documenting rage and anger, Jesus shifts back into healer and peacemaker mode. These are the three verses that directly follow Jesus's turning over the tables in the temple:

> The blind and the lame came to him in the temple, and he cured them. But when the chief priests and the scribes saw the amazing things that he did, and heard the children crying out in the temple, "Hosanna to the Son of David," they became angry and said to him, "Do you hear what these are saying?" Jesus said to them, "Yes; have you never read,

'Out of the mouths of infants and nursing babies you have prepared praise for yourself'?"[9]

To whom does Jesus draw near after his anger is made manifest? He is with infants and children, with people in need and with people with disabilities. Jesus is not angry for the sake of getting angry, nor is he angry because someone has insulted his manhood or threatened his power. Jesus is angry because people are making money instead of giving glory to God. Jesus is angry because the very real needs of ordinary people are being neglected, and people are using God for their own profit rather than providing real healing and care and support.

When we gaze back at the landscape of American Christianity throughout the end of the twentieth and beginning of the twenty-first centuries, we can see hundreds and thousands of monuments to American Christian greatness, from the opulent church campuses and grounds of places like Bill Hybels's Willow Creek in the Chicago suburbs, and Rick Warren's Saddleback in ritzy Orange County, California, to Christian academic ivory towers and manicured college campuses, from Westmont to Wheaton to Liberty in Virginia. Reading through these passages again, is it not imaginable that it would be these very places—holders of millions of dollars in property, wealth, tuition, and book sales—in which Jesus would overturn tables? And in their place, that he would invite in the very migrants and outcasts whom those institutions and leaders have tried so desperately to keep out?

The Kind of Man Jesus Wants You to Be

Let's spend a bit of time looking directly at some of the most popular literature and teachings about Jesus's masculinity in recent history, beginning with Seattle pastor Mark Driscoll, who based much of his fame on his purported ability to bring young men back into prominence in the Church in an increasingly secularized America.

In Driscoll's book *Real Marriage*, co-written with his wife, Grace, he paints a disturbing picture of the ideal Christian man and husband, ostensibly based on Jesus's example (though Jesus was never married).

One of the saddest sections of *Real Marriage* is Driscoll's dim view of male friendship. He writes of his and Grace's friendships: "Through it all, we have learned that friendships take so much time, energy and investment that *you can only have a few friends—maybe two or three real friends*. In the same way, Jesus had many foes, many fans, and only three real friends—Peter, James, and John—who had the most privileged access to him."[10]

As is often the case, Mark Driscoll tells us more about himself than he tells us about Jesus in this passage. *Real Marriage* was written at the height of Mark's popularity, when he was building a massive social media following for his sermons and his writings, speaking in stadiums for huge speaker fees, and becoming a "Christian celebrity." Reading his words about the paltriness of friendships in his life, and the presence of "many fans," you get a sense of the utter loneliness Driscoll must have been experiencing at the time. He obviously saw congregation members at his megachurch, Mars Hill, merely as fans, and not fellow disciples of Jesus, and he also clearly saw his colleagues and fellow pastors as "foes," rather than co-leaders in sharing the gospel. His was a competitive, lonely, and anxious existence. But don't foist that onto Jesus! The biblical evidence, again, just isn't there. Not only does the Bible list twelve disciples, whom Jesus later actually calls, verbatim, his friends,[11] but also the Greek word for "friend" used by Jesus throughout the Gospels is φίλος (philos), which refers to deep affection and brotherly love (the same word is the root of the name for the city of Philadelphia). Again and again, Jesus refers to his love for his friends, who included not just the male disciples but also women like Mary and Martha, the sisters of Lazarus, and Mary Magdalene—the women who were the first to share the message of the resurrection (more on this later).

What's important here for the emotional and social development of young boys and men is that Driscoll is forcing a description onto Jesus that doesn't fit Jesus at all—but it does fit Driscoll and many other egotistical male Christian leaders of our time. Because Driscoll's (and others') books and materials are specifically geared toward young men, the way they describe Jesus is particularly critical. They're not just trying to say how young men should be, but they're prescribing a kind of fatherly guidance that prioritizes anger, isolation, loneliness, and violence over the true example of Jesus, a man of many friends, and a man capable of deep, intense brotherly love.

Later on in *Real Marriage,* Driscoll says it directly: "The key to understanding masculinity is Jesus Christ." But he goes on to emphasize Jesus's "toughness" and to talk about Jesus "swinging a hammer as a carpenter," and "taking responsibility for us on the cross."[12]

Describing the atonement as Jesus's "taking responsibility" for humanity is a coarse and cheap way to describe God's greatest act of love for humankind. At root, God chose to become incarnate in Jesus, and to die and rise again not out of responsibility but out of love. The whole idea and grace and beauty of the atonement falls apart if it merely becomes God's action under compulsion. And, furthermore, if God acts out of compulsion, who or what is compelling God? Wouldn't that individual or thing be God above God if they had the power to compel God? Driscoll's view of Jesus's actions is not only reductive but also nonsensical.

Despite the lack of theological cohesion, however, Driscoll's depiction of Jesus and of God's actions in Jesus remains persuasive and influential, especially toward his target audience of young men, as well as the young dads and church leaders who will influence young boys. These readers understand that Driscoll's depiction of Jesus prescribes men who are led by a sense of responsibility, not of love, when it comes to other human beings. They are told that it's realistic only to have two or three friends—and, of course, those friends must only be other men, not women. Jesus is described for them as tough, and Driscoll leads with Jesus's job as a carpenter as the most important part of his identity, rather than his relationships or his service to the world. You can see the consequences of this view of manhood in young, white Christian men and boys growing up in the recent years after Driscoll and others like him published their books. They've borne fruit in a generation of young men who, even if otherwise well-adjusted and successful, have no idea how to build relationships or gain emotional maturity, to the extent that some pay thousands of dollars to attend a retreat at the "Confident Man Ranch," a unique experience designed to help men work through their emotions and their relationships together, a group therapy-esque gathering mixed with outdoor activities and cowboy culture.[13] Driscoll himself likely would have poked fun at retreats like that one, unless, of course, he was running it and making money off of it, but the truth is that rhetoric and books and sermons like the ones he preached resulted in emotionally inept, lonely, isolated, cynical, and lost men—much like

Driscoll himself. But that's just not a portrait that matches the Jesus of the Bible.

Another set of favorite texts of Christian leaders like Driscoll, who want to emphasize male hierarchy and overt masculinity, are the texts that talk about Jesus being the Head, and the husband being the "little-h head," of marriage and families (Colossians 1:18, 2:10, 2:19; Ephesians 1:10, 1:22, 4:15, 5:23).[14] What's critical though is that Jesus himself never says anything of the sort, and Jesus himself was also not married, nor a father. The Jesus of the Bible, much to modern-day Evangelicals' chagrin, just wasn't overly concerned with the structure of nuclear families, or even of marriage itself. Jesus was focused on the world and concerned with reaching and caring for those who had been left of out of society, marginalized for one reason or another. Whenever he had an opportunity, Jesus tore down hierarchies. He was such a threat to the established hierarchy of the Roman conquerors and the religious elite that they conspired together to kill him. While in a few instances the more systematically inclined Apostle Paul did attempt to elegantly lay out an arrangement for social and family life with Jesus at the head, it just doesn't make sense to make this hierarchy the centerpiece of a theology focused on Jesus's life, death, and resurrection; and it especially doesn't make sense to place such a critical emphasis on gender roles, again rooting them in the creation story of Adam and Eve (see chapter three).

The Fruits of Driscoll's Jesus, and an Alternative Path to Christian Parenting

In January 2024, I went to Scottsdale, Arizona—home to Driscoll's new congregation, Trinity Church, planted after the well-publicized blowup and collapse of his Seattle congregation, Mars Hill[15]—to see these kinds of fatherly and family values firsthand. What I saw at Trinity and heard Driscoll say in his preaching that Saturday night horrified me, but it also made me really sad for the boys, young men, young fathers, and young families in Driscoll's orbit. While Driscoll's early sermons and books at least sound like the work of a true convert, a zealous believer with real intentions to help people meet the Jesus he thought he knew (even if the Jesus he describes is inaccurately violent, angry, and hyper-masculine), the Driscoll I encountered in Scottsdale in 2024 was cynical, faithless, and concerned most with promoting himself and proving his own prosperous bona fides, sliding Jesus in as a sort of side dish to his main course of misogyny, anger, and self-congratulatory remarks. While I didn't see too many traditional "churchy" elements at Trinity, and the worship space was devoid of worshipful or holy markings like crosses or stained glass or holy water, I did see lots of mini-altars to Driscoll himself. Numerous digital signs and flatscreen TVs flashed ways to buy Driscoll's course material and visit his website. You could also buy his latest books outside the worship center, one entitled *Win Your War*, or t-shirts emblazoned with eagles' wings motifs and the words "More Fathers" or "Real Men." The bookcase with items for sale did not appear to contain any Bibles, nor any books written by anyone other than Driscoll himself and his wife, Grace. During his nearly hour-long sermon, which was followed by zero time for communion or musical worship, Driscoll at one point enumerated his son's reasons for dropping out of Arizona State University, in what appeared to be a cursory plaudit to fire up his audience's appetite for conservative culture wars.

"He couldn't do the pronoun thing," Driscoll said of his son, referring to the practice of listing your pronouns after your name, and then went on to share an anecdote about how one of his son's professors had assigned the class a reading from communist political theorist Karl Marx, whom Driscoll called "a mass murderer." For the record, the German-born Marx was dead thirty-seven years before the Russian Revolution, and while I suppose you could make an argument pinning mass murder in the Soviet Union and communist China on the communist system, the more accurate blame belongs to dictators Mao Zedong and Joseph Stalin, both of whom continue to be lionized and admired in authoritarian Russia and China. But Driscoll wasn't there to critique authoritarian strongmen, of course. He'd rather falsely accuse a political theorist who never killed anyone.

Disturbingly, while Trinity doesn't have an overly large worship space, the full crowd in attendance at that worship service (maybe two hundred people) didn't seem to realize Driscoll's lies about Marx. Instead, they cheered and jeered his culture war lines and seemed to awaken most during that moment, while otherwise somewhat restive during the lengthy sermon, which also contained long stories about

Driscoll's various world travels during his time at Mars Hill, about which he seemed to relish bragging, as well as to provide a sort of aspirational vision for his congregation, in a similar vein to what I'd heard from prosperity gospel preachers like Joel Osteen and Paula White.

Many of Driscoll's seemingly offhand remarks also sounded like dog whistles meant to evoke latent sexism, racism, or classism, or to spark in his listeners a reminder of what they'd likely heard on conservative radio, TV, or YouTube/social media earlier that day. At one point, when relaying an anecdote about a supposedly hapless young man he'd seen in a grocery store shopping with his mother, he needlessly added that this young man was wearing a mask. I highly suspect this anecdote was entirely made-up; however, did Driscoll stop to consider that maybe this young man had cancer or another chronic illness? No, he was utterly devoid of empathy for anyone except himself. And he used disease precautionary measures as a wedge.

At a time when boys and young men are desperate for belonging and assurance, Driscoll's scornful posture and depiction of an angry, violent God seems like a recipe for violence and despair. But I don't think he was healthy enough at this point to be thinking about the young fathers in the worship center who were hanging on his every word, outfitted in the Arizona conservative costume of cowboy hats, trucker hats, and copious facial hair, flanked by docile young women with uniform long locks, dresses, and heeled booties, and, after collecting them from the nursery staffed by more young women with braided blonde hair, lots of very young children. Battered by the defeat of public shaming and a fall from grace at Mars Hill, Driscoll came across years later at Trinity as preening and insecure, desperate for an audience to affirm him and even worship him. Humiliatingly, at the end of the sermon, while the audience was silent, Driscoll gave himself a sort of brusque double-clap, to which some listeners guiltily added weak applause.

Driscoll himself seemed to be a lost cause. But what about the families who had followed his teachings in their young marriages and early parenting days? Fortunately, earlier that weekend in Phoenix I'd met a family with three young boys who'd formerly followed his brand of complementarianism but had since chosen a different path.

Kara and Noah[16] met at an Evangelical church in Phoenix, where they were both close friends with the pastor and Kara briefly worked on church staff. A political science major who would go on to work at high levels in the Arizona Republican Party, Kara had seen firsthand how Driscoll's and others' angry brand of Christianity and depiction of Jesus as a militant, violent man had seeped into conservative politics in her state. In a state with a proud conservative tradition and independent streak, with reverence for military service, Kara watched in the early 2000s as "Impeach [former Republican nominee for president] John McCain" bumper stickers started showing up in parking lots for state GOP events, and people started calling longtime public servants and party members RINOs (Republican in Name Only), an epithet that Trump would later reclaim. Trump took on Arizona Republicans' former patron saint without hesitation or shame, and it ended in victory for a Trumpian, MAGA takeover of the Arizona GOP, the culmination of which was a slate of extremist, widely mocked (and losing) candidates fielded by the party for statewide office in the 2022 election cycle.

Kara's lack of connection to Christian groups on campus led her to the Evangelical church where she met Noah, a University of Southern California engineering graduate who was raised a Seventh Day Adventist in rural northern California, a part of the state that votes more like Alabama than Los Angeles. It was at USC where Noah became socialized as an Evangelical, joining a Christian fraternity where, he says, he expanded his horizons and met a diverse group of friends much different from his sheltered and homogenous, predominately white hometown. While Noah's family was politically conservative growing up, and Rush Limbaugh was a prominent family influence, he didn't necessarily think of his faith as connected to his politics. It didn't become personal to him until he built deep friendships with other Christian men at USC, and, secondly, until he got married and became a father of three boys.

When the couple first got married in 2010, their pastor was heavily influenced by Driscoll's teachings on masculinity, marriage, and parenting. The whole environment was one in which Jesus was a violent, angry warrior—an exemplar for husbands who ruled their churches, wives, and families with an iron fist, like Driscoll purported to do himself. Noah joined a men's group at church that sort of saw themselves as "warriors for God." They became cautious about using author and pastor Rob Bell's NOOMA videos in church classes, because Driscoll had called Bell "an apostate." Bell was too gentle, too "hippie-ish," too 1970s-era Jesus; not enough soldier Jesus of the early 2000s. But Noah's analytical nature caused him to carefully parse everything he was handed about Driscoll, and his suspicions were quickly raised. In Driscoll's *Real Marriage*, he "presented a version of complementarianism that didn't feel complimentary," Noah told me, mentioning how he'd been brought up in a family where men did a lot of cooking, and his grandma ran things in the household, while his mom served as primary accountant for the family business.

Kara, too, as she observed the rapidly changing and increasingly extremist Arizona GOP, felt uncomfortable with the message Driscoll was selling for her marriage and family. She'd been raised by parents who initially embraced the strict Christian parenting guidance of leaders like Wayne Grudem and James Dobson, but that thin facade of control and shiny, happy Christian family was shattered when Kara's parents separated when she was just a young teen.

She told me her dad was extremely possessive and dominating of her mother, even while suffering from alcoholism. Worse, their church pastors seemed to condone her dad's behavior, even approving of his desire to "have my mom's breasts fingerprinted so that he could be sure no other man had been there." In this Christian teaching, White Jesus protected the men's desires to subjugate women, but White Jesus didn't seem to care about how mothers and children were doing in the chaotic and angry households of these violent and jealous men.

A strong, outspoken, vibrant woman in her thirties, Kara told me, when we spoke that afternoon in her Phoenix kitchen, that the wounds suffered by her mom in the midst not only of the breakup of her marriage but also the mistreatment she received from the church pastors she'd revered still affects her mom to this day.

So, rightly, Kara was suspicious of integrating similar teachings into her own marriage, and Kara and Noah together shared similar misgivings. Fortunately, their church's pastor came to a similar conclusion and moved away from Driscoll-esque teachings by the late 2010s. Instead, their church turned to a focus on becoming more fully planted in their neighborhood, and embracing racial, cultural, and ethnic diversity: hiring a woman pastor and a Black worship leader, along with a diverse group of other staff members. Suddenly, Jesus wasn't White

Jesus anymore. The church reemphasized Jesus's biblical teachings about love, charity, humility, and justice. They acknowledged that Jesus wasn't white at all—per historical fact—but instead was a Middle Eastern, brown-skinned Jew.

By then parents of three boys, Noah was also chairman of the church board during the tumultuous years of the early 2020s, when the church faced division and attrition due to COVID-19 regulations and uncomfortable conversations about racism after the murder of George Floyd by the Minneapolis police in May 2020. Kara and Noah remained firm in their conviction that Jesus was not militant, violent, white supremacist, or hyper-masculine, and they were determined to raise their boys to be creative, open, loving, patient, and confident enough to be vulnerable. They felt they'd missed something in the past by attending only predominately white Evangelical churches, and they actively sought out opportunities to encounter more diverse worship and preaching. Their relationship and parenting were grounded not in strict, complementarian gender roles but instead in biblically prescribed mutuality, respect, honor, and deep listening.

"You are so incredibly lucky that you have the openness to learning to be challenged with knowledge," Kara said to Noah, when we talked about those difficult years he spent as church board chair.

"I want to be curious, not judgmental," he said, remembering again his time at USC but also time studying in China and in visiting farms in Oregon. "I learned to encounter new things by saying, 'Huh, that's new. I wonder what else is out there?'"

Noah's curiosity about the world and openness to newness matches the biblical stories of Jesus calling the first disciples, and it matches the Apostle Paul's openness to include Gentiles in what had formerly been a uniformly Jewish group following Jesus. But his was a humble posture, and one not often prescribed for young men and boys in the conservative Christian culture Noah and Kara were also steeped in. Their choice to step away from the White Jesus religion of decisive anger and fear didn't come without a lot of loss, including the loss of their close friends and former bridesmaid and best man, over a post Kara had made on Instagram that their friends thought conflicted with the teachings of their increasingly extreme Christian faith. The blowup happened as a result of a seemingly innocuous quote Kara had shared, from a conservative Christian parenting group, of all things. As a result of the argument between the two wives, Kara's friend insisted that her husband call Noah to reach a resolution between the men, which struck Noah as odd and uncomfortable, though it is the prescribed process in many conservative Christian communities. Nothing was resolved. Their friends seemed to have fallen too deep into a rabbit hole of exclusionary and extremist teachings to listen to pleading from Kara and Noah to come to reconciliation and understanding. The last they'd talked, the friends had moved to Nashville and were involved in a church heavily influenced by Pastor Doug Wilson, an acolyte of White Jesus and an infamous and prolific author and preacher from Idaho who supported "classical" education and strict gender roles, in addition to being implicated for helping to cover up sexual abuse of children in his community.[17]

Notably, in different ways, Kara and Noah's parents were also open to conversation with them about a new understanding of their Christian faith. Noah's father had been mayor of their small town and had learned that he had a responsibility as a politician to get things done, rather than just complain about things or spark controversy. He'd become "burned out" on politics as a result.

Kara, meanwhile, was figuring out how to navigate life in her chosen role as stay-at-home parent while also resisting the idea that Noah was always the "tiebreaker" and "leader" of their family. Instead, Noah and Kara wanted their boys to see them having conversations together and making decisions as a team, each deferring to the other's areas of expertise and strongly held opinions. They followed the example of a Jesus who frequently met with and ministered with women, rather than lording his power over them. In this new path, Kara and Noah didn't have hard-and-fast rules to rely on, which might have seemed easier at first, but instead they were learning how to do it together—as they went—invoking prayer, support of their church family and pastors, and extended family and friends along the way.

The couple still felt great sadness about the friends and fellow church members they'd lost. They sensed that a lot of their former friends and church members felt they needed to "protect" God and White Jesus.

There was a sort of war footing with which they approached the world. That wasn't how Kara and Noah wanted their boys to approach the world.

On their own, with the support of their church and pastors, Noah and Kara had chosen a different path.

"One of the biggest shifts we've made [in raising our three boys] is the emotional awareness. We discuss feelings and help with regulation," Kara said. "We want to make them aware of a bigger, broader world. We want to allow them to express themselves and their own unique versions of masculinity. They don't have to conform to a 1950s ideal."

Kara then shared a story about going into the American Girl doll store when her son was about three or four. He fell in love with a Black baby doll he called "Twinkle Buddy." But Kara said no. She said she was thinking that he was a boy, and a white boy didn't need a Black baby doll.

"That was a huge shift and challenge for me," she said.

Later that night, her son was taking a bath. He got a wistful look on his face.

"I hear something," he told his mom. "I hear Twinkle Buddy. She's crying because she doesn't have a home."

Kara and Noah talked about it. Noah said he brought up that if their boys played with dolls, maybe it would help them to be good with children later in life. They took their son back to get his beloved Twinkle Buddy. Later on, one of their younger sons asked for a Barbie doll, which the family also purchased.

Kara said sometimes going against the strict gender roles she had been taught was "weird."

"We're holding our cultural identities with open hands," Noah said.

Kara also remembered letting her son pick out a library book that featured the story of a transgender girl, even though she "really struggled."

But as their boys got older, they saw positive effects. Their boys were comfortable expressing and sharing emotions. They were kind to each other. They weren't as quick to melt down or to respond with physical aggression if they felt threatened. The voices telling Kara not to "emasculate your boys" had become "dampened." Jesus, for Kara and Noah and their family, was no longer a champion of the strong and the powerful; Jesus, instead, listened and embraced sensitivity and difference.

Kara and Noah didn't want their kids to look at others so often and think "that's wrong" or "that's weird," as they sometimes had as a result of more narrow Christian upbringings. Their boys attend their public neighborhood school, even though Kara had once been on the board of a charter school. They're trying to keep choosing openness, in response to a world that prescribed fear and violence and protectiveness—and in response to friends and family members who ask: "Don't you really have to watch the ideas your kids are exposed to [in public school]?"

To chart a path as Christian parents who are choosing openness and acceptance and vulnerability for their boys, Kara and Noah didn't get handed a lot of books to follow. Instead, they had to outright reject many of the influences beloved by their family, friends, and community. They had to reject White Jesus. In his place, Kara and Noah instead hold on to a deep faith in a Jesus who himself was open, accepting, and even vulnerable.

Jesus as Sex Therapist?

One of the most salacious parts of the Driscolls' marriage book—and maybe one of the reasons why lots of people decided to buy it—was that they promised to talk directly about sex. This was, of course, the era of the "smoking hot wife," where Evangelical pastors got regular laughs and applause lines at Christian conferences trying to one-up one another about the attractiveness of their wives.[18] This was another key teaching about manhood aimed at young men and boys: that masculinity was evidenced by the attractiveness of one's female partner, and that women existed primarily to feed men's egos and their (obviously more powerful) sex drives.

One of the most troubling passages of *Real Marriage* (and there are several) comes near the beginning of chapter nine, a chapter entitled, "Selfish Lovers and Servant Lovers."[19] If you only read that title, perhaps you thought: finally! Driscoll will finally talk about Jesus's example of a masculinity that seeks first to serve others. Spoiler alert: no such luck. Instead, the opening anecdote of the chapter tells the (probably made-up) story of a man and woman who have a "disappointing" honeymoon, primarily because the woman (who had never had penetrative sex before their wedding night, as prescribed by conservative Christian teaching and purity culture) found penetrative intercourse to be deeply painful.

Naively, as I read this story, I thought that Driscoll might be advising the man to be a "servant" lover and thus learn how to first pleasure his wife, thereby increasing her opportunity at pleasure in sex. How could the advice for men reading this chapter be anything other than an admonition to be servants to their wives, following the humble advice of Jesus, which Driscoll recounts on the following page: "Jesus also said, 'Whoever desires to become great among you shall be your servant'" (Mark 10:43).[20]

However, here's where the advice about masculinity offered by Driscoll and other conservative male pastors again becomes nonsensical and fails to follow a logical pattern. While spending most of the book claiming that Jesus is the ultimate (male) example for young men to follow, Driscoll shifts gears to suggest that, when it comes to sex, women are the only ones called to follow Jesus's example as servant leaders. This idea was made almost painfully clear as Driscoll recounts the wife's "helping hands" (which means she was pleasuring her husband with no opportunity for her own pleasure). He finishes the anecdote about the young, sexually frustrated couple by writing that "[w]hen we met, she was surprised to hear that she was selfish."[21] I bet she was! The poor woman had for years failed to be satisfied by her husband, after "saving herself" for marriage her whole life and being taught that sex was shameful, especially for women. She gave her husband "helping hands," in Driscoll's immature vernacular, and then when she endured painful sexual intercourse in order to provide children (again, as prescribed by conservative Christianity and purity culture) she is told she is selfish! It is not a far leap from this story to imagine, as was documented on *Christianity Today*'s podcast about Driscoll and his church,[22] that Driscoll would counsel sexual abuse survivors that they were in fact to blame for abuse, and to hold women accountable for men's sexual transgressions.

Many books, notably Sarah Stankorb's *Disobedient Women: How a Small Group of Faithful Women Exposed Abuse, Brought Down Powerful Pastors, and Ignited an Evangelical Reckoning*,[23] have documented the toll this type of teaching about sex and gender roles has taken on generations of women and sexual abuse survivors. Young men and boys also lose out when trying to follow this type of teaching. What the Bible actually prescribes in relationships is mutuality grounded in love, grace, and forgiveness. Whether physical, sexual, or emotional intimacy, all types of intimacy require this mutuality and shared trust, vulnerability, and love. Prescribing rote roles and privileging "responsibility" is a recipe for marriages lacking trust, intimacy, and love. When fathers set this kind of example for their young boys, boys grow up thinking that this is all they can hope for in their own relationships. All parties lose out. And sadly, it's clear that these kinds of prescriptions fall far afield from their stated example, Jesus himself.

Jesus Came to Save . . . Gender Hierarchy

I want to briefly mention a few more problematic references to Jesus found in influential texts targeting boys and young, white Christian men—references whose influence we can see in policies, attitudes, and actions of recent years.

Wild at Heart author Eldredge suggests that Jesus should be pictured less like Mister Rogers and more like William Wallace, of *Braveheart* fame.[24] In this bestselling book that many a teenage girl was advised to give to her boyfriend, Eldredge goes to great pains to depict Jesus as a "fighter" battling for "our freedom."[25] You'll notice it's not a far leap from that kind of language about Jesus to rhetoric that suggests Trump is in the service of the same kind of Jesus, "fighting for our freedom."[26]

In another troubling passage, Eldredge contrasts Jesus to a "pale-faced altar boy with his hair parted in the middle, speaking softly, avoiding confrontation, who at last gets himself killed because he has no way out."[27] *Wild at Heart* was first published in 2001, just a year before the *Boston Globe* published its groundbreaking report on sexual abuse within the Roman Catholic Church. It's troubling to read Eldredge's depiction today, shaming a "pale-faced altar boy," because even if unintentional, Eldredge's description of that altar boy brings to mind a male victim of sexual abuse. It's no wonder that generations of young, white Christian boys and men who were given this kind of literature and rhetoric from their parents and church leaders carried deep shame about instances of sexual abuse, especially within the church, by clergy.

This type of shaming of "weak" boys and men is part of a consistent pattern in rhetoric within Christianity that seeks to prioritize violent and powerful masculinity and gender hierarchy above all other teachings. Just as Eldredge wasn't above shaming boys who served the church as altar boys, Du Mez points out in *Jesus and John Wayne* that right-wing leaders were willing to go so far as to commit major theological heresy, and champion a hierarchical Trinity with a subordinate Jesus, in order to maintain their ironclad commitment to complementarianism and male headship.[28] Instead of one God in three coequal persons, a hierarchical Trinity places one, solitary God at the top, with Jesus and the Holy Spirit subordinated below. To make the Trinity hierarchical would be to upend an entire Christian theological history of coexistence and relationship and coequality and creation, as referenced in John 1:1–5, "In the beginning was the Word, and the Word was with God, and the Word was God. He was in the beginning with God. All things came into being through him, and without him not one thing came into being. What has come into being in him was life, and the life was the light of all people. The light shines in the darkness, and the darkness did not overcome it."

It's here, of course, that Christian leaders always run into trouble when they attempt to base their definition of militant masculinity on the example of Jesus. For every drawing of Jesus in military fatigues, or carrying a gun, or charging into battle like William Wallace—Christians have to come to terms with the myriad of texts where Jesus insists upon nonviolence, humility, and the primacy of love. It's for this reason that complementarian theologians run into problems with their Trinitarian theology. It's for this reason that Driscoll's explanations of servanthood end up prescribing following Jesus only for wives, and his advice becomes nonsensical when placed into context with the rest of the Bible's witness about Jesus's friendships and his commitment to healing, restoration, and love.

So what might a biblical instruction based on Jesus's actual example look like for our boys? We can start, as many churches and Christian institutions have done, by basing our images of Jesus—to the best of our abilities—on what Jesus likely actually looked like. He would have been short, at least by modern standards, and with dark brown skin and Semitic, Middle Eastern features. The unavoidable conclusion of performing this exercise—that Jesus is decidedly *not* a white man—strikes a huge first blow into the foregoing conclusion that Jesus sits atop a social and historical hierarchical history of the world, as many white conservative Christians assume (you might recognize this ideology as that of white supremacist groups as well). The more accurate depictions of Jesus's skin color also raise conversations and questions about assumptions many white Christians make about Black and brown men. Reminding young, white Christian boys and men that Jesus is not a white man forces them to take Jesus and put him into a seat often occupied by people who are oppressed and marginalized, and whose strength and power are seen more often as a deviant threat than as something to be emulated and admired.

Beyond Jesus's physical appearance, when teaching young white boys and men about Jesus and also about the kind of masculinity Jesus evidences, we can lean into the actual Bible stories of Jesus's life, death, and resurrection. Jesus's first appearance in the Bible is as a newborn baby, completely reliant on the care of those around him, vulnerable and inarguably needy. God does not avoid this aspect of humanity but emphasizes it in the incarnation of Jesus, being born not just a vulnerable baby but one who is born to poor, unmarried parents, part of a minority, oppressed ethnic and religious group.

As for Jesus as a young boy, we only have a story about his intellect and desire to learn about God in the temple.[29] Jesus did not shun being known as a teacher and as someone who had lots of questions and a desire to learn more. His disciples called him "rabbi," or teacher, not "boss" or "master" or even "coach." And, far from Driscoll's claim that Jesus was a man of few friends, Jesus prioritizes his friendships throughout the Bible, including to women. In her seminal sermon referencing the work of theologian Libbie Schrader, historian and Christian thought leader Diana Butler Bass suggests that Jesus's female disciple, Mary Magdalene (derisively called a "prostitute" by many male theologians and preachers), may have actually been his closest friend. She gets conflated by later male Bible writers into two separate women, Mary and her sister, Martha, instead of one, whom Bass calls "Mary the Tower," or Mary Magdalene.[30] It's this Mary who is with Jesus as he weeps over the death of his friend, Lazarus, and who makes this first brilliant confession of faith: "Yes, Lord. I believe that you are the Messiah. The one who's come into the world."[31]

We will never know how different church history might have been if, as Bass asks, "the faith hadn't only been based upon 'Peter, you are the Rock and upon this Rock I will build my church'? But what if we'd always known, 'Mary, you are the Tower, and by this Tower we shall all stand?'"[32]

What we can know, though, is that by offering young boys and men a window into a nonmilitant, peaceful, loving, caring, friendly, hopeful, vulnerable, needy, well-adjusted, occasionally tearful Jesus—we can offer young, white Christian boys and men a much fuller, healthier, and more accessible vision of masculinity: one that's more reflective of the wide spectrum of masculinity and femininity occupied by both boys and girls.

The misleading depiction of Jesus as warrior, man's man—as unsympathetic, lonely, and harsh was always a caricature. That White Jesus is always eventually exposed as a straw man, an Oz shouting behind a curtain, a president reliant on spray tan and tax fraud. Jesus as he was and is offers something much more powerful and relatable.

CHAPTER 5

Oppressors and Victims

As I dived deeper and deeper into research about young, white Christian men in America, it quickly became clear to me that two statements dominate discussion of men and boys today.

Men and boys are the problem.

Men and boys are in trouble.

I see these two overlapping truths about men and boys as central to understanding the role of radicalization in their lives, and also central to helping them step away from radicalization, isolation, and violence and into a healthier vision of masculinity, one which more closely mirrors the God and Jesus of the Bible, and not macho-male American Christianity, as discussed in the previous two chapters.

It's my hope that in covering these two truths together, we can perhaps find common purpose across sometimes disparate political interest lines. Stereotypically, more liberal Americans are more likely to emphasize the first statement, that "men and boys are the problem." More conservative Americans are more likely to emphasize the second statement, that "men and boys are in trouble." But it's also clear to me, in my intensive research and conversations with young men and boys and those who love them, that both of these statements are true, and we need to grapple with both statements in order to be of support and assistance in moving young men and boys away from radicalization, violence, and despair, and toward actualization as adults with intimate and loving relationships and healthy senses of self. Attempting only to "fix the problem" of men and boys ignores the need to reach men and boys through loving relationships, to understand their own internal senses of inadequacy or shame, which often find their way out in anger or hatred or substance abuse. On the other hand, if we only see that men and boys are in trouble, but don't address their roles in the problem, we risk infantilizing them and under-emphasizing the role of choice and agency among men and boys in choosing to step away from radicalization, violence, and brittle masculinity. We want to help them make the healthier and more fruitful, but difficult, choice to relinquish some status, power, and wealth in favor of improved relationships and more equitable and loving communities. This second choice, only to address that men and boys are in trouble but not to address the ways in which they're part of the problem, again often favored by conservatives, also makes a common historical error of privileging the emotional and physical needs of white Christian men and boys ahead of the emotional and physical needs of other human beings. This has led to all sorts of ongoing devastating consequences for human relationships, including the persistence of racism, sexism, classism, anti-Semitism, and Islamophobia. It's important, while caring for and researching the needs of men and boys, not to privilege their needs over the human needs of other groups and individuals, especially those who have been historically marginalized.

It's indisputable at this point that men and boys are both in trouble and also themselves the direct cause of many of their problems. In order to support and help the young men and boys who you love (or who you are), it's important to examine deeply both truths and how they're currently operating in America.

Over the past few years, I developed an extensive collection of major media clippings and reports documenting trends in coverage of men and boys in America, including a few books as well. I then gathered together these reports and data, spread them out on the floor, and attempted to distinguish whether they were writing about men and boys as the problem, or men and boys as being in trouble. I noted that I ended up with two fairly equal piles, which wasn't surprising to me. What was a bit surprising, however, was how little the two ideas overlapped, and how little discussion there was of how these statements relied upon one another. For example, those writing about the challenges and struggles of men and boys often didn't spend as much time writing about the ways those struggles and challenges for men and boys were threatening and damaging to the rest of humanity. At the same time, in coverage of the more despicable aspects of male behavior and violence, there was little space to examine how instances of men's misbehavior, violence, and hatred boomeranged back to create more problems for men and boys.

In beginning to unload and examine both of these piles, I want to then put them into conversation with one another, so that we can fully understand the plight and outcomes of the current state of men and boys, and help, support, and urge them into a better place—while also fighting tooth and nail against the violence, hatred, and abuse committed by men and boys against their fellow humans.

Men and Boys: The Problem

Let's begin by looking at a selection of news stories documenting the problems and issues ignited specifically by men and boys, in harmful ways toward their neighbors, friends, loved ones, and strangers. This is by no means an exhaustive list of incidents or individuals, but a sampling that attempts to cover a wide breadth of topics and people.

One of the biggest problems involving men and boys in America is the ways in which social media influencers and advocates of intense masculinity have made their way into positions of political power, particularly in conservative, right-wing circles. This is a problem because many of those same influencers and politicians often find themselves in overlapping circles of influences and ideology with white supremacist groups and leaders, which we'll explore more fully in chapters eight and nine.

Historian Heather Cox Richardson has been writing her near-daily newsletter, *Letters from an American*, since September 2019, documenting political trends and connecting them to historical events. On May 15, 2023, Richardson devoted her newsletter to a discussion of a recent speech given by President Joe Biden at historically Black Howard University, when he singled out white supremacy as "the most dangerous terrorist threat to our homeland."[1] For Americans of my generation, who were teenagers when extremist Muslim terrorists hijacked two planes and crashed them into New York City's Twin Towers, this was a radical shift—but also one that made sense for those of us who had watched neo-Nazis march on Charlottesville, Virginia, and viewed our share of Trump rallies. Still, it would be difficult to change most Americans' default image of what a terrorist might look like. Most people still envisioned Osama bin Laden, a man with brown skin and a long beard, speaking Arabic. Most people, when they heard the word "terrorist," didn't think of a young white man with a close-cropped haircut, well-spoken and calling himself a patriot, even after the attempted insurrection at the US Capitol in January 2021.

Richardson went on in that same newsletter to make clear the connections between some conservative Republican politicians and white supremacist groups. She referenced the breaking news that the digital director for Paul Gosar (R-AZ) was a "devoted follower of white supremacist leader Nick Fuentes," who had "openly embraced Nazism and Russian President Vladimir Putin's authoritarianism."[2]

Gosar's digital director, a man named Wade Searle, was also associated with a group called "Groypers," who referred to themselves as Christian conservatives but followed Fuentes's ideology of "[h]olocaust denialism, white supremacy, white nationalism, pretty strong anti-women bigotry," and a "return to Twelfth Century Catholicism."[3]

About a year before Richardson's writing, I had completed a long magazine piece about traditionalist Catholics,[4] so I had a pretty good idea of what all a "return to Twelfth Century Catholicism" might mean for women, and it didn't sound good. These were movements for whom male survival and thriving, and adherence to traditional Christianity, necessitated a loss of liberty for women and other minority groups. But young men and boys were nonetheless drawn to these groups, and also to their clear access to power in conservative political circles. Notably, Richardson's reporting also documented another Fuentes follower in Gosar's office, a young intern.

Thinking about these hate-based movements and their attraction to young, white Christian men and boys reminded me of reading about a movement within mainline denominations to return to a more "orthodox" version of the Christian faith.[5] As part of this movement, a number of churches found "95 Theses" posted on their church doors on Reformation Day (Oct. 31) 2023. The documents took a strictly fundamentalist and traditionalist approach to theology and church teaching, outrightly condemning "liberation theology" and making several oblique references to LGBTQ people, including No. 90: "[c]onvicting people of sin and demonstrating their need for Christ should come before affirming their lifestyles"; and No. 78: "[f]lags that reflect neither Christian significance nor national representation should not be displayed in or around churches, lest focus be shifted from God to politics"—the latter an ironic admonition—hinting at the rainbow flag—in an age of ascendant white Christian nationalism in the Republican Party that often entails political worship of the American flag.[6] In a discussion among ELCA Lutheran pastors, I learned that while these statements were ostensibly signed by people who were serving as representatives of particular congregations, in most cases the pastors of those congregations had not seen the statements nor approved them before the church's name was affixed to them. In multiple cases, the pastors said the signee was not a congregation member or active participant but an infrequent attendee; in some cases, a teenager! Most of these signees were sheepish when confronted by the pastors about using the church's name in this movement. It was also suspected by theologians reading the statements that they'd been produced at least partially with the help of AI.

As we attempt to hold up both the problem of male violence and also the corrosive effects of that violence on men and boys themselves, specifically when it comes to the enlistment of very young men and teenagers as foot soldiers in right-wing and white supremacist movements, I'm reminded also of the tragic cases of Kyle Rittenhouse and Daniel Penny, both of whom were young white men who killed people and were subsequently lionized and lifted up by right-wing movements. What did it feel like for Penny and Rittenhouse to be glorified for their violence and, ultimately, for their taking the life of another human being? Even if Penny and Rittenhouse would stand behind their actions, citing self-defense or protecting others against violence, the taking of another human life is an occasion for sadness and lament, not celebration—at least according to Christian tradition of honoring life in all circumstances. The celebration of acts of violence stands in contrast to long-standing US military conventions against glorifying killing or desecrating corpses. In my work with military service members and veterans, I have always been told that taking human lives, even in the line of duty, is a solemn responsibility and one that often weighs heavily on soldiers' souls. As Jesus told Peter in a warning against even retributive violence: "Put your sword back into its place; for all who take the sword will perish by the sword."[7]

In her writing on May 15, 2023, Richardson quoted historian Thomas Zimmer: "All strands of the Right—leading Republicans, the media machine, the reactionary intellectual sphere, the conservative base, the donor class—are openly and aggressively embracing right-wing vigilante violence. This sends a clear message: It encourages white militants to use whatever force they please to 'fight back' against anything and anyone associated with 'the Left' by protecting and glorifying those who have engaged in vigilante violence—call it the Kyle Rittenhouse dogma."[8]

The consequences of this violent vision of white masculinity were pertinent even for women close to the highest ranks of American political power. In this same May fifteenth newsletter, Richardson wrote about a lawsuit filed by former Rudy Giuliani employee Noelle Dunphy, who said that Giuliani never paid her a promised salary and also forced her into sex.[9] While working for Giuliani, Dunphy had a front-row seat for his descent from the role of America's mayor after 9/11 to that of a "chronically alcoholic sexual abuser prone to racist and sexist outbursts."[10] Giuliani, whose legal license is now suspended in Washington and New York, and who is facing state criminal charges in Georgia, is yet another example of the ways in which men who are part of the problem of the rise in masculinity centered on hatred and violence also become tragic cautionary tales about what happens to men at the center of these movements. Like Giuliani, they often end up shells of themselves, in poor health, mocked, humiliated, bankrupt, and—sometimes—held legally accountable for their actions, with their families and close relationships, not to mention their professional lives, in shambles.

What follows is a further catalogue of the problems of men's and boys' investment into a violent and self-serving masculinity, problems that end up harming their lives and relationships as well as those they victimize. This catalogue ranges from the serious to the absurd, but all of the examples are important to note.

A *Los Angeles Times* article from August 2023 told the story of Laura Ann Carleton, a sixty-six-year-old woman who was killed in her resort community hometown by a man who didn't like the fact that she flew a rainbow flag outside her store. Prior to shooting and killing Carleton, her killer had made disparaging and angry remarks about the flag.[11] Tragically, Carleton was remembered as one who was particularly invested in and "good at" bridging the politically divided world of Lake Arrowhead, where liberals and conservatives lived next door to one another.

Carleton "loved speaking with people who disagreed with her and trying to change their minds," friends said.[12] She also brought together local shop owners to set up a "free store" to supply free food for people in need. Carleton was a mother of nine. She was beloved by many in her small community, but she also endured verbal assaults and complaints from neighbors and strangers alike who didn't like her flag.

It's ironic that right-wing masculine movements so heavily emphasize strength and power and confidence in order to attract young men and boys. How insecure and weak does your masculinity have to be, though, to be threatened enough by a rainbow flag to take a mother's life?

The flip side of the violence unleashed by male activists supporting militant masculinity and white supremacy is the huge amounts of money and wealth earned by some of the movement's most visible acolytes, one of whom is Turning Point's Charlie Kirk, who was able to purchase a $4.75 million estate in Arizona at age twenty-nine with the profits he made touting far-right politics and traditional white Christian masculinity.

Shortly after Kirk's purchase of the mansion, Brian Slodysko of the Associated Press ran an investigative piece about the finances of Turning Point, quoting conservative commentator Erick Erickson, who called it "a grift."[13] Despite Turning Point's lack of success in Arizona elections, Kirk's brash embrace of right-wing politics and traditional masculinity won him access to elite Republican circles. He first served as a personal aide to Donald Trump Jr., and then practiced his culture war talking points on cable TV.[14] The year before purchasing his $4.75 million mansion in Arizona, Kirk had purchased three other properties, all worth over $1 million.[15] There is a great deal of money to be made in selling traditional masculinity and so-called strength to young white men and boys and their families. But as Slodysko pointed out, the movement had little communal achievements to show for itself—just a lot of yelling and a lot of loud men who had gotten rich off their yelling and posturing, through what often seemed to be dubious and even illegal financial practices.[16] Still, during the 2020 campaign, Turning Point consultants kept recruiting teenagers, most of them boys, to "spread false information online about voter fraud and the COVID-19 pandemic."[17]

Kirk and Turning Point weren't the only ones getting rich off of right-wing, traditional masculinity talking points and media. Prior to his removal from Fox News after being subject to a lawsuit for sexual harassment (notice a pattern here?), commentator Tucker Carlson produced a documentary called *The End of Men,* written about in *Rolling Stone* by Nikki McCann Ramirez, who called it: "light on substance and heavy on shirtless dudes."[18]

The documentary attempted to tell the story of the current state of men, but instead of data or personal stories it delved deep into the weird and grifty, with a (maybe unsurprising) focus on male sexual organs.

"Carlson's long-standing obsession with masculinity—and tangentially, testosterone levels—is rooted not so much in a concern for the physical well-being of his viewers, but a right-wing worldview that centers physical ability as a cornerstone to the maintenance of a society on the verge of collapse," Ramirez wrote.[19]

While the special touched on the challenges facing men and boys, which we'll delve deeper into in the second half of this chapter, Ramirez wrote that it didn't offer policy or communal solutions, instead "offering up physical dominance as a solution to those widespread systemic issues." Reading her article, I'm reminded of the tendency of teen boys who are bullied to first consider ways that they can "bulk up," often trying out protein shakes or weightlifting for a relief from social exclusion or physical attacks. But as educators and parents know, the solution to bullying must be a socially rooted solution that addresses the problems of the bully, not the bullied.

Bullying, especially among young boys and men, is yet another issue that finds its roots in a vision of masculinity grounded in competition and scarcity. In my time as a sports reporter covering professional athletes, I spent my fair share of time in locker rooms. What I noticed was that men who had excelled in the highest levels of physical competition, who had achieved elite levels of physical strength, and whose bodies comported most closely with the ideals envisioned by adherents of traditional masculinity, were also men who were generally unconcerned with the physiques and relative physicality of other men. Sure, they might joke around—but there wasn't a lot of bullying or scrambling for dominance. In fact, professional sports have been a field where you can see increasing gender parity or an openness to lifting up female strength as well as male strength. I'm thinking of the support shared between NBA and WNBA players during the anti-racism protests and Black Lives Matter movement in the summer of 2020, and I'm thinking of the increasing popularity of women's sports and media coverage thereof.

In response to the rise of women athletes, we can, however, also see a backlash from insecure men. Recall the story of Luis Rubiales, former president of the Royal Spanish Football Federation, who forced a kiss on the lips of star Spanish midfielder Jenni Hermoso, who had just helped the Spanish women's soccer team to its first ever World Cup in August 2023. After initially saying the kiss was mutual, Hermoso later said that the Spanish soccer federation had pressured her to do so, and she had in fact not granted consent for the kiss.[20] Hermoso went on to say that she felt "vulnerable" and was "the victim of an impulse-driven, sexist, out-of-place act without any consent" on her part.[21] Instead of backtracking and apologizing, Rubiales shifted into victim mode and claimed those who were upset with him were "overreacting false feminists."[22] And in a demonstration of how mothers of men and boys can contribute to the worst effects of traditional masculinity and its mistreatment of women, in response, Rubiales's mother "reportedly locked herself in a church and went on a hunger strike until everyone stopped being so mean to her boy."[23]

Meanwhile, the kiss unleashed reporting of a long history of Rubiales's misbehavior and undervaluing of women's soccer. He was shown grabbing his crotch in a macho gesture moments before the women's victory, and he picked up another player (Athenea del Castillo) over his shoulder.[24]

Ultimately, Rubiales faced consequences and was forced to resign. But his actions again demonstrate the tight hold traditional masculinity has on the actions of many men in power, and the ways in which those actions sideline, diminish, and mistreat the accomplishments of women in their midst.

It's on the topic of abortion, however, that male pursuit of traditional masculinity and brute strength and control is likely most damaging to women, and to humanity in general. In the wake of the Supreme Court's reversal of federal abortion rights formerly granted in *Roe v. Wade*, reporter Sofia Resnick documented the role of men's movements in "a nationwide quest to end abortion."[25] In her investigative article, Resnick painstakingly documents the role of men's groups in the anti-abortion movement, despite the broader messaging from a Christian pro-life movement that claims to be "pro-woman," "pro-mother," and "pro-family." One of the male activists Resnick interviewed was a father of more than ten children, and he took pride in the fact that his wife, who wore a head covering, had never held a public job.[26] He was hoping his daughter, whose age he declined to share, would wed soon and have twenty children.[27]

But as Resnick pointed out, it's not the most visible extremist protesters and conservative Christians who are the men driving the anti-abortion movement. Instead, it's the ordinary-looking men, dressed in suits and ties and generally without long beards or wives wearing head-coverings, who are making and approving the laws that will limit women's rights to reproductive health care, in some cases even to the point of the risk of death to pregnant women. Many male anti-abortion activists, like the ones Resnick interviewed, claimed biblical support for their positions, relying on many of the same tropes supported by the pastors we studied in chapters three and four. But, as documented in those chapters, a broader view of Scripture makes clear both Jesus's relationships with women who were not his mother—women who were valued for much more than just their status as reproductive vessels—as well as God's insistence on protection of *every human life*, not just those who are being formed in women's wombs.

Men in the anti-abortion movement focus their attention not on support of families and mothers in poverty, who will be in greater need without access to reproductive health care, but instead on access to guns and ammunition. Resnick quoted a Wisconsin minister named Wendell Shrock, preaching from the pulpit of lead pastor Matthew

Trewhella, who has long advocated for a return to traditional gender roles, and a masculinity rooted in violence and control.

"It's not being a protector to your family that God has called you to be. Get yourself in shape. Cultivate some physical strength. Buy guns. If you need to, buy a lot of guns. It's no limit on gun purchases; you have my blessing . . . And if you buy a gun and you buy ammunition, train with it, and get around a group of men that you can train with. Get around a group of courageous men who will fight, bleed and die with you, for you, and for your families and for your liberties," Shrock said in a sermon.[28]

Listening to Shrock's words about guns and violence, and the responsibility of men to be violent and own guns, is haunting in context with stories like Dylann Roof's, who was just twenty-one years old when he committed mass murder at Mother Emanuel AME Church. Shrock and voices like his inspire young men to idolize guns and commit acts of violence, and they don't seem concerned about unintended consequences, leading one to wonder if the reason they don't care is because those killed are often not white men.

Beyond churches and political rallies, Resnick found that the men's groups working to end abortion were also involved in camps, like the Manhood Restored Bootcamp for boys and young men held in Frankfort, Indiana, put on by Operation Save America, which produced a 2021 YouTube video "featuring suggestive and violent imagery involving scenes of a man with an assault rifle, then cutting to a Planned Parenthood facility, while reciting the biblical verse that begins, 'To everything there is a season' and includes the line, 'a time to kill.'"[29]

American voters have been pushing back against this message of militant masculinity and against control of women's reproductive freedom, with referendums on access to abortion even in red states like Kansas and Ohio. Still, as late as November 2023, American Catholic bishops voted to identify abortion as the ongoing "preeminent priority" for American voters.[30]

It's clear that men and boys, and their ongoing embrace of traditional and militant masculinity, are a problem for the rest of humanity, as well as a threat to themselves. In the wake of coverage of Rubiales's forced kiss after the World Cup, Elizabeth Spiers wrote for the *New York Times* about the need to "beware of the men who double down" in her recounting of a sexual assault inflicted on her on her way home from work in New York City, an assault made worse by those who insist such assaults weren't really assaults, that men's infringement on women's bodies and women's autonomy wasn't really an issue. "The double-downers offer a test for how much abuse society thinks a woman should tolerate, especially from someone in a position of relative power," Spiers wrote. "They encourage others to widen the sphere of what's acceptable when it comes to mistreating women. They do it with confidence and model an extreme entitlement with few consequences. And so they ensure it will happen again."[31]

What might be even scarier is the documented unstable position and temperament of the men closest to the center of these violent and destructive movements of militant masculinity. In September 2023, feminist writer Lyz Lenz interviewed Amanda Moore, who had embedded as an undercover reporter with alt-right movements during the January sixth attempted insurrection.

Moore told a story about being approached by a man with "tears pouring down his face" while they marched toward the Capitol around 12:45 p.m. on Jan. 6, 2021. He told her he had just punched a police officer who he thought was "trying to hurt some lady."[32] He kept telling her he wasn't crying, that it was because of the tear gas.

I think that vignette from Moore is so instructive in our study of white masculinity and its effects both on those it seeks to diminish and destroy and also on white men and boys themselves. You can see how some misguided sense of chivalry and traditional gender roles had inspired this man to react violently, even against law enforcement. His tears signal that something was very wrong. Maybe they were partially due to tear gas; I suspect he was also emotionally overwhelmed. But he had to make sure everyone knew he was not crying.

Moore went on to talk about how the true power brokers, the right-wing politicians and movement leaders, would always deny and disavow connections to extremist and white supremacist groups. But their connections were inextricable, and the politicians and leaders had no problem taking the money and votes of those with white supremacist sympathies; neither did they have a problem appealing to the same traditional gender roles and militant masculinity.

There's a huge cottage industry of male so-called comedians and influencers who appeal directly and especially to white boys and young men. And again and again, these same men seem to show up in stories about abuse and mistreatment of women, from Andrew Tate's arrest in Romania for sex trafficking and rape, to the Ring camera video showing conservative host Steven Crowder berating and belittling his eight-month-pregnant wife for not showing him adequate "discipline and respect."[33]

Otherwise obscure young white men have been able to make huge amounts of money and gain access to political power in recent years for amplifying far-right rhetoric and even conspiracy theories, like the case of twenty-seven-year-old Garrett Ziegler, a former Trump White House staffer who started a nonprofit, Marco Polo, attempting to "take down" Hunter Biden.[34] In her *Washington Post* article about Ziegler, reporter Meryl Kornfield combed the activist's social media accounts, finding "posts of inflammatory memes and conspiracy theories, rhetoric that says Christians are better than others, and that White people have been particularly persecuted."[35] He has accused Biden allies of being "Bolsheviks," which the Anti-Defamation League notes is often code for "Jew,"[36] and he "shares photos of his targets' daughters wearing bathing suits or partying with friends, ridiculing the girls' appearances."[37]

From Ziegler to Tate to Crowder to men's anti-abortion activists, to the insurrectionists on January sixth, to Spanish soccer figurehead Rubiales, to Paul Gosar and Tucker Carlson and Charlie Kirk and Daniel Penny and Kyle Rittenhouse—the common threads are clear. Militant masculinity forces men to abandon softer emotions like compassion, empathy, or sadness—and it encourages them to buy guns, get bigger muscles, and abuse and diminish women. This is an unequivocal problem for humanity, as well as for American politics. But where does it leave the young men and boys influenced by such men toward hatred and violence, and is there hope for their recovery?

Men and Boys: In Trouble

It's time to transition to looking at what violent masculinity is doing to men and boys themselves. A late-2023 TikTok trend encapsulated, in a humorous way, the sometimes perplexing state of modern-day manhood. In viral videos, women asked the men in their lives how often they thought about the ancient Roman Empire. To their surprise and confusion, the men often answered: multiple times a day![38]

As a fun object lesson that I suggest trying with the men and boys in your life, I ran down to the basement, where my husband, Ben, was playing video games, to ask him how often he thought about the Roman Empire. For reference, he works in a male-dominated, science-and-math-related field, and he's in the thirty-five to forty-four age group.

When I asked the question, Ben stared back at me. Like the engineer he is, he squinted and tried to figure out if I was going to trick him.

"The Roman Empire? I don't know. Probably more often than I should. Maybe every few years, or when I'm worried America is going to fail... why?"

I explained the viral TikTok trend to him. He laughed and shook his head.

"A few times a day?"

Obviously, the trend isn't fail-proof. My brother, who works in education and is in the twenty-eight to thirty-three age group, said similarly, "pretty much never." And my dad, who, to his credit, was taking care of my kids at the time, didn't text me back. I didn't bother asking my male friends, many of whom are pastors and/or academics who think about the Roman Empire in terms of religious or academic history, and thus, I thought, might taint my sample.

Still, the idea that men are often thinking broadly about the Roman Empire—despite my male family members' claims, all of us did watch the movie *Gladiator*—does suggest a certain yearning for a violent past in which, at least according to popular history, white men carried undisputed political and social power.

For our purposes, in examining in particular young, white Christian men, it's important to note that the Roman Empire was the empire that crucified Jesus, and, 300 years later with the deathbed conversion of Emperor Constantine, the same empire that co-opted a formerly persecuted religion made up primarily of marginalized Jews, turning it into the Western world's most powerful religion, and later, Europe's wealthiest and most prolific landowner.

It's amusing to think about a bunch of modern-day men, holding their smartphones and driving cars, thinking back to a relatively primitive time in history, to an empire whose fall was great and preceded an era of plague and death: the Dark Ages. It also signals to me that, at least to a certain extent, men and boys in America have been socialized to think that a more violent and primitive, and less-equal, era might bring them greater happiness and fulfillment.

For Christian men, again, this longing for the Roman Empire ignores the ways in which the Roman embrace of Christianity also led to the faith's complicity in violence and mass murder, from the Crusades to later Western Christians' participation in anti-Semitism, colonialism, and racism.

For some men, the affinity for ancient Rome, or other more violent periods in the past, goes beyond just thinking. The *Washington Post* traced the TikTok video trend back to a thirty-two-year-old Roman reenactor and history influencer (yes, that is a thing!) from Sweden, named Artur Hulu, whose social media accounts feature photos of Hulu in Roman military garb looking stern and powerful. A few months before the Rome TikTok trend took off, the *Los Angeles Times* ran a lengthy study of the resurgence of a medieval sport called "buhurt," from the old French word for "to wallop."[39] Participants in the sport, who do include some women, wear up to one hundred pounds of armor and fight against one another with blunted steel swords, axes, and maces—"until someone goes down, gives up, or loses on points."[40]

Males seeking dominance, competition, violence, and hierarchical power is nothing new. I was fourteen when the movie *Fight Club* first came out, and my fellow hormone-drenched male classmates spent the next several years chiding each other, "We don't talk about Fight Club," and then laughing with certain furtive glances at one another.

These trends toward violent outlets for boys and men might seem harmless, and most of the time they are. Some churches, who regularly feature men's programming that emphasizes physical activity and the great outdoors, even encourage the sense that men must first compete with their bodies before being able to open up to one another in their hearts and their minds. This doesn't have to be an overtly harmful idea. Sometimes boys (and girls) can open up more after physical activity. After attempting to sit through movies with my youngest son, during which he has to be diving off the couch or leaping into the air at least once every three minutes, I can even give some credence to the idea that kinetic learning and movement are uniquely important for boys, something we'll revisit in chapter six when we focus on education and schools. Still, as a point of argument, it's clear also that we have far too little cultural understanding and too few popular examples of boys who shy away from physical contact and prefer quiet, intellectual or emotional discussions (and, for that matter, too few examples of girls who require a lot of physical and sensory input to thrive). When less active and more quiet boys and men are featured, they're often portrayed as nerds or outcasts or as somehow defective men, aberrations from the norm of physical activity and violence. By socializing all men in the same way, we risk othering men and boys who don't fit this stereotype. If they can't find their "niche" in some culturally approved way—for instance, via music, drama, or academics—these men and boys end up being the ones so frequently mentioned as troubling and problematic in my research and in scary stories about young, male perpetrators of violence and hatred. It's also clear that there's a real race and class dynamic here. In most of the post-2016 election stories about white cultural despair, including those I myself reported, the main characters were blue-collar or lower-middle-class white men, often living in rural areas where the economy had slowed down and opportunity was at a lull, where addiction and alcoholism were on the rise, at a time in America when nearly 70 percent of deaths by suicide involved white, middle-aged men.[41] White, middle-aged men are also most likely to come from families holding traditional religious and cultural values, and to live in communities that are overwhelmingly politically conservative. This means that the social and cultural costs to being a man or boy who doesn't fit into masculine stereotypes about athleticism, violence, and machismo are higher than for men and boys living in more urban or culturally diverse areas, which tend to be less invested in traditional masculinity. A caveat it is important to note here is that this tends to be truest for white men and boys, who are the focus of our study. Black and Latinx American men also face a range of cultural and social pressures to conform to traditional masculinity, albeit in different ways, and their rates of suicide remain lower than white men's, even while they face greater challenges when it comes to economic opportunity and racial and ethnic profiling from law enforcement.

Lenz, whom I covered earlier in this chapter for her interview with neo-Nazi undercover reporter Amanda Moore, in the same time period also wrote a lengthy essay called, "Male Loneliness is Killing Us," in which she reviewed the book *The Unplugged Alpha*, by YouTube "Entrepreneurs in Cars" creator Richard Cooper, who touts himself as a successful debt advisor and "high net worth" coach. As of this writing, Cooper had nearly 650,000 subscribers on YouTube and more than 1.2 million likes on TikTok, though his subscriber count appeared to have fallen by almost 40,000 since Lenz wrote about him in her newsletter. Cooper appeals to the egos and attentions of young white men and boys with promises of unfettered wealth and influence, putting himself forward as a man with great success pursuing women romantically, despite his baldness. Still, as Lenz documents, behind the facade of wealth and influence, Cooper is revealed to be sad, lonely, and pathetic—a poor example to young boys and men seeking fulfillment and satisfying, intimate relationships.

Lenz points out that even Cooper's factually correct writings about men run into false and problematic conclusions, like when he claims that the world is skewed against men because men are more likely to be victims of violent crime than women (Lenz rightly documents that this is because men and women are both likely to be victims of male violence), and when Cooper suggests that men have it worse because they're likely to be killed in war, compared to the way in which "women were just made to be war brides."[42] Lenz, in response: "Sir, that's rape."[43]

While Lenz's takedown of Cooper's book is revealing and funny, her title also reveals that, at its base, Cooper's lonely and one-dimensional depiction of modern masculinity is sad. Cooper is offering to young men and boys an "explicitly transactional" view of manhood and adult relationships, full of hatred and lacking creativity, beauty, and love.[44] Lenz laments that while women are often called upon to heal male loneliness, with even media outlets like the *New York Times* encouraging women to "just have sex with men,"[45] men are rarely called upon to look internally for remedies to their loneliness and anger.[46] Books like Cooper's make clear that many men are without a compass, adrift in a sea of get-rich-quick grifts, protein shakes, and penile-enhancement drugs. Again, it's amusing until you think about the vulnerable young men and boys, often ones who least fit the hard-core masculine stereotypes foisted upon them, who fall into these online worlds of indoctrination and hatred. Maybe Cooper is just looking to make money from his writings and salve his own wounds of rejection from women. But young men and boys will often quickly move along the algorithm from Cooper to things like incel message boards and white supremacist neo-Nazi groups.

As much as women, like me—and maybe you, reading this book—deeply love the young men and boys in our lives, this doesn't seem to be something we can fix for them. Solutions lie within the world of masculinity itself, though loved ones and mentors—both male and female—have important roles to play.

Lenz quotes bell hooks at the end of her newsletter about Cooper, and I think it's instructive to repeat that quote here at length:

> Usually adult males who are unable to make emotional connections with the women they choose to be intimate with are frozen in time, unable to allow themselves to love for fear that the loved one will abandon them. If the first woman they passionately loved, the mother, was not true to her bond of love, then how can they trust that their partner will be true to love. Often in their adult relationships these men act out again and again to test their partner's love. While the rejected adolescent boy imagines that he can no longer receive his mother's love because he is not worthy, as a grown man he may act out in ways that are unworthy and yet demand of the woman in his life that she offer him unconditional love. This testing does not heal the wound of the past, it merely reenacts it, for ultimately the woman will become weary of being tested and end the relationship, thus reenacting the abandonment. This drama confirms for many men that they cannot put their trust in love. They decide that it is better to put their faith in being powerful, in being dominant.[47]

I wrote at length in chapters three and four about the ways in which the Church and influential male pastors spent much of the early aughts and 2010s attempting to bring men back to church by emphasizing the traditional masculinity of Jesus, even attempting to claim him as vitally angry and violent. Many American conservative Christians, as evidenced by their ongoing support of former President Donald Trump, continue to subscribe to a faith in brittle and brutal masculinity. But that's not the only option, writes Matthew Loftus for *Christianity Today* in an opinion piece that starts out promising in its critique of extreme manhood influencers but ends up falling flat in its call to traditional complementarianism and limited gender roles.[48] In response to "manosphere" influencers, Loftus suggests that the church will always be destined to fail—that men and boys will always be more drawn to bullish, muscular media figures than to bookish missionaries and Christian writers like himself. He rightly criticizes the ways in which the Christian Right's embrace of ultra-masculine figures deviates from the peaceful and pacifistic Way of Jesus Christ. But Loftus is still caught in a conservative Christian tradition that was built upon essential gender differences, allowing only men to occupy the Church's highest rungs of power. Even his admonition to young men to "do the dishes after dinner" in order to find a "Christian wife" rings out as patronizing, like when dads suggest they "babysit" the kids in order to give mom a break. Loftus's prescription to the Church to mentor and build relationships with young men, and to value genuine connections, opening doors and making space at our tables, is a worthy prescription. But like too many American Christians, his allegiance to the strict gender roles of complementarianism and heterosexuality leaves him unable to fully combat the power of brutal masculinity. Only when the Church fully rejects the idea that gender tendencies were ordained by God in creation, as discussed in chapter three, will the Church be able to embrace the full breadth and uniqueness of all men and boys in our midst, offering them a chance at full personhood whether or not their "manhood" is deemed sufficient by grifty influencers and pastors.

Sensitive, emotional, vulnerable, gentle boys and men are a gift to the world, as anyone who has held a newborn baby boy in their arms can attest; and as anyone who has comforted a grieving, crying father or husband can also attest. Forcing sensitive, emotional, vulnerable, and gentle boys and men to suppress their natural tendencies and fit into some kind of contrived and prescribed box of traditional masculinity only leads to feelings of inadequacy, loneliness, depression, and despair. In this context, it's not surprising that many men and boys who fit these descriptors turn to drugs or alcohol. Writer Jared Yates Sexton documents these truths poignantly in his memoir of masculinity in his own life and in the life of his sensitive, repressed father—*The Man They Wanted Me to Be*.[49]

Growing up poor in rural Indiana, Sexton spent much of his life trying to overcome his own emotional, sensitive tendencies in order to win the love and affection of his often-distant father. It wasn't until much later in life that Sexton saw that his dad, too, was naturally sensitive and emotional, traits he covered up and repressed at great cost to his relationships with all his loved ones, especially his son and his wives. In response, Sexton prescribes increased care toward young boys and men, and also an unabashed truth-telling about the dangers of traditional and violent masculinity. He rightly notes that men and boys need to heal and be embraced in community, while at the same time being held accountable for their own participation in the kinds of violent masculinity that hurt them as well as those around them: "I've had to come to terms with my own failings in achieving the masculine model and accept that it was unattainable in the first place," Sexton writes. "It took the support of loved ones reminding me and assuring me that they loved me despite my failings and shortcomings, not to mention calling me on my overcompensation bullshit, and still telling me it was okay if I wasn't invincible, to even stand a chance of escaping the vicious cycle of toxic masculinity. Realizing I could be vulnerable and that my suffering wasn't a sign of weakness, but actually a display of strength, made all the difference in the world"[50]. The powerful thing about Sexton's story is that it's not an outright rejection of his own masculinity. Instead, it's a redefining of what healthy manhood can look like and, more importantly, feel like.

The Problem of Troubled Men and Boys: Where Do We Go from Here?

Those who are not white men and boys, who are victimized by the dominant groups' propensity and glorification of violence and anger, suffer its consequences quickly and painfully. Their suffering grounds our shared responsibility to combat gun violence, mass shootings, domestic violence, and hate crimes. For my purposes here, I also want to make clear that violent masculinity, despite its popularity on social media and in the Church and right-wing politics, isn't good or helpful for young, white Christian men and boys either. In an April 2023 study, the *Washington Post* showed that men in the United States were likely to live nearly six years fewer than women, the largest gender-based gap in life expectancy in twenty-five years.[51] Men had higher rates of mortality from COVID-19, diabetes, and cancer, and the death rate for boys and teens ages ten to nineteen was twenty-three points higher than for girls of the same age.[52] Nearly three-quarters of motor vehicle crash death victims were male, as were 87 percent of bicyclist deaths and 92 percent of motorcyclist deaths.[53] Men's under-utilizing of the health care system, and their hesitancy to seek health care, only exacerbated these trends.[54] But why would you hasten to the doctor if you've been told to avoid weakness or vulnerability at all costs?

Three months after that study came out, *Washington Post* columnist Christine Emba wrote a lengthy essay about the challenges facing men and the dearth of mainstream responses about what a "healthy masculinity" might look like.[55] She rightly points out the tendency to think that attention to men and boys might limit resources for continued needed focus on women and girls, a point also made by author and researcher Richard V. Reeves in his 2022 book-length study on masculinity, *Of Boys and Men*. Anecdotally, I can affirm the difficulty of pointing out the challenges and troubles facing white men and boys, in a world that is still skewed in favor of their privilege, at least when it comes to economic and cultural advantage. What I've attempted to show in the second half of this chapter is that we have overlapping reasons not to ignore the current state of white Christian men and boys—the danger they are to others when they embrace hatred and violence, and also the danger they currently are to themselves. It's inescapable that young, white Christian men and boys are both often the problem in modern-day America, and they're also in trouble and in need of care and support in ways that don't ignore the truths about the dangers posed by traditional masculinity, which is too often conservatives' only solution to the problems facing men and boys.

As Reeves told Emba, regarding his own admitted difficulty with finding solutions to the problems facing men and boys, "As soon as you start articulating virtues, advantages, good things about being male . . . then you've just dialed up the risk factor of the conversation," he said. "But I'm also acutely aware that the risk of *not* doing it is much greater. Because without it, there's a vacuum. And along comes Andrew Tate to make Jordan Peterson look like a cuddly old uncle."[56]

As evidenced by the personal stories about himself and his father shared by Sexton in his book, combating the damages of rigid masculinity is difficult, and when that work doesn't begin until adulthood, it is sometimes too late. Influencers like Tate are targeting younger and younger boys, especially on YouTube and social media, as evidenced by the fact that my then-fourth-grade son told me that all his friends knew who Tate was, and they were all watching videos about 'rizzing,' or the art of picking up girls and women. As researcher Peggy Orenstein, author of the 2020 book *Boys & Sex: Young Men on Hookups, Love, Porn, Consent, and Navigating the New Masculinity* told host Jo Piazza on the podcast *Under the Influence*, whose listeners are mostly moms of young kids, the trajectory of hyper-masculine influencers among young boys follows a well-worn path, from boys laughing and joking about the videos and influencers, to the influencers steadily gaining a foothold and going on to have an insidious impact on the ways boys think about themselves and about relationships with others.[57] To Piazza's horror and shock, Orenstein went on to tell her—and the audience—about the popularity of violent masculine influencers. In response, Orenstein advised honesty and compassion, a mix between taking the influencers seriously and avoiding terms like "toxic masculinity," which sometimes makes young boys see themselves as toxic.

The path away from a masculinity whose violence and emotional vacuity is literally killing people and destroying lives every single day, as many of us know personally, is not an easy one. It involves a refusal to look away from the carnage of many of our traditional teachings about masculinity, especially within the church and conservative culture. But it also involves a stubborn willingness to engage with conversation about the well-being of young, white Christian boys and men, offering them positive and healthy ways to be gentle, vulnerable, to express their emotions openly, and to build intimate and honest relationships with others. Besides parents, few people are as well-positioned to enact these social changes among boys and young men as educators, many of whom are also unfortunately underpaid and overworked, edging toward burnout in American schools today. It's there where our attention must turn next.

Chapter 6

Schoolboys

I grew up believing in the magical power of the American public school system—comprised of recess and playgrounds and wooden desks and carpet squares and lunch pails and the three Rs. In the 1980s and '90s, the dream and (valuable) myth of the American public educational system still endured, and not just because my mom was an elementary school teacher at a public school. I vividly remember writing poetry that we presented while scrambling across the monkey bars in third grade; painting posters of American states for the fourth-grade recorder concert, which was complete with random squeaks and a performance of "Fifty Nifty United States."

I remember school lunches that cost $1.30 and band lessons in the freezing cold entryway where we learned the *Star Wars* theme for trumpet. I remember throwing our bodies down the frozen, snowy hill at recess, and bringing extra pants to change into afterwards.

Memories of school can be idyllic if you had a privileged experience. They can also be traumatic, complete with bullying and embarrassment and harassment. American students and teachers have learned, in fits and starts, since the 1990s, that it was wrong to glorify Christopher Columbus and spend months learning the names of the European explorers who "discovered" the world, while teaching Native American history as though the tribes were mere relics of the past, not vibrant people living throughout America today, in spite of European American efforts to exterminate them.

We've learned that teaching about Martin Luther King Jr.'s "I Have a Dream" speech during Black History Month should not have given white schoolchildren the impression that racism ended in the 1960s. Or that white men—and some women—were the only authors worth reading the other eleven months of the year.

We've learned about "social and emotional learning," about emotional regulation, about disabilities and neurodivergencies. We're learning about gender and sexuality, and we're still figuring out how best to teach kids about those things—though maybe they are the ones teaching the adults in their lives.

But as you can see, school no longer looks the way it did just a few decades ago in America. For many reasons—among them social, political, and economic—American schools have become rhetorical battlegrounds. Tragically, while politicians and parents are arguing over the ideologies in American schools, American students and teachers return each day to school buildings where they fear they might encounter a real gun battle, a real mass shooting, and witness or experience violent death in a place parents have always considered to be among the safest for their children. Unlike during the school bombing drills of the Cold War, in American schools today the enemy is no longer Soviet Russia but instead that brooding teenage boy who stole his father's gun.

We cannot understand the problems of radicalization among young, white Christian boys in America, nor fully grapple with the challenges and troubles facing these boys, without understanding what's happening in American schools. And without consulting that most underpaid and too-often scapegoated American professional, the public school teacher.

Again, when I was growing up, public school teachers were generally viewed positively. Some of the era's most popular films glorified them, albeit in a white savior sort of way, in movies like *Dangerous Minds* and *Mr. Holland's Opus*, both of which I watched multiple times at home and as required viewing in school. Public school teachers weren't expected to get rich, but they could earn a solid middle-class income, with good benefits and a pension, offering many baby boomer parents like mine an opening into the middle class after childhoods that veered toward the poverty line—childhoods in large families with lots of kids. This was the case for both me and my spouse: both of our mothers ended up as public school teachers after growing up in families without a lot of money and with lots of mouths to feed.

And even when your parent was a teacher, teachers in general remained sort of otherworldly beings whom you were shocked to see outside the classroom or to learn had families of their own. They were mostly treated with respect and honor, with parents generally deferring to the teachers' best interests.

It was around this time in my childhood, in the 1990s and early 2000s, when that polarizing stimulant Ritalin, or sometimes Adderall, was starting to be prescribed to young students who had trouble sitting still in class. At the time, these seemed like wonder drugs, especially in families who were adjusting to the idea of having two parents working outside the home, and thus had more stress and less time to focus on children's educational travails. Attention-deficit disorder (ADD) and attention-deficit/hyperactivity disorder (ADHD) became common parlance among middle schoolers and high schoolers, and college students started to experiment with Adderall not just to study for tests or pull all-nighters, but also as a sort of party enhancement drug, sometimes as a precursor to the harder prescription drugs of the era, like OxyContin, other opiates, and Xanax.

These trends were pronounced among boys, especially white, middle-class or upper-middle-class boys, who have long been diagnosed with ADHD three times as often as their female peers.[1] As more adults have explored ADHD diagnoses in recent years, the adult rate of ADHD tends to be closer to one to one among men and women.[2] The reason for that difference is instructive for our study: researchers have determined that boys tend to present ADHD symptoms that are more external, more physical, and more disruptive than girls, especially at younger ages. One can see how this might manifest in elementary school classrooms, whose numbers have ballooned in many settings in recent years. Thus, teachers found themselves managing increasing numbers of prescriptions and increasing numbers of students presenting with preexisting traumas and diagnoses. More and more students were placed on what are called "individualized education plans" (IEPs), which designated particular accommodations that the students required. I realized this in a striking manner when I spent an afternoon filling in as a substitute English and journalism teacher at our local, urban public high school. I asked another teacher what I could do about the number of my students who appeared near-comatose in class, many of them wearing earpods and listening to loud music.

"Nothing," the other teacher told me. "Most of them are on IEPs."

As public school teachers reading this book know well, here is where the pendulum swings back-and-forth, back-and-forth in an ever-evolving educational system. On the one hand, it's a positive change that individual needs of students are being prioritized in particular ways in schools that were formerly "one-size-fits-all," and that left too many students behind—especially students who came from marginalized backgrounds, who grew up in poverty, or who had multiple disabilities. A more empathetic, understanding, and personalized educational system is a good thing. And on the other hand, you can see how drastically these changes have transformed the jobs of public school teachers, who were formerly narrowly focused on strictly academic, and maybe some disciplinary, aspects of their jobs. Now, teachers were expected to function also in roles similar to those of social workers or medical workers, managing diagnoses and complex medical and social-emotional needs. Many teachers were not prepared for this kind of environment in their own education. And they were being asked to manage these additional changes often at the same time as they were asked to accept pay cuts and dwindling benefits, and at the same time as they were also being asked to function as minor security officials, running their kids through active shooter drills and being forced to contemplate whether each morning that they entered the school building would be the day that their classroom faced an armed assault.

These are not the fairy tale, myth-making classrooms of an idealized American educational past (we are not even addressing fully here the long-running inequities in public education and the shame of segregated schools and American Indian boarding schools).[3] These are classrooms and teachers that are often in a constant state of flux, being challenged by would-be saviors and for-profit education innovators, educators with aims that are altruistic but that sometimes compete with traditional public schools and teachers (entities like Teach for America, or charter schools), as well as those who enter education strictly with a view to how much money might be made: businesspeople without educational experience, right-wing ideologues with donor money who open fortress-like schools that deny many of the needed innovations of the past few decades, as well as disallowing admission to the very students who most need individualized education and additional help.

Of course, all of these changes and challenges were well underway before public education in America went through the difficult years of the mid-2010s and early 2020s. President Donald Trump, elected in 2016, would nominate as Secretary of Education multi-level-marketing heiress and private school champion Betsy DeVos. Apparently subscribing to a tradition in which politicians nominate as heads of governmental departments people who aim to utterly destroy such departments,[4] Trump's nomination of DeVos sent alarm bells ringing in public school districts. She and her family, named by *Forbes* in 2016 as the eighty-eighth richest in America, had spent decades and millions of dollars advocating for government money to be diverted away from traditional public schools and toward private schools by the use of voucher programs, which tended to benefit America's wealthier families and also to exacerbate trends that public schools were trying to move away from, like segregation of schools by race, wealth, class, and ethnicity—as well as denying education to disabled students. After being confirmed—for the first time in Senate history—by a fifty-one to fifty vote (Vice President Mike Pence cast the tiebreaking vote)—DeVos went on dismantle the department's staff, attempting to purge anyone she thought might be an Obama loyalist, and also weaponize the department against vulnerable people, including sexual assault survivors, disabled people, and undocumented immigrant children.[5]

You might imagine that DeVos's policy changes were good for white Christian boys, but that would assume that policies that impact vulnerable students don't also affect all American children and families, even those who don't attend public schools. Attending a private school does not protect you from being a victim of a school shooter, as students, staff, and teachers at Nashville's private Covenant School, affiliated with the conservative Presbyterian Church in America, tragically found out on March 27, 2023, when a former student entered the school with two rifles and a pistol, killing three nine-year-old children and three adults.

DeVos would also end up serving as secretary of education during one of the most difficult and perilous periods for American public schools, perilous due not only to the impending threat of school shooters but also to the COVID-19 pandemic, which closed school buildings across the country in 2020 and 2021 and forced unprepared teachers and students to temporarily move all instruction online. Even as American public schools had been defunded and understaffed and were at risk of violence and crumbling buildings, America also saw firsthand during the closing of school buildings how central public education and schools and teachers remained to the well-being of students and families. Teachers in districts across the United States, from rural western outposts to inner-city schools, raised the alarm about—in many cases—the majority of students who relied upon the schools for at least two meals a day. What would they do with the closing of school buildings? Overwhelmed districts and staff hastily organized breakfast and lunch meal pickups, and teachers tried desperately to connect with their students via online video classes, but they found out just how many students lacked working devices or internet connections. Again, as in the case of food, schools and teachers and staff were then called upon to provide devices and internet. In this time of crisis, so many stepped up and went above and beyond their job responsibilities to care for American kids and students, including parents, many of whom ended up serving as de facto home teachers, instructors, and technology support professionals, while also attempting to hold down their own jobs. Parents, kids, teachers, and staff alike all made the best out of a difficult situation. But when the pandemic dragged on and on, into fall 2020 and the beginning of another school year, fatigue and frustration set in. Many families pulled out of public schools, who were subject to state regulations around masking and online instruction, in favor of private schools, many of whom continued in-person classes throughout the pandemic and did not require masks.

Many other families, though, did not have the financial resources or wherewithal to put their kids in private schools during the pandemic. Many families were just holding on for dear life, trying to survive, including families with parents who were working on the front lines of the pandemic, whether as medical workers or in other frontline positions dealing with the public and/or caregiving. With all the stress requisite to a global pandemic, adding in the national reawakening on racism after the May 2020 murder of George Floyd at the hands of the Minneapolis police, many parents, families, and teachers felt that they were living in a pressure cooker. No one could handle additional stress and changes, but the changes and stress kept coming, as pandemic waves buffeted the country and schools found themselves reopening and closing according to infection and death rates. Millions of students, teachers, and staff lost family members and loved ones to COVID-19, and millions of others witnessed loved ones hospitalized and suffering immensely due to the disease. Others saw loved ones fall back into addiction or mental illness during the pandemic, or suffered from them themselves, due to upheaval and lack of routine care/support for their addictions and mental health.

White students, many of whom had been told rosy stories about the civil rights movement and racial progress in America, some of whom had watched the first-ever Black president inaugurated twice in their lifetimes, were now learning that the pernicious evil of racism was still alive and well in America, and sometimes they watched their family members react to this truth with shame or with indignation, expressing fear and anger over the racial justice protests that swept across America in the pandemic summer of 2020. For Black and brown students, Floyd's murder was confirmation of experiences of racism they'd long known well, including in American public schools. Many Black and brown families at this time considered homeschooling or leaving public education, often for different reasons than their white counterparts, but nonetheless adding to the historic totals of American children who were opting out of the public school system.[6] For educators and administrators who run public school systems that are often funded on a per-student basis, the loss of these students usually meant a requisite loss of funding and staff, sometimes meaning classes or positions would be cut just a few weeks into a new school year, necessitating class changes, again—another arrhythmia—for young children and their families.

Heading into the 2020 presidential election, American voters accustomed to the chaos and uncertainty of the Trump years opted, narrowly, for the apparently steadier hand of President Joe Biden, who promptly named a new secretary of education who came from a traditional public school background, Miguel Cardona, who grew up speaking Spanish and was commissioner of the Connecticut State Department of Education from 2019–2021. But COVID-19's school interruptions continued well into the beginning of Biden's term, and Cardona had his hands full just trying to retain funding for public schools and also rollback some of the culture war initiatives that had started under DeVos, especially regarding LGBTQ students and rights of sexual assault survivors.

It didn't take long for the right-wing de-funders of public education to roar right back, however. Less than a year after American voters chose Biden as their new president, voters in Virginia, who had voted for Biden by a margin of more than ten percentage points, elected as their new governor Republican Glenn Youngkin, who ran hard on a campaign emphasizing "parent rights" in education, which would become a right-wing rallying cry in later elections. Youngkin's first three orders all dealt with educational policy: (1) a requirement that only parents determine if children wear masks to school; (2) forbidding teaching of "inherently divisive topics, including critical race theory"; and (3) an investigation of a wealthy northern Virginia school district that, according to the *Washington Post,* had "been embroiled in high-profile controversy for more than a year over allegations related to critical race theory and transgender rights, as well as administrators' bungled handling of two sexual assaults."[7]

Looking back at this time in American history, I am sympathetic to parents for whom each of those three orders seemed attractive and desirable. Our children were living through a global pandemic. Their lives had been almost completely turned upside down. Many parents, especially white, middle-class, Christian parents, became radicalized during this time. Perhaps understandably, they were seeking a return to a more innocent and idyllic school environment for their kids—the environment so many of us had romanticized from our own early school experiences, which, of course, had to include a hefty dose of willful blindness about the bullying, violence, racism, injustice, and classism that was rampant in many of our schools. Still, families were understandably exhausted. They were vulnerable to the siren song of a return to a simpler era, and they were recruited by well-trained and well-funded organizers, like the right-wing group "Moms for Liberty," by innocent-sounding platitudes like a return to parent rights or appeals to the innocence of children.

It's important to recognize, though, that beneath the shiny slogans and appeals to innocence from right-wing parent groups—overwhelmingly led by white, affluent moms—only some children were allowed to be innocent, according to these groups. Certainly LGBTQ children were viewed more as threats, and as more dangerous than innocent. And Black and brown students were classified as "dangerous" when teaching, or even mentioning, long-standing truths about the history of race and racism in America was disallowed. Right-wing parent groups also sought to ban books en masse, especially books that were written by LGBTQ or Black authors.

Where did all this leave young, white Christian boys? And how about their teachers? The answers might surprise you.

Joe,[8] fifty-nine, is just the kind of teacher that hard-core advocates of traditional masculinity might dream up as their ideal educator for young, white Christian boys and men—at least at first blush. Joe, who has been teaching for thirty-six years in total, and thirty-three years in the Minneapolis Public Schools, stands six foot, five inches tall. When it comes to physical education instruction, which he has led for twenty-three years at his current school building, Joe is no-nonsense and almost stern, cutting a strong, athletic, and disciplined figure, a product of his Marine veteran father, who worked for decades in underground pipelines after leaving the military.

Joe spends his winter days at an upper elementary school in a relatively affluent neighborhood of Minneapolis, with a student body that's more than 85 percent white;[9] only to drive across the Mississippi River after school to St. Paul's Central High School, where he works as an assistant basketball coach at a school that is 59 percent minority students, including 29 percent Black students, in a neighborhood where 18 percent of residents live in poverty.[10] It's a fitting dual existence for Joe, who describes his childhood as a life in two worlds. His dad was a member of the Red Cliff Native American tribe, and the family lived together on the reservation near Bayfield, Wisconsin, even though Joe's mother was white. He recalls that sometimes he was bullied on both ends, about his Indigenous ancestry by the white kids, and from the Native kids, called an "apple," suggesting that while he was "red" on the outside, he was really "white" on the inside. Joe thought maybe that was because his teacher mom encouraged her four boys to do well in school, something that wasn't always popular on the reservation, for myriad reasons.

So Joe and his brothers found their salvation in sports, excelling in basketball and baseball, some of the only sports available at the high school in Bayfield, which didn't have football or hockey but did field a downhill ski team. He initially entered college intending to try and become a sportscaster, but when he saw the limited opportunity in that field, Joe decided to follow in his mother's footsteps. He started teaching PE in Minneapolis right around the same time his dad died, the result of a tragic accident on a worksite, when his dad fell backward without a hard hat and suffered a brain aneurysm. He never came out of the coma afterward. Joe is confident nonetheless that his dad would be proud that his two oldest sons followed their mom into careers in education, even if he might have wished to see them also enlist in the military.

Teaching PE and coaching basketball enable Joe to continue using parts of his skill set and personality that some advocates of gender absolutism might consider contradictory. He retains much of the "tough-love," "old-school" military mentality that his dad instilled in the boys. And at the same time, Joe also saw the ways in which that hard-core masculine identity led his dad to a life of physical pain and even premature death, in a situation where the hospital that cared for him after his work injury didn't have the necessary equipment to potentially save his life. Joe saw the strengths and limitations of a masculinity that's only rooted in hardness and discipline. So he brings a bit of his mom's more nurturing side to his role as an educator and coach as well. After all, Joe says the best parts of his day are often the hours he spends in physical education with a smaller group of students with disabilities and cognitive delays. These students, who are often withdrawn or quiet or uncooperative in public settings, seem to innately trust Joe, something I saw firsthand when I served as a substitute teacher in his classroom. They know the rhythms and routines of the gymnasium; it was a place they clearly felt accepted, loved, and known—something achieved by an educator rooted in discipline and athleticism but also in emotional connection, patience, and kindness.

Given his popularity among many of his students and student athletes, and his continued commitment to athleticism even into his fifty-ninth year, you might think that Joe is supremely confident and undeterred in any school setting. But he knows that washboard abs or biceps would be no match for an AR-15 in a potential school shooting situation.

"That scares me more than anything as a teacher," Joe told me, when we discussed the potential of a school shooter coming to our shared neighborhood. "Even who I am, there is very little I can do to stop that situation. The best thing we can do is just barricade ourselves."

Joe says he thinks about it often, imagining himself in the shoes of fellow teachers and educators who have faced active shooters in their buildings.

"They probably thought the same things I do," he said. "Your senses are so heightened as a teacher. You're making sure all your doors are shut. You're following the proper procedures for code red. What do you do? What do I do? What if I'm at prep? What if it's happening in another area of the building? Of all the things, that's the one that scares me the most."

I'm struck at this moment by the seriousness and vulnerability and sadness that has come over Joe's face. This is a man who deeply loves being a teacher. He told me he tries to follow the example of his mom, a third-grade teacher who always tried to have new ideas every single year as a teacher, even up to her retirement. In her honor, he says he adds a new unit each year, trying to include ideas like kayaking, sailing, pickleball, skiing, dance competitions, jump rope, etc. He knows he's in a privileged situation, in a school where sometimes outside funding and access to nearby lakes and ski hills gives him the chance to try new ideas and new equipment with the kids. He usually finds willing partnerships with parents, even if he does note that it sometimes seems like many of his students are rarely told, "No."

By nature of his work with disabled students, among whom boys are overrepresented, and his role as a boys' basketball coach, Joe does tend to spend a bit more time with boys as an educator and coach, though his office is also filled with cards from former students that are divided equally between boys and girls. He's also the father of a twenty-something son, whom he watched attend school in the same district where he teaches. He says the two of them will talk about those boys who seem to fall through the cracks, the ones for whom traditionally masculine outlets like sports or mathematics don't seem to fit, but who also don't find their place in outlets like music or drama. He and his son recently together discussed the fact that two of his classmates— despite their relatively privileged backgrounds—had recently died of drug overdoses. Joe talked also of watching the boys who used to run with joy and abandon around his gym classes, pelting each other with balls, turn into sullen, withdrawn, and angry teenagers. Sometimes seeing them makes him feel sad and powerless.

"When you, as a teacher, can pinpoint those students out, you try and let them figure out a way for themselves, and also serve as advocate for them and help them find a way," Joe says. "Sometimes they just need an ear to bend. Sometimes parents will ask me about younger kids and help them find a group, or a place to fit in."

For his part, Joe tries to make the gym and PE class a place of "escapism."

"I think that's what they want," Joe says, specifically of the young white boys he teaches who might have trouble fitting in. "They want to get away from all the other noise that's going on around them. Whether it's good or bad noise, for fifty-five minutes they can focus on whatever we're doing in here. They can put all their worries behind them."

He says that's why he's sometimes toughest on the youngest grades. He wants to set a tone: that this is a safe place for everyone where he is in charge, and the activity of the day sets the tone.

"I'm one of the few teachers who has you every year," Joe tells his students. "I get to know who you are. I probably know half of your parents out there. That's really big. I just hope for fifty-five minutes I can have you come in and be a kid."

I realize, in talking with Joe, that it's not his height or his athleticism or his perceived traditional masculinity that makes Joe a favorite among his students, or that has enabled him to have such longevity as a PE teacher in a challenging time for public school teachers, especially in inner-city, urban school districts. For Joe, for his students: the key is trust and relationship. He has been able to carve out a unique sense of both in his role as teacher and coach in Minneapolis. But it doesn't escape me that even in this ideal school, Joe still faces the fear and anxiety of the violence of the wider world, the ominous threat of a school shooting.

What about Rural Schools, Teachers, and Students?

I wanted to understand a fuller breadth of what's happening for boys in American public schools, in an environment very different from

Minneapolis, but also an environment that likely shaped Joe's youth. So I headed nearly three hours west, to a school district bordering the Lower Sioux Indian Reservation, to speak with a teacher who works with some of the district's youngest students—as well as being a mom to a teenage boy in the same district, and wife to a pastor in one of the town's largest churches.

Linda,[11] forty-two, holds an undergraduate degree in business, and she came into her role as an educator in response to the drastic need for teachers in the rural Midwest. After working for a few years as a preschool assistant in her small Minnesota town, she got a phone call from the superintendent, offering her a position in early childhood special education. Linda says she's a "poster child" for the Grow Your Own grant program in Minnesota, which helps fund education for teachers. She was just working toward the conclusion of a master's degree in education through the program when we talked in the fall of 2023, but she said many of her urban and suburban counterparts in the program, as well as her instructors, didn't quite understand her role as a rural, early-childhood educator who worked with a population of students and families who were predominately Indigenous. Instead, many people assumed that because she was working in rural America, her experience was predominately white. And even though Linda is pursuing proficiency in the Dakota language to help in her work with Indigenous families, she said that most of her diversity education instruction focused on Black and white contexts, ignoring other forms of ethnic and socioeconomic diversity.

Linda's comments highlight the ongoing gaps between educators' needs and the instruction in education they're offered, whether it's at the undergraduate or graduate level. American public schools have, in many cases, become "majority-minority," with huge numbers of students identifying as biracial or multiracial, as well as coming from backgrounds that are Latinx or Asian-American. Additionally, many of the white students whom Linda works with have biological parents who are or have been incarcerated, or who are struggling with addiction and have lost custody of their children. Her context throws many preconceived notions about American families and students out the window.

Like Joe, Linda also works as a coach, serving as an assistant for five years to the area high school cross-country team, whose boys' team qualified for the state tournament in 2023. Recently, her son has been a member of the team. She's a mother of three, with two teenage boys and a younger daughter. Thus, Linda experiences kids at the very beginning and very end of their interactions with the local public schools.

Her work as an early childhood special education teacher brings her into contact with students and families with a long history of trauma and often abuse, addiction, and legal issues. For her students who come from Indigenous backgrounds or live on the reservation, Linda also knows that they're grappling with generational trauma and historical violence and abuse against Native Americans. Known for its proximity to fertile farmland and its picturesque waterfalls, her small town is also located just seventy miles northwest of Mankato, Minnesota, where thirty-eight Dakota men were hung on December 26, 1862, before a crowd of an estimated 4,000 onlookers,[12] in the largest one-day mass execution in American history—just two days after white Minnesotans gathered in churches for Christmas Eve services.[13]

As a white schoolgirl in Minnesota growing up in the '90s, I learned a lot about lynchings of African Americans in the "racist" South. But I never learned about the Dakota War, much less about the fact that I'd grown up less than two hours from America's largest one-day mass execution. It's not only this tragic history, then, but also its erasure among most white Americans that Linda confronts as she works with young students with special needs in the local district. At the same time, she attends the large Lutheran church in town where her husband pastors, in a community so rooted in German and Scandinavian Lutheranism that the town's other large congregations are not Evangelical or Baptist but Catholic and other strains of Lutheran. So, much of the community remains rooted in a sort of rural whiteness that is still figuring out how to confront its violent past with the Native American tribes that first inhabited this land. It's not easy to say what effect this history is having on the young white boys who are growing up in the area. (I'll interview a few of them in the next chapter.) For Linda, in her role as mom and cross-country coach and pastor's wife, she notices the same common trends among young, white (and rural) Christian boys and men that others I interviewed had mentioned to me: specifically, that boys tended either to be involved in lots of extracurricular activities or none, in the latter case succumbing to isolation and occasional diversions into online rabbit holes that prioritize brutal and violent masculinity and sometimes right-wing Christianity. She watches how generational trauma and incarceration runs in white families, too, noting that she'll often recognize family names from county jail rosters. As is typical in rural America, mental health resources are often hard to come by.

"We have one licensed psychologist in the area," Linda told me. "And she was the president of my husband's congregation." The interconnectedness of small towns sometimes means confidential health care is tough to find. But it also means that the couple can work together to help get resources to people in need, by utilizing their shared connections through church and the school system.

Linda has also experienced parents, even of preschoolers, pressing her about right-wing talking points often spread to parents online by groups like Moms for Liberty.

"[The culture war stuff] is sometimes the one thing they can control," Linda said, noting that sometimes parents whose kids were having trouble in the school system would grasp for anything they could think of to explain what was happening, an understandable impulse in the chaotic recent years of pandemic and intense political division, flames fanned by right-wing political leaders in order to solicit donations and ramp up GOP voting blocs in rural America.

While the right-wing Evangelicalism that makes up much of the Republican Party's base in the rural South and West is almost nonexistent here in rural southwestern Minnesota, Linda says it's sometimes boys who've attended the conservative Lutheran K–8 school who she sees struggling the most to square their experiences as teenagers with the socially conservative worldview they were taught in school, including an emphasis on traditional masculinity and femininity. On the other hand, when it comes to issues of transgender students, the Indigenous students in the area bring with them a particular understanding of transgenderism, rooted in the Indigenous tradition of Two Spirits.[14]

And even here, hours from the Twin Cities, educators, students, and families face the impending fear of a potential school shooter. Linda says that for the first time, they recently added a secured entrance at the school where her kids attend. And she's relieved, even though parents complain about lockdown drills in the schools.

"There were days in the past when I was like, 'Shoot, I have to send my kid to school for something,' and it doesn't feel safe," she said.

Her own boys are still relatively early into their teen years. She hopes they can look to their dad for an example of masculinity that's grounded in love, dignity, kindness, and respect. But she also knows that their growth into men goes beyond just their dad's example.

"I want them to see that masculinity isn't necessarily the only piece," she says. "Who you are doesn't have to be rooted in some piece of masculinity that this world has said. Be very confident in who you are. If we are all created in Christ, then everybody has a place. It's not all the same, and that's OK."

Like Linda, Amy,[15] thirty-seven, is a rural educator and also a mom of boys. She formerly coached volleyball in the schools as well but is taking a break now and "only" officiates volleyball and softball for extra money. The daughter of a longtime PE teacher and single mom, Amy brings athleticism and energy to her job teaching middle school science in a rural Midwestern district where 30 percent of students are nonwhite and 20 percent are considered economically disadvantaged, as well as nearly 10 percent as English-language learners.[16] Most of the school's racial and ethnic diversity comes from a large population of Latinx students, some of whom are family members of migrant workers who work at the nearby Seneca Foods processing plant. As a result, a significant number of Amy's students "head south" for weeks or months out of the year, sometimes to Mexico or Central America, but often to Texas. This means teachers, students, and families are often coordinating different school curriculums and standards, or even, in the middle school setting, different subjects altogether, like biology vs. chemistry or earth science or life science.

It's important to spend significant time learning about these rural educational settings when studying young, white Christian men and their potential radicalization into right-wing violent or white supremacist groups, because one of their most fertile recruiting grounds is found among young white boys and men in rural America, where conservative politics are already dominant, and Christianity still holds strong social influence among white families. It's also important to consider how the growing racial and ethnic diversity of rural communities is changing the experiences of white boys in schools, and how school systems are having to make adjustments and adaptations in real time, on dwindling resources.

Despite the limited financial renumeration and occasional challenges of working with young teens in the midst of puberty, Amy—a mom of four, including two boys—says she still loves teaching students at "the most awkward, hardest, weirdest times in a kid's life." After working briefly as an emergency medical technician, Amy followed her mom's path into life as an educator and coach, saving lives in a whole different kind of way.

She says she loves watching kids grow and mature: "I look at these kids I had four years ago and see them as juniors and seniors . . . I am not as worried about you now," she adds, chuckling.

Amy, like Joe and Linda and, I imagine, like many teachers and educators you're thinking of as you read this, got into education out of a sense of love and relationship and desire for connection with all her students. She says the hardest part is figuring out how to leave work behind when she goes home to her family, especially when she's thinking about students who leave for break without being sure they'll have enough food to eat or a safe place to sleep at night. Post-pandemic, she said her district is seeing "really, really low reading levels," which makes teaching other subjects difficult, as many lessons rely upon students reading and understanding directions. Add in students who are still learning English, and students who miss one to two months of school every year when families head south, and Amy has her hands full attempting to help her kids meet the district and state "grade level abilities."

Among the middle schoolers she works with, Amy also notices more absenteeism, a lack of self-motivation or self-gratification, a lack of patience with learning difficult and detailed concepts. And then as we're talking, before school starts, a student comes to the door asking for help.

"He's worried," Amy says, a look of concern on her face. "He doesn't want to go south; he's worried about going to a new school, and he's worried about having enough food."

But she's grateful this student is sharing his concerns with her because Amy also says she has lots of male students who don't.

"It's harder for them to show the emotion or ask for help."

In a district where Amy says students come with an average of five to six adverse childhood experiences,[17] and many students have parents who are or have been incarcerated, while others deal with domestic violence in their homes or alcoholism among caregivers, one of the new innovations added to school buildings is a place called the Calming Room, a space right by the counselor's office where students can go to calm down, or possibly color or read picture books: stepping away from stimulation and regrouping.

A place like the Calming Room might be an easy innovation for right-wing traditional masculinity influencers or politicians to mock, but in a chaotic environment filled with change and uncertainty, it seems like a needed resource, especially for boys who might have a hard time verbalizing their emotional needs. Amy says some students are starting to have Calming Room access written into their IEPs, and she says she's a personal advocate of the increased use of IEPs, although it's challenging for teachers because often all students with IEPs are grouped into one section of the day, due to lack of staffing for classroom aides.

Accordingly, Amy too sees a majority of middle school boys, more than girls, who are diagnosed with ADHD or autism. She sees the benefits of medication for these students, but she also sees students who are "overmedicated," or students acting drowsy or erratic due to changes in medication, something teachers aren't always notified of until the behavior changes. She worries about the kids who sit silently, day after day, and she wonders if she's reaching them, or if she's meeting their needs. Often, the medications cause lack of appetite, too, which increases feelings of tiredness and lack of mental attention among her students.

When it comes to hot-button social issues, especially around sexuality and gender, educators I spoke to in rural areas sensed a preemptive concern about lawsuits that sometimes caused school districts to make sweeping decisions in the absence of actual student or family situations in their districts. I sensed that the greatest gift of teachers and educators was their ability to see each student as an individual, and to cultivate trust and relationships with them. District administrators didn't have that same gift or ability, and their policies sometimes made it harder for teachers to use those relational gifts. More opportunities for shared listening and decision-making among educators, administrators, students, and families would likely result in better outcomes, even if the process might seem more fraught in the beginning.

Finally, when I ask Amy about that ongoing topic, of young white teen boys who seem aloof, distant, and lonely, she brings her innate sense of compassion and energy to talk about boys she obviously knows well. Amy talks about her district's Science Club, Art Club—and even about scheduling students to come and see her so they can talk one-on-one. She also mentions an area for board games or playing chess, which she says has been a "great outlet" for the kids who haven't found their niche or clique in other areas, especially music and sports, which tend to form the center of rural kids' social lives.

But educators and schools don't have to be the only social resources and communities where young, white Christian men and boys are formed in a more empathetic and understanding version of masculinity. The church, especially in rural communities, has often served as that "third place" where community happens. But how can churches help young, white Christian boys and men find compassionate masculinity, when so often American Christianity has instead championed a violent, angry, hierarchical masculine God?

Chapter 7

To Fear and Love God So That?
Confirming White Boys in the Faith

First, they came for the Koreans.

I had been telling a rural, Midwestern pastor about my work and research into young, white Christian boys and men. This pastor too was a parent of boys and had spent more than a decade in a rural Midwestern church, where the pastor was beloved in town and known for speaking boldly and prophetically about divisive social issues.

As I told this rural, Midwestern pastor about my study of young, white Christian men and boys, the pastor got a far-off look in their eyes. The pastor was remembering a story.

It happened about fifteen years earlier, in the pastor's previous congregation, in another small Midwestern town. The boys were now, as the pastor told the story, in their late twenties and early thirties, beginning to have children and families of their own. But they were young teens when this story took place. The pastor remembered them as good, kind boys. They were faithful church attendees and hard workers. They were respectful and engaged in the study of the Bible, particularly in this Wednesday class, known as "Confirmation," where they spent time with the pastor learning the basics of their faith, in preparation for the rite of Confirmation, which would be celebrated in front of the entire congregation.

These were boys we'd all be proud to call our sons. They were captains of the sports teams and leaders in the school band. They helped local farmers bale hay and operate equipment, working late in the night on their families' or neighbors' or local friends' fields. They opened doors for women and said "please" and "thank you." These weren't the boys we worried about, the ones who slunk around in the corners of doorways smoking cigarettes or surreptitiously sipping liquor, staying out late and ditching class. These were the "good boys."

The pastor had first been a youth pastor, working with kids and teens for almost ten years before pursuing additional theological education and becoming an ordained pastor. They were one of those people who just had a knack for asking the right questions and keeping kids on task, getting them to open up and share stories and "be themselves," in a way that teenagers often aren't with adults, especially authority figures. So the pastor knew and loved these kids, including the aforementioned boys.

"I couldn't believe the words that came out of their mouths," the pastor told me, remembering, shaking their head.

The pastor was teaching a lesson about creation, a basic one really. It was supposed to be a fun exercise, a throwaway thing that serves as a kind of icebreaker, before the kids all opened their Bibles to read and learn and laugh together as they had on Wednesday after Wednesday after Wednesday for generations, in a town where the school sports coaches still ended Wednesday practices early so that kids could get to church.

"We did this exercise," the pastor said. "I asked them: 'If you were God, what would you include that God didn't? What kind of world would you create?'"

The pastor walked over to a group of girls discussing the question. They brought up ideas like breathing underwater. A world without diseases.

The pastor walked across the room to the boys' table. They were snickering, blushing.

"What if we had invisibility so we could look in the girls' locker room?"

The pastor attempted to move the conversation along, to open the Bibles and get to the "real" lesson. But the boys were getting into it now. They started talking about North Korea and the dictatorship there and its ruler, Kim Jong-Un, who had recently succeeded his father.

One of the boys just said it: "If I was God, there would be no Koreans."

Another one nodded accordingly: "No Russians, obviously, either."

"Definitely not any Mexicans. No Hispanics."

The mood in the room shifted. It got personal. Their desire to eliminate North Koreans and Russians was abstract and political, but their *reasoning for eliminating Mexicans or Hispanics came from much closer to home—simply because of a few kids at school they didn't get along with.*

"No African Americans either," someone said.

There was internal debate.

"No, no, no," another boy said. "Take that back. [The African Americans] can be the ones who clean and cook the food."

The boys—all of them white—continued planning their white utopia, assuming that White Jesus would agree.

"I just let them keep going," the pastor said, looking stricken. "I was internally just like: 'Holy shit.'"

At some point the group had also banned all Jewish people, though the pastor was doubtful any of them had ever met a Jewish person. There were no synagogues or Jewish temples for at least sixty miles.

Eventually, they got to the coda of their new creation: the shining White City on a Hill.

"Women can be there, but they all have to be naked!"

They sat there grinning, proud. They'd made a plan. Now, the pastor would tell them to open their Bibles and class would go on, right?

The pastor stopped them.

"I was just really animated, really over-the-top," the pastor recalled.

"WHOA! You guys! Holy cow!" the pastor started out, the boys looking at the pastor expectantly. "Do you know what, you guys? I totally know this. What you've created. It sounds so stellar to me. So similar. You have actually described the requirements of a super elite exclusive club of people."

They just looked at the pastor, some of the boys starting to furrow their brows. Maybe the pastor was mad they'd also banned a fellow high school student, a frequent church volunteer and attendee who was known for speaking his mind. He had to go, too.

The pastor looked back at them, caught in a moment of heartbreak almost hinging into despair. What happened to all the lessons on God's love, God's acceptance? What of the Jesus who came to save the world? Hadn't they heard a single one of the countless sermons the pastor had preached?

One of the boys cleared his throat.

"Are we like the KKK or something?"

"Yeah, well, or the Nazis," the pastor affirmed, a lump in their throat.

The pastor took a deep breath and dived in, realizing that that night's planned lesson would never be taught, because this was the moment, the moment when hatred and love diverged in the truth, and God was almost traded in for a cynical, violent bully. It wasn't too late for these boys. The pastor loved these boys.

The pastor held their swelling tears at bay, kept a stoic face, asked the boys: "Do you really believe these things? Are you really racist? Sexist? Anti-Semitic?"

The pastor had been teaching them about the Bible for three years.

"I was just heartbroken. Shocked," the pastor told me. "It started out joking. Some of it came from a real place."

The pastor pointed out to the boys that while they banned white individuals, they were quick to exclude entire groups of people who weren't white. The boys, just teenagers, trusted the pastor enough that they kept going with the conversation. They stared at themselves in the mirror the pastor held up to them.

"They were able to name that it was racist. We talked about the KKK and the Nazis and about how these ideas were the same ones they have. And about how those groups (and so many others) acted on those hatreds. And what it did to the world."

The boys stared down at their hands, hardworking hands, hands that held their mommies' hands when they were dropped off at Kindergarten for the very first time, looking through eyes flocked by long, still-boyish eyelashes, eyes that held tears and sensitivities that—in this time in their lives—they were trying so desperately to hide away. They painted over their pain and love and emotions with the easily accessible white male hatred, asserting themselves at the top of the social order. Because the vulnerability required to do otherwise was impossible, now that they were becoming men. Someone would call them a "pussy."

There were other influences, too, though. Dads and grandpas and pastors and moms and uncles and aunts and older kids. People who were gentle and kind no matter their gender. A church that had taught them of a God who loved first, who turned the other cheek.

They beseeched one another, admitting their culpability, grasping for their humanity, desperate for God to be God, for the relief of not *having to make themselves into little white male demigods of guns and violence.*

The pastor took a deep breath.

"The ultimate conclusion was that they were super glad that God was God. And God had done the creating, and not them," the pastor told me, their eyes far-off again, remembering that day. *"They were glad that they hadn't done the creating, because they would have created something bad."*

The pastor first told me this story months before I began working in earnest on this book. But it never entirely left my mind, because it said so much in a single anecdote. These were the boys we didn't think we had to worry about. It turned out that the hatred was latent in them, too. The creation story, fallen and thwarted and perverted by white men thirsty for power. Of course, the story didn't end in that place, not this time. The story kept going, and I have to wonder if those boys didn't think of it from time to time today while they raised their own sons. That group of Confirmation students allowed what could have been a devastation, a declaration of war and rage, to be a turning point, perhaps. It was a time to step back, to see and lament the ugliness within, offer it to God, and change.

I'm sharing this story at the start of this chapter about catechism and faith instruction in the Church for young, white Christian boys and men because it's such a critical place of instruction and maturation for boys. It's here, on these worn-out, faded, and patched couches of church youth group rooms permeated by the smell of burnt microwave popcorn and raging teenage hormones, that so many young, white Christian men develop their own sense of faith and God.

In these youth rooms, retreat centers, camps, mission trips, conferences—some youth pastors, seeking their own fame, attention, and glory, abused young people and taught young men to abuse young women, suggesting that women were only valuable as silent, sexual objects. Long is the list of pastors, priests, teachers, and volunteers who have used the churches as their personal grooming grounds, exploiting the vulnerabilities of young people and shaping a mistrust of God, an incalculable loss of love and trust that for many would be a lifelong hurdle. Still others, with good intentions brimming, would teach God and Jesus and Christianity as merely smokescreens for white American patriotism, a sense that white Christians alone were the "chosen people," and that God's love was exclusive and violent and inscrutable—calculating.

I tell this story to remind us all that the wreckage of these youth rooms and youth pastors and purity retreats and abuse, perhaps the wreckage we know in our own lives, is not the only story about Christian education of young, white Christian men. There are other rooms, other spaces, other teachers, where boys might hear and see and sense and feel God, and then turn toward love and acceptance and peace, in the freedom to be vulnerable and loved themselves.

The truth is that most of these spaces, these church youth group classrooms for teenagers, fall somewhere in the middle. And churches, mired in a world where they're either irrelevant or evil for many young families, are simply desperate for anyone who might come and learn and teach. But we discount the power of these spaces at our peril. It's here where transformation can take place, where the Holy Spirit might intervene in the violence and radicalization of boys, if only we come and see.

Teach Your Children Well: Confirmation Stories

I have my own years of experience teaching catechism and Confirmation classes to teenagers in the church. And while I spent years teaching youth in large-church settings, where pastors get the luxury of speaking to teenagers from a stage following band-led music and excitement, the place I learned most about teenagers was the little rural church where I was on my own with a group of as many as ten seventh-, eighth-, and ninth-grade students.

In the first year of my time with them, they got dropped off by the school bus across the street from the church building, in a tradition that likely began decades ago when it was taken for granted that most students would spend Wednesday afternoons at the church. When I first started teaching in 2019, the kids told me that most students in their schools still attended Confirmation classes, but in actuality, "a lot of them don't believe in God."

I journeyed with these kids through Confirmation classes at that church in the rural Midwest from December 2019 to January 2023, during the chaos of the COVID-19 pandemic, the horror of the murder of George Floyd at the hands of the Minneapolis police, and the carnage of the January sixth attempted insurrection at the US Capitol.

We were together nearly every Wednesday afternoon from 4 p.m. until 5 p.m., except for the weeks when we met virtually due to the pandemic. Some of the memories from that time make me smile even to this day, like the time when the kids were horsing around and knocked over a big plant in the education room. After getting out the ancient vacuum and cleaning up the dirt spill, a few of them made it their mission to nurse the plant back to life. Even throughout the pandemic, occasionally they'd check in on the plant. It brought us a sense of community, somehow, in a perilous world.

I remember with fondness the boys who would tear up to church on their four-wheelers, fearless and undaunted, and then whip off their helmets to reveal the still-maturing boys underneath. I remember turning on the Zoom Confirmation class to meet virtually, only to see one of the boys Zooming in from his ice house on the frozen lake where he was going ice fishing. I think he was much more focused on the fish than the lesson for our day, but still, I was touched. Everything in the world was upside down in that moment, but he still made the effort to tune in to Confirmation, with his friends in the ice house looking on.

I remember lots of cameras pointed up to ceilings, and I remember realizing how awkward it felt for self-conscious teenagers to have to stare at themselves on camera all day, and how much they hated having to do online Confirmation after days upon days of online school.

I remember how happy they were when we came back together for in-person Confirmation, and how for so many weeks I tried to cram in too much content, too much Bible-reading. It took years before I learned that the most important part of our time together was often our practice of sharing "highs" and "lows," and really listening to one another, as they came to trust me and trust each other.

I remember the tall, blond boy, the eldest of four in his family, the one who always helped carry things or volunteered to usher at the Sunday services or answered the question no one else wanted to answer during class. I remember his wide smile, and I remember the unspeakable sadness in his voice when we talked on the phone after he'd been in an accident on the school bus on the way to an athletic event. In the moment of the accident, he'd been there, present, alert, and poised, helping other kids and keeping everyone calm. But the driver of the other vehicle, a young woman, had died in the crash. He couldn't get the sadness out of his head. I was so thankful that occasionally he'd talk to me, and that his parents were able to access other support for him. He was going to be OK. But so many of these kids had suffered trauma and accidents of one kind or another, and they didn't always get the support they needed.

From a distance, these kids—like the ones in the story I mentioned earlier—were the "all-American" good kids. They played sports and did music and worked on the farm. Some of them wore Crocs, and some wore cowboy boots. They were wrestlers and football players and set designers for the school musical. They were brothers and sons and sisters and daughters and grandchildren, and when they got confirmed in front of the church, they were the pride of the entire congregation. I remember one bashful boy sharing about what he'd learned in the Bible, and another brave girl talking about her commitment to her faith. Sometimes they surprised me when we met one-on-one before the Confirmation service to go over their written faith statements. Their faith in God was burgeoning, rich, inviting, and questioning.

There are other memories, too: more painful ones. That first group of ten kids was the first time I'd been the primary teacher to teenagers, with no other adults in sight. It was a much tougher gig than standing on stage in front of hundreds at those larger churches. I was earnest and energetic, and I probably didn't listen enough. I had multiple students, mostly boys, with disabilities in the group, and I didn't always know how to engage them or handle the times they got frustrated or didn't want to participate. I learned as I went on, but one of them pulled out of the classes before getting confirmed, and as a pastor, you kind of always feel like it's at least partially your fault (kind of like being a parent, or a teacher). That boy wasn't close to his mom; she had moved to another state without him, and sometimes I wondered if there was something about me that reminded him of her. He got especially angry when I talked to the class about George Floyd's death, and about the role of racism in Minnesota. I got another angry phone call from a different parent that week, too. Or actually, my church council president got the call, about me.

Still, that same student would often send me Zoom messages. Trust built up slowly. Each fall, I got to meet with the kids individually and hear them share with me about what they believed about God. I got to pray for them and "confirm them" in their faith, a rite of passage sometimes also called "affirmation of baptism." In Christian traditions that baptize infants, like my own, this rite is an opportunity for teens to take their own initiative when it comes to their faith, after the guidance of their families and church communities. Sometimes, Confirmation equaled graduation, and we rarely saw the kids again. But more often, they remained in the church's orbit, and upon high school graduation, they were sent off with a handmade quilt.

The last few months before I left that rural congregation, I had a little group of students that was all boys—plus one girl who joined us in their second year. I felt like I was finally hitting my stride as a teacher of teens. One night in November 2022, I was asked to share a message of hope with junior high students from a nearby small city and its surrounding area, about an hour's drive from where my church was located. I told my Confirmation students they could just have the night off, and maybe watch it on YouTube if they got a chance. But to my surprise, their parents got together and offered to drive the kids two hours, round trip, to join in the event. I remember looking out into that sea of church pews to a bunch of unfamiliar faces, only to look at those four kids with a swelling in my chest that could only have been immense pride. I still remember that feeling when I think about it today, when my chest gets that same puffed-up feeling, and when I look at the wall and see a painting one of them gave to me.

Anyone who teaches or coaches middle schoolers (or parents middle schoolers, for that matter) will tell you it's one of the most difficult and also one of the most rewarding things you'll ever do. I remember driving home at 5 p.m. on icy roads for fifty-five miles at the end of teaching confirmation that first year, with ten kids, at least eight of whom I was pretty sure didn't like me at all, and definitely wouldn't be there if their parents weren't making them. It was thankless work some days. But there was nothing like looking into their faces years down the road and seeing that maybe they trusted me, that I had listened to them, and that together God had changed something in our hearts, urging us toward patience, love, and understanding—even across our urban–rural political divide.

Raising "Pure" Teens

I was on a research trip in the rural Midwest, to a town where a white supremacist organization had purchased a former church building in order to hold gatherings and, apparently, spread its hateful ideas.

Just five blocks away from the white supremacist "church," I noticed there was another church, this one Roman Catholic. It was part of a large, rural parish group, and, in an age of ongoing priest-shortage, especially in rural parishes, one ordained Catholic priest was expected to cover six parishes, across an area of sixty-plus miles.

Unlike in days gone by, when my dad went to a Catholic school taught primarily by nuns, most of these rural parishes didn't have much in terms of staffing and programs. So I was surprised to see a whole horde of kids, backpacks in tow, marching into the Catholic church when I drove past on that orangey harvest-time afternoon.

An hour later, after conducting interviews in the nearby town, I went back on a whim and walked up to the door of the church. Unlike with many church buildings, this time when I walked up, the door was open. I walked right in, and I heard the kids and teachers wrapping up lessons in the church basement.

I think I approached Jane,[1] forty-four, maybe because she just looked like someone who could have been a friend of mine. Tall, with a frank, open, welcoming face, her voice encouraging but authoritative with the kids, Jane didn't look too annoyed by my unannounced visit.

"We're just finishing up," she said, inviting me to take a seat upstairs.

I watched as the kids filed out. They were younger than the Confirmation ages I was used to teaching, maybe more upper elementary school. But they too were working toward what Jane called their "sacramental years," milestones in the church like first communion (usually in second grade) and Confirmation (usually around eleventh grade).

Jane told me that it was her first year teaching here, that previously the kids had to drive to the neighboring town. But everyone preferred going to their "home parish," and the kids walked over straight after school.

Jane's own kids made up a sizable portion of the group. She was mom to six, three boys first, followed by three girls, ranging in age from thirteen to just one year old. Her eldest son often babysits, she said, and he's at ease taking care of his younger siblings, despite being, in her words, "cynical and conservative," and frequently challenging his teachers at school.

Jane and her husband, Sam,[2] raised their kids to be that way: centered in their faith and maybe a bit suspicious of others who would challenge that teaching. Jane homeschooled the kids during the school's mask mandate, and she told me she'd be happy to keep doing it. But her husband is a school board member, and she said they're generally happy with the local public schools.

Women like Jane, who is contracted for ten to fifteen hours a week at the church but said she often works more than forty, are a lifeline to rural churches strapped for staff and funds. She previously worked as a teacher and is experienced preparing lessons for kids. She brings to the job the organization and experience of a trained educator, as well as the zeal of a fairly recent Catholic convert. Jane didn't grow up in the church; in fact, her mom told her that "if you pray you're stupid or brainwashed." Still, Jane had spiritual experiences even as a girl, like the time her friend prayed for her while she walked between hulking dairy cows in the barn. And when she fell in love with Sam, they went to mass together. She was drawn to the Eucharist, what Catholics call the bread and wine of holy communion, Jesus's body and blood.

When Jane and Sam first wanted to start a family, she had trouble conceiving. As she sought out church resources for infertility, Jane also found herself drawn to the church youth group. She and Sam started teaching classes about sexuality and gender to single-sex groups of boys and girls. She talked to the girls about all the things that the other adults in their lives were possibly too squeamish to bring up, and she shared her personal story with them: how she didn't grow up going to church, how she did have sex before marriage, and how she regretted it. Eventually, Jane had an operation at a Catholic institute in Nebraska intended to help her be able to become pregnant. Miraculously, the treatment worked. I had never heard of it before, but Jane said she was referred by a pro-life women's health clinic in the Twin Cities metro area. That same clinic advertises "abortion pill reversal" on its website. As for the institute, its founder, Dr. Thomas W. Hilgers, a clinical professor in the Department of Obstetrics and Gynecology at Nebraska's Creighton University, writes on the institute's website about his dismay over "a distinct move at various locations throughout the United States in an attempt to reclassify the gender with which we were born . . . the conflagration of genders at younger and younger ages is becoming a serious problem and one definitely needing a response."[3] Hilgers goes on to rail against Planned Parenthood and its "highly perverted and distorted view of humans."[4]

As I talked more with Jane that afternoon, I was struck by her generosity and openness. She shared about her relationship with her sister, who had come out as a lesbian a few years ago. Jane said that when her sister first came out, she was "really promiscuous." It was hard for Jane to keep introducing her kids to her sister's many partners. But even though the two remain separated by a large gulf of politics and religion, she admitted: "My sister seems healthier now than she has been for a long time." Jane said her sister told her that when she first came out as a lesbian and started dating women, she "didn't do it right at first."

When you sit with Jane, like I did, after all the kids filed out, and her son went home to babysit, and her husband finished up work in the fields before attending community meetings, you come to understand how people get drawn into right-wing Christian movements. Jane experienced, in her telling, a miracle through her treatment at the institute. She now has six children to show for it. In a childhood marked by chaos, parental alcoholism, and loneliness, her commitment to the Catholic Church and to her faith has brought her a grounded sense of comfort, peace, security, and safety. When Jane tells me about her passion for teaching teen girls—and her husband's passion for teaching teen boys—about sexual purity, I can see it comes from a genuine place. She wants to protect these girls from the struggles she partially attributes to her own lack of religious guidance. She wants these girls to have what she has now: the husband, the kids, the family, the church—without the pain it took to get there.

Without knowing Jane and her story, I might wonder why she lets her son frequently wear "Don't Tread on Me" shirts to school. Or why she so quickly dismisses the stories of women who died or suffered immensely because of antiabortion laws in conservative states that prevented them from access to life-saving medical treatment. Jane hesitates when I ask her about these stories, given her staunch antiabortion stance.

"I think . . . maybe those stories are exaggerated," she says, looking uncomfortable.

The reason I think it's important to hear Jane's story in a book about young, white Christian men and boys is because it's often women like Jane who are mothering and teaching these boys. Women like Jane who are pulled into right-wing movements to ban books or to limit LGBTQ rights. And I say "women like Jane" not as a pejorative because, like I said, I liked Jane. I sensed we could have been friends. I heard her story and could see how she got to the conclusions she drew. She told me that she wanted to teach her sons, and the boys in church, about chivalry and how to treat women. She doesn't let her oldest son, or any of the kids, watch YouTube, and she said she wouldn't want them to be influenced by the young men on there who encourage "rizzing" or picking up girls, and treating women like sexual conquests.

Jane said she asks her oldest son each day what he wants to offer his day for, and lately he's been saying that he wants to pray "for an end to abortion." She said she doesn't like politics, doesn't want to overly identify herself with one party or another. But social issues like abortion and LGBTQ rights "make you have to look at the party by their name," and like so many other rural, white Christians, this makes voters like Jane vote Republican almost axiomatically, especially in the absence of Democratic Party organization in much of rural America.

Ironically, though, while Jane is overtly focused on her family and students' moral lives, she said she doesn't think much about the "personal lives" of politicians, like former President Trump.

I'm struck by this enduring truth in right-wing politics, that men get to have "personal lives" and "indiscretions," while women get to be called "sluts" and "abortion-seekers" and "lazy" and "selfish."

Jane said she does worry about the teen boys who "aren't involved" at school. Her oldest does jazz band, football, and drives the tractor almost every night in the fall. He doesn't seem to have time to get into trouble. But she sees the other kids, the ones who are on the outside of the town's social circles.

"They're already drunk . . . I wonder what we could do to get them more involved. Maybe more tech stuff. Maybe they could run the scoreboard at a football game. Anything to stop them from being alone, bored, with nothing else to do," she said.

This is Jane, and other moms like her, at their best: innovating and thinking of solutions. Showing empathy and care and consideration. She told me that she wants all kids to know they're loved by God, even the eighth-grade girl who got pregnant a few years ago, or students who might come out as gay or transgender.

"I want them to know they're not who society says they are . . . not gay or transgender . . . But a son or daughter or the King. You're amazing. You have gifts and talents."

I wish I would have asked Jane, but I wonder now, as I read back her quote, if it's possible in her worldview for kids to be children of God and *also* gay or transgender. I suspect that, ultimately, she'd get there, like many American Christians who have come around to acceptance and affirmation of LGBTQ people. God's path always seems to lead toward greater inclusion. But people have to take time to get there, and they have to be surrounded by others who encourage them to question prevailing right-wing social and conservative thought.

Jane and I talked a little more about troubled kids, the boys especially, and Jane told me that she knows the suicide rate is highest among white men (actually, middle-aged white men).[5] Suicide is a worry here, especially with lots of local farm failures, rare access to mental health care, and lots and lots of guns.

But Jane quickly moved on, in her energetic way, to sharing with me an armful of books and pamphlets to take home. There's a DVD called *Green Sex*; a "Pure Commitment" card with space for a signature and a date from chastity.com; and books called *Pure Manhood, Pure Love, Male, Female, Other? A Catholic Guide to Understanding Gender, Raising Pure Teens, How to Find Your Soulmate,* and *Theology of His Body: Discovering the Strength and Mission of Masculinity.* The author is Jason Evert, a forty-eight-year-old Catholic author and "chastity speaker."

I asked Rebecca Bratten Weiss, digital editor of *U.S. Catholic* magazine, journalist on religion and social issues, and former classmate of Evert's at the ultra-conservative Franciscan University of Steubenville (she said the two didn't know each other there, though), what she thought of Evert and his work.

Weiss called Evert a "Catholic influencer" who "has successfully repeated a number of the same culture-war mantras, all of which have to do with an obsession with chastity, purity, and virginity . . . and with rigid heterosexual gender roles."

"[Evert] is not offering anything new or unique. He is not an intellectual, a philosopher, an ethicist, or a psychologist . . . he is a product of the same culture war machine . . ." she added.

Looking at Evert's books and pamphlets, in comparison with Weiss's unsparing words about his ideology, I'm reminded of the soft-focus, "all-are-welcome" megachurch websites that bury their anti-LGBTQ and anti-women-in-leadership, retrograde teaching in catchy slogans and pop music, with smiling headshots and a racially diverse staff (though the lead pastors are usually white). Weiss said that Evert and others like him don't lead with their most divisive ideas; instead, they "repackage traditionalist ideas to make them sound more appealing, more progressive, with a faux-intellectual veneer."

I think about how attractive these ideas and teachings might seem to well-meaning parents of white Christian boys. I think about how it seems almost forward-thinking, compared to the purity culture and demonization of girls' sexuality that I was raised with in the late '90s and early aughts. Weiss says that Evert calls LGBTQ people "delightful" and "worthy of love," but also says they have an "intrinsic disorder" and are "against nature." She worries about young LGBTQ people being lured in by the seeming "niceness" and then getting thrown into conversion therapy, manipulated into seeing themselves as "disordered."

Jane comes to mind when Weiss says that Evert's teachings appeal to "people who want to live virtuously."

"It's a misleading system," Weiss says. "And even when the rules are good ones (e.g., don't pressure someone to have sex), they are built on faulty premises."

A lifelong Catholic with a degree in philosophy and English literature, who was raised as a conservative homeschooler in Appalachian Ohio where she still lives, Weiss said she speaks out against Evert and "the system that produced him" because, unlike conservative critiques of progressive Catholics might suggest, she cares deeply about truth and goodness. She's just tired of these moral goods being twisted by profit-makers that dehumanize people, especially women and LGBTQ people.

I suspect Weiss has also known friends and family members like Jane, zealous and committed likely because of personal experiences, with energy and goodwill and work ethic to spare, who are nonetheless spreading the gospel of conservative influencers and traditionalist social teachings more than the gospel of Jesus Christ. The rigid teachings might give boys a framework from which to approach the world, but what about when they, or people they love, inevitably step out of that framework. Then what? Sometimes, they respond with anger, fear, and violence—toward others or themselves—leaving their moms and the ones who worked so hard to teach them the "right" way, to cry and pray alone.

What Do We Know about Jesus? A Garage, Teen Boys, and Mixed Blessings

Deep in the prairie of southwestern Minnesota, just a few miles east of the Roman Catholic church where I met Jane, a group of rural middle and high school kids had gathered in the garage of their pastors' home, a tidy, yellow, clapboard-sided abode with a red roof and a sign proclaiming welcome to the farm. Dan[6] and Janine[7] had been teaching confirmation classes here, often with snacks and gathering time before and after, and fresh eggs from the chickens, for a couple of years now. They had a refrigerator full of two-liter bottles of pop (as people in this part of the country call it), and a large green chalkboard at the center of the garage for lessons on the Bible and Martin Luther's small catechism. The chalkboard was surrounded by a circle of metal folding chairs. Both military veterans, and parents of four adult children, Dan and Janine first met in Munich, where they'd worked together at a center debriefing political refugees, mostly from the then–Soviet Union. They'd been around the world, working on highly sensitive operations. Dan had deployed overseas just before COVID-19 and experienced horrific loss as a part of his military service; Janine had stayed home to deal with the calamities of church and children during a global pandemic. Their lives had been rich and, at times, incredibly difficult, meaning that their Christian faith had weathered more than a few storms, been changed in the midst of traumatic circumstances. But still somehow the couple kept pastoring, out here in the heartland. And there were few things more important to them than the faith of these teenagers who gathered with them on that night for confirmation class.

"What do we know about Jesus?"

"WHAT DO WE KNOW ABOUT JESUS?"

The voice is a bit of a bark, authoritative and raspy, and it made sense that it was coming from Pastor Dan, though when we'd talked earlier in the day, he'd struck me as a little bit shy. Dan was in his element now, though, far away from the deployment to Iraq in 2019, right before the pandemic, that still rang in his ears, along with the memories of the guys who died and all the ones who lost their faith, even his fellow chaplains. He was in a whole other world, then, while Janine stayed back here in the rural Midwest and tried to pastor and raise their kids, including a nephew whom they would later adopt, and to tell the truth, both Janine and Dan had fought to stay alive and to still believe.

It would make sense if they'd grown too tired and left and moved away, or if they decided they were sick of jobs that required them to serve and give until it felt like there was nothing left, for their country or their church or their God, much less one another. Instead, though, there they were: grilling hot dogs on a charcoal grill and hosting parishioners for dinner in their heated garage, which was hung with drawings the teenagers had made that reminded them of God.

Dan and Janine were fifty-eight and fifty-five, born right smack in the middle of the war that would forever shake America's confidence and moral compass. Dan spent some of his growing-up years in Germany, where he learned German while his dad was a contractor for the German Navy. But he went back to graduate high school in the rural Midwest, and then on to the state flagship university, where he failed out. Dan joined the army and became an interrogator in Germany in the late '80s, where he'd interview exiles, refugees, and immigrants who were leaving the Soviet bloc.

"I wanted to be Ernest Hemingway," he says, with a wry smile.

At the Allied Forces Coordinating Center, Dan met his Catherine, though Janine was a fellow intelligence officer rather than a nurse. It would be years later that she'd have to nurse him back to health, just as he'd held her up in some of those early years.

The two of them were bright and ambitious, but they wanted to get out of the military and to go back home to the rural Midwest. So Dan and Janine, now married, got degrees at a smaller public college, while Dan worked as a reporter for small local newspapers, and Janine became a teacher specializing in English-language learners. Eventually, they bought a newspaper in South Dakota. And even though the market for journalism was quite different from what it was when Hemingway got his start, the couple was making it work. Kids came, three of them, and in the midst of it a persistent church leader kept asking Dan and Janine if they'd ever thought about being pastors.

First, Dan laughed.

"Eighteen-year-old Dan was scoffing," he said. "But I guess what made me do it had more to do with Confirmation. I actually sort of enjoyed middle school students and trying to explain it to them in ways they could understand . . . in a way they could hear it."

He used a fishing analogy, or was it a journalistic one?

"If you don't have a hook to put it on, it ain't gonna land."

Dan was one of those people who had an innate sense for who people really are, deep down inside. He saw past the artifice and self-presentation. He didn't care for all that. Maybe it was his military years or being a kid whose parents got divorced in the '70s. Whatever it was, he got straight to the point.

"I wanted to work on language that soldiers and kids and general people can understand [about God]," Dan said. "Or maybe they can't admit that they do know about God, because they're embarrassed."

He told me he remembers everything, so much so that he rarely studied in college or graduate school. These memories, unlike the other ones, served him well.

"Maybe God gave me this background so I could do what I do now," Dan said, in a softer moment of introspection.

As it had been with Dan and Janine from the beginning, though, they would do this thing, ministry, together, too—if slightly differently. Janine took a more traditional path to ordination, earning a master's in divinity and going to serve a small-town church. She was in school, raising kids, and working through a difficult time trying to help raise her sister's son as well, a boy who would end up becoming her fourth child, after her sister was unable to parent him. Dan opted to return to the military for his ministry training, joining the National Guard as a chaplain candidate. They were so short of candidates that, given his experience, Dan got a battalion right away. He was gone all the time for training and drill. Janine supported his mission, and she also felt like she was drowning.

They served churches together in their rural area for just eight months before Dan's first deployment. The military had a severe chaplain shortage, and Dan was a prized candidate. So he went to Kuwait, where his troops faced bombardments and heavy losses. His fellow chaplains, in some cases, publicly lost their faith in the face of so much tragedy. Dan held it all together, like he always did, but he felt the heaviness of the soldiers' needs, and his own relative impotence.

"It beat the shit out of me," he said, four years later. "The need was so great. It was like throwing a cup of water on a house fire."

"I'm not the same as I was," he continued. "I'm not as connected with anything as I was before."

I listened to Dan, and I thought about all the time I'd spent in churches on Veteran's Day and Memorial Day and the Fourth of July. I thought about how we had the soldiers and veterans stand, and we honored them and we thanked them for their service. I thought about the faux-fawning attitude I've seen so many pastors put on before the flag, about how they act like they're the only *real* Americans and that patriotism means being rough and tough and bragging and *winning* and Trump.

It was a real disconnect: a diagnosis of PTSD and trauma for so many soldiers, and the Church wrote a prescription for Christian nationalism and fireworks. It was like white American Christians knew there was this big need, but in order to meet it, we'd have to talk about the vulnerability and weakness of so many tough men—so we pushed it aside and grilled hot dogs on the church lawn and set off fireworks, the loud bangs ringing in the ears of the local veterans.

"When I was a kid, it was easy to know what it meant to be a man," Dan said. "Now, I say that, and I just laugh. There's no clear, defined road map. A lot of [young men and soldiers] will crush themselves and one another with their own expectations. I worry about veterans more than I did when I was a soldier."

Back home, as COVID-19 raged and Janine's youngest son kept running away from home, again and again, struggling with his disability and feeling lost, her husband away on deployment, Janine faced an unsupportive congregation. Whatever she did—however hard she worked—nothing was enough. As so often happens, church people put their anxiety about the very real dangers in the world onto their identified leader, usually their pastor.

Janine had been so brave, in different but no less courageous ways than her husband. She grew up in a conservative branch of Lutheranism that doesn't allow women to be pastors or even serve in most leadership roles or vote in church elections. Yet here she was. Ultimately, when Dan returned from deployment, the two of them were able to find new churches to serve together, a parish of four churches in the rural Midwest. Their kids were growing up and out of the house—doing OK. Janine found a way to muddle through.

"About the time that I'm feeling the most discouraged, depressed, wanting . . . life is so incredibly hard . . . then I'll get a card or a letter or someone will tell me my ministry matters to them," she said. "It's a reminder. It's as if God is saying: This is why I need you. That's been my entire call story."

I told Janine her description of her ministry journey reminds me of the contrast between Christian nationalism's theology of glory, which suggests power and riches to all those who follow God, and the theology of the cross, which reminds us that God draws nearest and does God's most powerful work when everything seems lost and hopeless, and we are most rejected, as Jesus was on the cross.

And as I looked back up at Dan, standing there red-faced and beseeching, staring out at those middle school kids whom he loved, I saw that same contrast in him, too. War beat him up. It wasn't about simple victory or God being on his side. He came back a wounded man. But there he was, in the middle of nowhere, doing exactly what he'd been created to do.

Gazing up at Dan were a group of eighteen middle schoolers and high schoolers from the surrounding towns and schools. Sprinkled in their midst was one mom and a couple of high school boys whom Dan and Janine said came back most weeks to help with the younger kids.

At one point in the night, Dan yelled at me to give my car keys to one of the middle schoolers, and I wondered if my car was going to be roped into farm service across the road, but it turned out he just wanted to give me two dozen eggs from his chickens.

The kids all came early to Confirmation. Not that they didn't also have sports or music or farm chores that night—but they came anyways, because here in this garage, and down the hill by the pigs and the chickens, this was their community. There was no sound system, no band, there were no screens, no slides—just Dan's booming voice and a pinkish-orange sunset over the prairie.

"WHAT DO WE KNOW ABOUT JESUS?"

The kids raised their hands. Quite a few of them had shirts with American flags or patriotic slogans. Wrangler jeans. Vans.

"WAS JESUS WHITE?"

"No," they said, this group of white Midwestern kids.

Dan replied that Jesus had olive skin, like the Iraqi people he met when he was deployed. But he gave the kids a piece of candy if they said "brown."

"DID JESUS HAVE LONG HAIR?"

Dan explained that Jesus had long hair to distinguish himself from the Roman colonizers, who had short hair.

"DID HE HANG OUT WITH THE POPULAR CROWD?"

He hung out with the sinners. The tax collectors.

"DID JESUS CRY?"

Yes, he did.

"We did this because I need you to see Jesus as a real person. A historical person. Someone who lived. He had a stepdad. Some of us have stepdads and stepmoms."

Dan stepped off to the side for a moment and coughed several times in succession. He had a chronic, hacking cough. I imagined the young man he was at age nineteen, shipping off to be a uniformed interrogator. I saw the toll that the work, the service, the years had taken. Theology of the cross, not theology of glory.

The boys there hung on his every word, though. They were all sitting together on the right side of the circle, with one girl in their midst. They had biblical names, like Jake and Levi and Aaron, and German and Scandinavian last names, with the long o's and a's common to this area of the country. One of them told me that his parents weren't farmers, though his mom worked at a turkey farm, and he was going over to his friend's house that night after confirmation class to help in the fields. There was a collegiality there to farming that was unique to rural life, an interdependence that had to be comforting in the harshness of freezing winters and rugged American individualism.

Levi, thirteen, kept me guessing all night. He was a questioner, a challenger. He broke against the grain of the rest of the boys when asked about controversial topics. He told me he thinks it's important to try and be friends with everyone, even "the people who don't like you."

To a person, nearly all the boys present told me they wanted to work on the farms with their families and neighbors when they get older. Sometimes that involved going to college first and coming back. They carried a strong sense of family and community duty; the only deviation from farmwork was one boy who wanted to work in the medical field.

It was so interesting to me to watch and listen to this collegial, community-oriented group, and then to contrast their clearly collective values with the voting patterns of this area of the country. Overwhelmingly, especially in recent elections, these counties have voted for individualistic, libertarian-leaning, stubborn Republicans. They've voted for people who've promised to cut welfare benefits and any form of "entitlement," except tax cuts for "the rich," a class these folks don't fall into. There's a sharp contrast between the cooperative farming spirit of these boys and the conservative political vision of individualistic, greedy manhood.

When I asked them about politics and social issues, they were open but noncommittal, talking about a few kids in their school who had identified as transgender in about the fifth grade. It was clear that these boys saw the LGBTQ students at their school as outside their social group, but they also talked casually about the presence of transgender kids in their midst, without much judgment, as, in a sense, it wasn't anything out of the ordinary the way it would have been at my suburban high school twenty years ago.

"They wanted to use a separate bathroom and a guest locker room," one of the boys told me. "We just mind our own business."

I ask the boys about the church building just a few miles up the road that was purchased by a white supremacist group.

"We didn't know who they were," Aaron said, looking embarrassed. "We didn't want people to get the wrong idea about us. We don't know anyone who goes there. They're from out of town."

One of the boys, a high school student, went to school in a nearby town with a much larger Black population. He said sometimes it's tense between the school's different races. He said they know white kids absolutely can't use the N-word, but they don't like being called crackers all the time.

"The diversity is good, for the most part," he said. "We have a bunch of different types of people, and we get along. There's definitely times that we don't—but at least in sports when we play together it's one common goal."

In this part of the country, racial integration has come very slowly. Much of the Upper Midwest, especially Minnesota and the Dakotas, is still predominately white, especially in rural areas—notwithstanding the forced migration and massacre of many Indigenous peoples who lived here prior to European colonization. I got the sense that those young, white Christian boys were clear on what they couldn't do in racially diverse settings, and they knew it was "bad" to be racist, but maybe they weren't fully clear on why. Maybe they hadn't learned the history of white supremacy in this country, even in these areas that many think of as home exclusively to mostly German and Scandinavian immigrants. I know I didn't learn that history growing up in school. I think these boys needed to understand more about what had happened: that anti-racism isn't about saying they're "bad," but about atoning for past wrongs and ongoing present discrimination, which often occurs at structural, more than personal, levels—like discriminatory housing or land-purchase agreements, or unjust hiring or policing practices.

Like the adults I spoke to in their community, these boys identified a few of their classmates, especially the ones who don't play sports or do music or plays, as being in trouble. They said those boys played a lot of video games and vaped in the school bathrooms. They said the school bathrooms always smelled like blueberries and bananas, and kids told the teachers it was water vapor, but often it was marijuana. Sometimes kids who couldn't accurately mete out the vape dosage got sick or got too high, and they threw up.

These boys, when they weren't outdoors or sitting in Dan's garage, said they did watch YouTube and TikTok. They liked the Millennial Farmer on YouTube, and they watched videos from a local farmer a few counties away. There was also Life on the Farm and the National Farmer's Association on YouTube. They said they've come across Andrew Tate and other influencers who talk about masculinity and "rizzing" on TikTok, but they said it's mostly a joke to them. Their male role models were football players and wrestlers and their dads and grandpas.

I asked the boys to tell me what words describe what it means to be a good man, in their view. I expected them to say things like strong or courageous or successful. But maybe Dan's lessons about Jesus were sinking in.

They looked at each other quietly.

"Kind."

"Respectful and responsible."

"Standing up for others"

"I always think about people in heaven up there watching me and what I do."

"My dad... he always works hard... so we don't give up on ourselves."

What I saw powerfully that night in Dan and Janine's garage was the potential role the Church could play in shaping the lives of adolescent boys and young men toward love, sensitivity, and humility, especially when the church is working in partnership with parents and caregivers and with the community at large. These boys seemed to feel secure that they could trust not only their parents but also their pastors and other adults in their community. Thus, online manhood influencers and extremist pastors had much less space to maneuver and to assert the worldview of White Jesus. In parts of rural America, those bonds of trust between the churches and community members and families seem to have survived intact, and perhaps stronger than they have in large suburban churches where pastors are more often seen on a screen than in their garage. This bond of trust and community and church is also commonly found in urban Black churches. But at the same time, in urban, rural, and suburban communities alike, these little churches and pastors are becoming fewer and farther between due to economic and social pressures, and so this formative experience of Confirmation class with your friends in the pastors' garage (or the humble church basement) is an all-too-rare one for American teenage boys.

CHAPTER 8

Innocuous White Supremacists and Midwestern Small Towns

Water has no color. It flows through mountains and valleys and trickles through arid brown riverbeds, seeking its own way, sculpting the land. Water picks up and holds on to the colors of the sky, reflecting a bright and clear blue, unapologetic, still and placid in the morning of a Minnesota lake.

Water is gray like the gathering storm clouds, green and mustard yellow in the wake of an approaching tornado, swirling up out of a stifling June evening, as brown and black cows flare their nostrils, put their heads down and mosey toward the barn.

In 2021, a tornado tore through western Minnesota's farm country, and a young volleyball player was gathering up the cows when she suffered a traumatic brain injury. That same night, I huddled in a southwestern Minnesota church bathroom to shelter from the storms, not knowing the tragic news, and my church council members and choir director and I laughed nervously and prayed and listened to the wind, believing this building built by the church members' hands would stand.

Joy and tragedy come fast here, in this land where the roads were once impassable for almost half the year. In the winter of 2022, in desperately frigid temperatures, an old farmer with a delicate, humble heart and thick, burly arms and legs suited to working long days and nights to bring in the crops and feed the animals, fell down in the snow outside his house in town, where they'd moved away from the fields when it became too much to manage at his age. He loved the land, but now the snow almost took his life, until a neighbor helped him up, and he was transported in the storm to the hospital the next town over. Numerous hospitalizations and months of healing black and frostbit fingers would follow. Somehow, though, he rarely complained, and he always said "thank you" when the local pastor came by to see him.

The water could turn deadly, when it froze on the roads and cars careened wildly into one another, sometimes after their drivers had indulged in a night of beer and pull tabs. Or when the rain fell in sheets and hail destroyed the crops. Or when it didn't rain, not at all, for a long time, and everyone sighed and waited out the drought.

The people here knew the water. Loved the water. Here in Swift County, in west-central Minnesota, less than fifty miles from the South Dakota state line, three rivers formed the edges of the county borders: the Minnesota, flowing southeast; the Pomme de Terre, flowing south-southwest; and the Chippewa, which flows south-southwest until it empties itself into the Minnesota just to the south of the county line.

The people who owned the land and farmed the fields and drove the ambulances were mostly of German and Scandinavian origin, and the towns all around the county still post signs for lutefisk dinners at the Lutheran churches, or pork chop lunches at local restaurants, often with beer. The names of the rivers tell of a slightly more distant past— the *pomme de terre,* French for potato, reminiscent of the fur traders and explorers who paddled these rivers when this land was still property of Emperor Napoleon Bonaparte, before the Louisiana Purchase created much of the America that today lies west of the Mississippi.

Then the other names—Anglicized now, making you think of Vikings and cold weather and "You Betcha," but instead denoting a more ancient people, the *Native* Americans, the Indigenous peoples from whom this land was stolen by the supposedly "nice" white people.

"Minnesota" comes from a Dakota phrase, *Mni Sota Makoce,* which means, "land where waters reflect the sky." The Dakota people had been driven from their homes, and the Civil War–era American government failed to provide promised annuity payments, leading to desperation, starvation, and immense suffering among the Dakota. Finally, in 1862, they fought back against their captors, and the battles and bloodshed reached the new European settlements in northeastern Swift County.

Hundreds of settlers died over the course of these five weeks, but the conquering white American government did not see fit to count the deaths among the Dakota. Instead, the Dakota people were again removed from their land, this time to desolate reservations, far from "the land where waters reflect the sky," in what is today South Dakota, North Dakota, and Nebraska.

Water has no color, so it turns red with blood.

At the end of the Dakota's desperate fight to save their people and their land, America and the new state of Minnesota retaliated with the nation's largest ever mass hanging. On the day after Christmas in 1862, the day of the birth of the white male Savior, thirty-eight Dakota prisoners were killed by hanging in Mankato, Minnesota, almost 150 miles from the Swift County seat of Benson.

When I was growing up, I learned about the valor of the First Minnesota Infantry Regiment at Gettysburg in the Civil War. I imagined that myself, my family, and our fellow Minnesotans were the "good guys." After all, we defeated the evil and racist South and we—yes, *we*—helped set the Black people free. We were so nice and good. I never learned that just six months before Gettysburg and the courage of the First Minnesota, my fellow Minnesota Lutherans were cheering the mass hanging of the Dakota in Mankato while we built churches and sang hymns and confessed our sins—just not that one—on their land.

Water has no color. It flows and filters out the sin within it, so despite all the death and bloodshed, and the excrement and disease we defecated into the rivers and lakes and clear, cold springs—in time, the twenty-four lakes and nine rivers and streams that flow through Swift County again ran clear, reflecting the blue, airy, blameless skies of the "land where waters reflect the sky." They ran so clear that when my grandma, Beryl, my mom's mom, was born in Benson in 1931, she knew the water only as a source of life, buoying the pioneer spirit of hope and possibility and manifest destiny, even in the midst of the Great Depression.

My grandma's people were Norwegian and German and Polish and Scotch-Irish, so far as I can tell. They came to Minnesota near the end of the nineteenth century, so maybe, like so many of us do, I can tell myself that we are not culpable somehow for the atrocities committed on these lands. But to cut myself off from those stories is like trying to cut yourself off from humanity in general, and, of course, that is impossible. So instead we bury our guilt with niceness and hard work and duty and religion. But what is it doing to our boys?

The White Supremacists Come to Murdock

Before I came to do research in Murdock, Minnesota, where national news outlets swooped in to cover the purchase of an abandoned former Lutheran church by a white supremacist "folk" organization, I did not know that Murdock was only twelve miles from the picturesque small town where my grandma grew up. It made sense, though, because as I left the bustle of Minneapolis on a brisk October day, and I watched as the "little boxes on the hillside" of the suburbs faded into rolling green hills and brown row crops, ready for harvest, a part of me felt like I was coming home. This was where my great-great-grandfather came from Germany to serve as a Lutheran pastor, amidst his ministry travels to Canada and the Pacific Northwest. His son, my great-grandpa, would settle in St. Paul, and *his* son, my grandpa, would become a Lutheran pastor, too.

Fifty miles from Murdock, in German Catholic Stearns County, my father's relatives would settle, too, and they would suffer and ultimately die from their military duties to their new country: my great-grandfather from complications due to mustard gas in World War I; my grandfather, decades later, from complications due to lifelong wounds, both physical and mental, the result of a devastating abdominal injury on the Pacific front of World War II. He was just a teenager, and he was never the same.

When I realized that my family surrounded the tiny town of Murdock, the story I read in the *Washington Post*[1] and the *New York Times*[2] was no longer just "a story." I didn't want to see my connection to the story right away, because it's always easier when complicated stories aren't about you. But this story, of the white supremacist organization that came to the "land where the waters reflect the sky," was unmistakably and uncomfortably close to my story, to so much that I held and hold dear, to the two white boys I carried in my womb and was raising in my home, to the churches where I preached and pastored, to the God who flows like water, taking on our sin and stories, cleansing and shaping our world, baptizing us into sin and death before resurrection.

I drove up to Murdock from Sherrie's Cafe in Kerkhoven, where I had a BLT for lunch with a couple of pastor friends. I kept not knowing how to refer to the place where I was going. Like we white Midwesterners do when something is guilt-inducing or uncomfortable, when we talked about the Asatru Folk Assembly, who had purchased the former Calvary Lutheran Church, established in Murdock in 1903 as Fridhem Evangelical Lutheran Church, we referred to the Asatru group with blank stares or knowing nods. We didn't want to call it by name, and I found myself thinking of it as the "white supremacist church." Of course, a church it was not.

A colleague of mine, Mike Carlson, served as administrative pastor when Calvary was closed. He wrote on Facebook in 2021 that closing the church was "easily the hardest thing I have been a part of." Initially, according to Carlson, the church was sold to a Christian ministry from the metro area who wanted to create a rural retreat. Those plans never came to fruition, and so the ministry sold the building to a family that was going to make it a home, as often happens to now-closed, small-town churches all across America and Europe. But the family couldn't make a go of it, and then the building was sold to the Asatru Folk Assembly, despite loud protests and attempted roadblocks from the town of Murdock.[3] Ultimately, the town determined it could not withstand a First Amendment challenge if it blocked the sale to the group.[4]

Google Maps, to its credit, won't give you directions to Asatru Folk Assembly in Minnesota. But once you're in Murdock, or if you zoom in on the map of Murdock, a cathedral-like icon will pop up at the corner of Paulina Street and Highway 12. "*Baldrs Hof,*" it reads, then in smaller print: "place of worship." Worship of what, though? Whiteness?

No one I spoke to in Swift County wanted to talk much about *Baldrs Hof.* It seemed they'd rather pretend it didn't exist, that it wasn't there at all. I understood the impulse. After the town's determination that it was forced to allow the sale on First Amendment grounds, there wasn't much they could do, maybe. But I also recognized a tendency, inherent in the "Northern European" white people whom the group wanted to recruit, to erase our memories about the movements that did not directly challenge or kill us.

I noticed this in myself, too. I felt odd, parking next to the former Lutheran Church building, whose cornerstone plaque still graced the side of the white clapboard church. In front was a red swing on a gently swaying oak tree, as if to entice children to come and play.

There was an old-fashioned wooden plow adorned with white, yellow, and orange fake flowers by the side of the church. Some kind of red walkie-talkie with musical note buttons lying next to the sidewalk. A shed, open, with a red gas can and funnel, a nice-looking Craftsman riding lawnmower, along with a push mower, a bag of charcoal, and a green Menards bucket. There were no swastikas, no overt symbols of hate, but as I looked again at the photos I'd taken, I was struck by all the red and black in this seemingly pastoral scene.

I heard from a person in the neighboring town that some people found the white supremacists kind and responsible because they'd "cleaned up the property," and they'd also given away all the crosses and Christian symbols that were once inside. Asatru itself merely means "belief in the Germanic gods," and refers to an "Icelandic pagan faith grounded in universal inclusion."[5] But the AFA co-opted the term and the pre-Christian Norse gods to "describe ethnic and racial exclusivity."[6]

"I have one person who refuses to believe it's a hate group," a local pastor told me. "She says, 'They're just such nice people, and they take such good care of the property.'"

I couldn't help but think of bucolic scenes I'd once read about in a description of the Berghof, Hitler's vacation home in the Obersalzberg of the Bavarian Alps near Berchtesgaden, Bavaria. There he and Eva Braun and the other Nazi officers and wives frolicked in the sun and ate rich food, singing and smiling as the smoke rose up from the gas chambers of Auschwitz.

When Murdock held a town meeting about the sale of the church to the identified hate group in October 2020, at the height of the COVID-19 pandemic in Minnesota, a representative of the AFA came to defend it.[7]

Allen Turnage, a member of the AFA's board, told the assembly, "A hundred thousand years from now, I want there to be blond hair and blue eyes . . . We happen to believe that Asatru is specifically a northern European religion, and that's it." Turnage told the Minneapolis *Star Tribune* that the AFA would not admit a Black person, "because they're not of northern European descent."[8]

Black resident Christian Duruji balked: "'I fail to see how a group that would reject me on sight and view my daughter as an aberration not to be celebrated' could contribute to the well-being of Murdock, he said."[9]

Murdock would become the AFA's third hall, following one that has operated for several years in California and another that opened in 2020 in North Carolina. Turnage said they only had about twenty members in or around Minnesota at the time, and several residents reiterated to me that "no one local goes there."

While I walked around the AFA, I didn't see anyone else. I did notice that those who drove past, in work trucks and pickup trucks and minivans, didn't make eye contact with me or wave, unusual for Midwestern small-town politeness. It occurred to me that, with my blonde hair and blue eyes, they likely thought I was a member of the group.

The inability of the locals to openly discuss the AFA or talk about what particularly made it so abhorrent didn't surprise me. After all, I was born and raised in the German/Scandinavian, Lutheran/Catholic, white culture of Minnesota. The worst someone will say to your face is that something is "interesting," which may as well mean it's the worst thing they've ever heard. White people here have a hard time saying how we really feel. It's why we're so "nice," and it's also why white Minnesotans often carry within ourselves a heavy dose of unexamined racism.

I noticed that the bright, blue sign denoting the *Baldrshof* building in Murdock was clean and undefaced. Maybe the group kept it that way, or maybe people were too polite to deface it. I wondered how Duruji felt about that, or if he still lived in town. And as the brilliant October sun beat down on the green grass, shining rays through the yellow leaves that had already changed on the nearby birch trees, I realized that this "*Hof*"—rather than representing something that the white Christian residents of the town wanted to outright destroy—instead maybe represented something abhorrent within ourselves, something we'd rather keep far below the surface.

Change is Hard

Swift County has become a much more racially diverse place than it once was. At the Catholic church just blocks away from the *Hof*, an after-school catechism program included several non-white students, most of them from Latinx families who had come from Mexico and Central America to work in the large dairy farms outside Murdock. Some of these young Latinx adults spoke little English, and they were hesitant to fill out registration forms due to their immigration statuses. The teacher at the Catholic church I spoke to was proud of the group's diversity. She noted how hardworking and committed the Latinx families had been to their church and their town, often returning to volunteer for church projects after working long days on the farm. She said she had wanted the town to forbid the white supremacist AFA from coming to Murdock.

Still, "change is hard," a refrain I have heard and repeated myself in white Christian circles for much of my life. I was surprised, upon driving into Benson, just a few miles up the road from Murdock, to see a large group of Black kids and adults playing at the local park and riding bikes up and down the streets. I actually saw more racial diversity in Benson than I often saw in the heavily white, urban, progressive neighborhood where my family and I lived. I recalled a *Washington Post* study that noted that small towns "don't vote like other rural areas," and they tended to be much less Republican—and less white.[10]

Kids of different races and ethnic backgrounds were attending school together now in Swift County, 161 years after European settlers stole land from Indigenous people, forced them into starvation and suffering, and killed them in a mass hanging in Mankato. Change is hard. Change is slow, and at the same time, unmistakably, change is coming to Swift County.

While the small towns diversify and kids grow up and attend school together, in some cases, a white backlash whips up. Swift County was once a Democratic stronghold. Former President Barack Obama won the county by 503 votes in 2012, a margin of nearly 10 percentage points.[11] But Trump roared back in 2016, defeating Hillary Clinton by a whopping 25 percentage points.[12] In the same election, longtime Democratic–Farmer–Labor congressional Rep. Collin Peterson (D-MN), former chair of the House Agriculture Committee, lost his seat after thirty years in the US House of Representatives.

A local pastor told me that "my farmers can't believe they lost Peterson in Congress. And it's all because of this 'Trump stuff.'"

This "Trump stuff" can't be understood in rural America, particularly rural Minnesota and the rural Midwest, without mentioning Trump's particular appeal to white men at a time when their overall share of the population in rural America is declining. David Duke, a former KKK grand wizard and one of the most well-known white supremacists in America, spoke at the deadly rally in Charlottesville, Virginia, about Trump's appeal to white supremacists.

"We are determined to take our country back," Duke said from the rally, calling it a "turning point." "We are going to fulfill the promises of Donald Trump. That's what we believed in. That's why we voted for Donald Trump, because he said he's going to take our country back."[13]

That kind of language resonates in places like Swift County and Murdock. It's an undeniable reason for the shift in voting records. It's likely why the AFA found Swift County an attractive place to host its next Hof, the townspeople's protests notwithstanding.

The thing is, what's most dangerous to America and to America's young white men and boys is not the overt hatred of Duke or the AFA. It's easy to disavow that which is easily marginalized or "othered." What concerns me more is the appeal under the surface to people for whom "change is hard," and who carry deep ancestral memories of cruelty toward non-white Americans, particularly Indigenous people.

White supremacist online recruitment, especially of young white boys and men, has grown so intense that the Anti-Defamation League produced an online guide to help parents, educators, and supportive adults identify ways that the young white boys and men in their lives are being targeted.[14] One parent mentioned in the ADL's guide, Joanna Schroeder, "explained how she followed her two teenage sons' digital lives and saw a steady stream and infiltration of sexist, racist, and heterosexist memes, infographics, jokes, videos, etc."[15] Schroeder wrote a viral Twitter thread on the subject and a later article that quickly garnered almost four hundred comments, many from other parents seeing similar phenomena in their sons.[16]

Former white supremacist Christian Picciolini told Boston's NPR station that the groups target boys at a young age: "Fourteen is a really magical age when it comes to extremism or radicalization."[17] Picciolini said he was susceptible to targeting because he "grew up fairly alienated and bullied, and it empowered me at first."[18] He found a "sense of purpose" in white supremacist groups, "at a time when young people are really trying to develop that sense of identity, community, and purpose."[19] This happens as teens are "breaking away from their parents for the first time."[20] That sense of "breaking away" I imagine is familiar to all parents of teenagers. But it happens at a critical time of recruitment for hate groups, who are ever-more accessible on the internet. Michael German, who infiltrated white supremacy groups for the FBI, told the Senate Judiciary Committee that the content is so rampant that it's "nearly impossible for law enforcement to separate internet ramblings from dangerous, potentially violent people."[21]

While these online memes and social media postings may seem like an escape for teen boys analogous to video games or virtual reality play, increasingly—as in Murdock—these groups are coming into real-life physical presence, especially in rural areas. One member of a township board in rural southwestern Minnesota told me that his group recently had to endure a meeting with a militia group advocating for "overthrow of the Constitution and the government." This was in 2021, after January sixth. Later, the same township board member told me that he'd heard his fellow (white) board members use the N-word in a meeting. And shortly after I visited Murdock in 2023, Sheriff Richard Mack, who sits on the board of the right-wing Oath Keepers, whose leader, Stewart Rhodes, was sentenced to eighteen years in prison in 2023 for his role in the insurrection at the US Capitol on January 6, 2021, came to Minnesota for a statewide tour and rallies. Mack founded the right-wing Constitutional Sheriffs and Peace Officers Association (CSPOA) and advocates that sheriffs have constitutional authority to refuse to enforce federal laws, in essence elevating individual sheriffs' jurisdictions over those of the federal government and even the President.[22] Mack's 2023 tour took him throughout the state of Minnesota, to mostly rural towns and outer-ring suburbs, including southwestern Minnesota towns Freeport and Brownton, both less than eighty miles from Murdock.

The pitch of white supremacist groups might not sound all that unfamiliar to young white boys and men in rural, predominately white areas where Fox News is often playing on TV screens all day long. As Picciolini told WBUR, "The rhetoric that I'm hearing today in our society is very similar to the rhetoric that I used to say 30 years ago that was part of our white supremacist neo-Nazi movement. Everything from the word 'invasion' to the idea that people are going to replace whites . . . those are all ideas that I used to spout when I was a neo-Nazi in the '80s and '90s."[23] Picciolini said what pulled him out of such groups was genuine relationships and interactions with non-white people and communities, something that might be more likely today in the rural Midwest, but also difficult in an area long marked by white and European dominance, with a legacy of violence against Indigenous people, and their forcible removal from these lands.

While white Minnesotans did not enslave people of color in this state, at least on the organized scale of the American South, white Minnesotans did succeed in creating a mostly "whites-only" place, where Indigenous peoples had once lived in large numbers.

According to the 2020 Census, just twenty-six Native Americans lived in Swift County, compared to 8,618 white people. While the county has become more diverse in recent years, it's still more than 85 percent white. A local woman I interviewed in the next town over from Murdock told me that she had never seen a single Black person until she moved to the Twin Cities from Swift County as a younger adult. The senior church ladies I talked to in Kerkhoven, a few miles from Murdock, told me that they'd noticed the men in their lives had gotten increasingly angrier over the past few years.

"The older I get the more I notice politics. It's all politics and it's all so negative."

Carla,[24] sixty-four, raised her two kids, one boy one girl, in Swift County as a single mom. She got married later in life.

"One thing I would say is before you get married, you should ask your spouse what Party they are," she joked. "He's one way . . . I can't understand it. It's all machoism. Fox News is on all the time. They're always cutting each other down and calling names. But he does listen to me. And he has moved, or slid, a little."

Carla's friend and fellow church member, Dee,[25] eighty-one, moved back to Swift County after spending much of her adult life in Bloomington, a Minneapolis suburb and home to the Mall of America.

"There's a lot of Scandinavians here . . . change is hard for them to accept."

But then Dee's voice drops, and she tells me that her son is married to a Korean American woman.

"One of their little girls, you know . . . she gets called . . . slurs at school. So it's really hard."

Dee's son and family live in an outer-ring suburb of Minneapolis, far from Swift County.

The senior, white Christian women I talked to in Swift County were all quick to share about their pride in their children. I asked them especially about their sons, and they told me about watching them grow up, about their playing sports and doing music and sometimes working in the fields. Most of the kids went to college. Carla told me about learning to go deer hunting and duck hunting so that her son would get those experiences with her, despite his biological dad not being present or involved.

I heard about basketball and football and grandparents and choirs and traveling and family pride. The women told me, too, though, that sometimes they worry about their grandkids or about the young white families in Swift County today. They said parents today are more worried about what their little kids wear, or how they do in sports, and they see parents on social media seeming to live vicariously through their children. They talked about the pressure on kids to succeed, and the increasing difficulty of doing so.

"I don't like it when parents think their kids should be perfect," Carla said. "There's more pressure."

The women also noticed more "partying" among young families, saying that alcohol use seemed formerly to tamp down once adults had kids, but now it seemed to go on even after the kids were born. Opposite overly involved parents who lived vicariously through children, the senior ladies also lamented the kids they knew who "didn't get the attention . . . because mom and dad are going out and partying all weekend. It's like they never quit."

I noticed that the senior ladies I spoke to that night, as the sun sank down over the nearby chicken coop and pig pen where we ate hot dogs and drank Diet Mountain Dew just outside Kerkhoven in Swift County—had hit upon so many of the pressures and trends facing young, white Christian men and boys in America. They'd noted economic and family pressures, the role of substance abuse, economic challenges, divorce, and increasing ethnic diversity (a good thing! But one that often is seized upon by white supremacist groups looking to increase anxiety in white Christian men and boys).

The ladies I spoke to had seen a lot over their decades living in and around Swift County. And while they worried about some of what they saw, they also noted positive trends.

"Oh yes!" said Carla, when I asked her if she thought young dads had become more active and nurturing fathers than those of the previous generation. "I told my daughter, 'Your husband is such a blessing.' It is so nice. They cook, and they wash, and they help. It's not just one parent. They're all really involved. The dads."

We all laughed when thinking about the older men who bragged about "never having changed a diaper," and I saw in these women both a wistfulness and an earned wisdom over the years of having parented and grown older in a changing America.

I drove back to Minneapolis that night mostly along the railroad tracks that follow US Highway 12 east to west across Minnesota. Fifteen miles southeast of Kerkhoven, I stopped in Willmar for a two-cheeseburger meal and a Dr Pepper for the ride home. Earlier that day in Willmar, I'd seen evidence of the changing demographics of southwestern Minnesota. I drove past a sign only in Spanish for a tattoo parlor. A block or so further, I saw a large painted sign for the local Black Lives Matter organization. Along the sidewalk, I saw an older Latinx man in a western shirt, boots, and a cowboy hat walking down the street, looking as if he had been transplanted from a snapshot of an old western film set in Mexico. Another block down, I saw an older Black man, in a full khaki suit and tie, walking in front of the Presbyterian church.

Trump won Willmar's county, Kandiyohi, by more than 25 percentage points in 2020. Maybe that was typical of the rural-American COVID-19 backlash against masks or shutdowns. Maybe it was a "white" lash against an area shamed and sorrowful about the murder of George Floyd ninety-five miles away in Minneapolis—an inability to reckon with the racism under the surface in Minnesota.

I drove back east on Highway 12, from the rural farmlands of Swift and Kandiyohi Counties to the urban sprawl of the wealthy suburbs west of Minneapolis. I tested out the long "o" vowel sounds on my tongue, those common to the Dakota language. Orono, named for a Native American leader who led his people in battle against Britain with the colonists thousands of miles away in Maine. Minnetonka, "great water," home to the area's wealthiest lakeside properties, where the Minnesota Vikings football team infamously took a "sex cruise," and four players were later charged with misdemeanors related to the events. Like Minnesota, Minnetonka's first sound, *Mni*, is taken from the Dakota word for water.

Two and a half hours after leaving Swift County, I arrived back in Minneapolis: a hybrid word, of Greek and Dakota origins, meaning city of waters. I am surrounded here by water, but what does it reflect? What kind of skies will the white Christian boys of this land inherit? Will they seek peace or acrimony, change diapers or march to Unite the Right and seek to overthrow the government with the right-wing sheriffs?

I think of the possible turns off Highway 12 West in Swift County, how I could turn down one road and journey into the shameful past, where Scandinavian and German immigrants displaced and killed the people of the land, and then erected whitewashed churches, where we never fully confessed our sins, only pointing to the racial sins of others. Our boys could turn in front of the well-kept lawn at the white supremacist *Hof.* They could talk about how they were just proud to be white. How they wanted to keep blond, blue-eyed people in existence. And they could assuage their fears and insecurities. They could be angry and drunk.

Or they could keep driving west. They could arrive in Benson, the county seat, where century-old buildings are still standing next to the railroad, and you can still buy cookies and bars at the Benson Bakery, est. 1931, where I bought a salted nut bar that was equal parts buttery, salty, and sweet. But maybe instead they'd drive to the park and sit by the playground, where Black kids and white kids and Latinx kids play, and their parents and other adults watch. They could band together to demand fair wages and better working conditions at the big dairies and factories around town. They could push for immigration reform and a path to citizenship for the workers who came from Mexico so they wouldn't be afraid to register their kids for Sunday school at church. They could fight for funding for their schools, and they could back up teachers. They could talk to each other and listen, and they could change diapers together in the men's public restroom.

They could clean their hands with water taken from the nearby lakes. They could repent and make reparations to the Native people of these lands, the Dakota. They could raise the clear, cool water in their palms and see the reflection of the sky—or their own reflection—and think of the God who made this baptismal water, and all people who see themselves in it, holy.

Chapter 9

Wild West, Wild Men, and De-radicalization

Desert Springs Bible Church of Phoenix is 1,600 miles and a world away from the white supremacist *Hof* in Murdock, Minnesota. Here, the landscape is unsoftened, dry, brown, red, and harsh—with none of the respite provided by the waters of *Mni Sota Makoce*, where the bright blue of the lakes and rivers seems to touch the cerulean sky.

Desert Springs has stood right here along Tatum Boulevard, the main artery of this part of north Phoenix, since 1988, almost ancient in nondenominational church years. The congregation began back when this part of Phoenix was wild country, desert, and the phone lines didn't reach into the neighborhood, as a church plant of then–Bethany Bible Church in 1977. Like many exurb and suburban churches of its era, DSBC grew up with the city. As new residents flocked to Phoenix from places like Texas and Kansas and Ohio and Indiana, they also filled its churches. Ten years after Desert Springs was first planted, its leadership built a campus here on this site, complete with a preschool, contemplative water garden, and worship center—including bolted-down metal seats with fabric cushions and covers resembling those in a movie theater, and in the style of Chicago's Willow Creek, which was pastored by church-growth guru Bill Hybels, and which built its first building in North Barrington, Illinois, just eight years earlier, in 1981, after famously starting its services in a suburban movie theater.

Desert Springs was such a success story that its longtime lead pastor, Rick Efird, retired after thirty-plus years only to go on to serve as a church leadership consultant and director of church partnerships for Phoenix Seminary. But for all Efird's prowess as a pastor, he was also a beneficiary of circumstances and population patterns. The '90s and early 2000s were a boom time for north Phoenix, before the threat of climate change and drought and inflated housing costs and burgeoning homelessness had afflicted the city's sunny disposition. The future still looked bright when current Lead Pastor Caleb Campbell, Efird's handpicked successor, took over as lead pastor in September of 2015. There was no way Campbell could have known all that was to come, not just for Desert Springs or this corner of north Phoenix, but for Christianity, America, and the world, over the next eight years, until I first came to visit Desert Springs in January 2024.

Caleb grew up mostly a Phoenix kid, aware of the intricacies and interconnectedness of the Valley in ways non-natives take years to understand. He told me that sometimes people get confused about Desert Springs and its neighborhood, because this part of Phoenix is called "Paradise Valley Village," and sometimes people think that means they're going to Paradise Valley, Arizona, a suburb just south of here that's known as Arizona's wealthiest municipality, home to opulent golf courses, luxury clothing stores, and unaffordable desert homes with mountain views. Paradise Valley—the suburb, not the neighborhood of Phoenix—is totally different from the ethos and vibe Caleb wants to lean into at Desert Springs, in a jaded Evangelical America where, when you tell someone you pastor a "Bible church," they might assume you hold frequent anti-gay protests or force women to wear skirts and dresses.

That kind of Evangelical Christianity, the kind that puts Trump and violence on par with the gospel of Jesus, just didn't appeal to Caleb anymore. He knew it too well. He knew where those roads would lead. He'd already traveled them, in fact, going the opposite direction, from being a part of a group of racist skinheads to being a fanboy of Pastor Mark Driscoll and White Jesus, before rejecting all that and nearly losing his pastoral position for his opposition to Trump and his preaching of anti-racist sermons after the murder of George Floyd.

I told Caleb that what I knew about his teenage years and the skinheads he ended up falling in with I'd taken directly from the 1998 film *American History X*, starring Edward Norton as a white power skinhead and neo-Nazi[1] named Derek Vinyard. I remember watching the film for the first time with my college boyfriend and crying, because even when Derek stepped away from the hatred and violence of his past, his younger brother, Danny, still ends up getting killed in an incident sparked by his racist hatred. The film seemed to say so much about the underbelly of the American dream, the hope and promise we still believed in during the 1990s, even after the civil rights heroes we read about in school had mostly been assassinated, and racial inequality was still the law of the land.

Caleb described his initial attraction to the skinheads as being driven by a few different motivations: his alienation from the fundamentalist Christian faith being preached by his parents and teachers, which seemed superficial, inauthentic, and "soft"; and his attraction to the punk culture, music, and general mayhem and violence embraced by the skinheads, a movement that began among working-class British teenage boys and young men in the 1960s and experienced a revival with British punk culture in the 1980s.[2] The British skinheads initially operated more like hooligans[3] creating public nuisances than ideologically racist neo-Nazis.[4] In the 1990s, the neo-Nazi version of skinheads became popularized in America, especially in the Southwest, as an outgrowth of prison gangs like the Aryan Brotherhood, the nation's oldest major white supremacist prison gang and a national crime syndicate founded by Irish bikers.[5] The Aryan Brotherhood is the deadliest prison gang in the United States, with more than 20,000 members inside prisons and working the streets, according to the Southern Poverty Law Center.[6]

At the time he joined the neo-Nazi skinheads in Phoenix, Caleb was isolated from his family and his faith and looking for a new source of community, one that appealed to his sense of antiestablishment anger and hunger for street violence. As a working-class white teenage boy, much like many white prisoners who are drawn into the Aryan Brotherhood or other white supremacist prison gangs, Caleb saw the neo-Nazi skinheads as his only option among the street gangs of Phoenix, and he took on the racist ideology attached to the skinheads as part and parcel of finding his identity within the group, without being able to articulate what the ideology meant to him at the time—except a sense of identity, community, belonging, and power, in a family and fundamentalist Christian community where he often felt powerless.

Caleb told me that *American History X* was pretty accurate, though he thought the film missed in one big way.

"They acted like the racist hatred came first," he told me. "It was the other way around. They offered belonging and safety in a scary world. The racist ideology was in service of the belonging. What I got was more important than what we believed."

As he said this, I thought back to all the reporting I've done on young white men and boys in the church, and about the forces impelling them toward radicalization, violence, and extreme views about masculinity and gender roles. I think Caleb has it right here. The ideas are in service of the belonging. So merely refuting the ideas isn't what pulls boys and men away from the destructive groups and ideologies. It's the community piece, the belonging.

Similarly, in order to understand how Caleb got here—leading one of Phoenix's longest-standing Bible churches by way of skinhead groups—we have to start with his traditional Christian upbringing, and the belonging he lacked.

Born to young, working-class white parents who hailed from Phoenix and Kansas, Caleb was brought up not too far from Desert Springs in Phoenix, before moving to Dallas from about ages eight to twelve. His dad was a tool salesman, and the company said he could move to either Vegas or Dallas. So the family moved from dusty Phoenix to the outskirts of dusty Dallas, on a three-acre property off a dirt road where Caleb and his friends rode bikes in the woods, played football on the street, and engaged in lots of Super Nintendo. His was basically the typical '90s-kid childhood, with his dad, and sometimes mom, scraping together a variety of jobs to make ends meet. But beneath the veneer of dirt roads, bikes, and Nintendo, Caleb was also raised with a worldview that taught him to fear the outside world. He said the family mostly went to church in Holiness movement churches, where the theology was relatively progressive when it came to gender roles (he remembered a few female pastors) but relatively regressive when it came to the teaching about evil. Caleb remembers a pastor who wore a suit and preached lots of "rules and regulations." In children's church he was told that if he didn't first ask for forgiveness, God wouldn't even bother to listen to his prayer. And if he didn't pray for repentance, then he'd be going straight to hell in light of his inevitable sins.

Caleb's parents scrimped and saved to send their kids to private Christian schools, and among their rules for their children included no R-rated movies and no drinking. But Caleb remembered going to his pastor's house in Texas as a young preteen. He noticed the pastor's family was watching *The Terminator* on VHS. Something inside Caleb recoiled.

"This is all a show," he thought.

By the time the family had moved back to Phoenix, unevenly, with his mom going back first, Caleb was almost thirteen and suspicious of all authority and everything his parents had taught him. It was 1994, and Nirvana frontman Kurt Cobain had just died by suicide. The music of the time was grungy and gloomy, an inheritor of the punk rejection of mainstream society but with a darker edge and none of punk's neon hopefulness. Teenaged Caleb was listening to Rage Against the Machine and heavy metal music filled with white male loathing and despair. His parents, distracted by his mom's father's recent illness and death, tried anyway to keep their oldest child on a straight and narrow path. They showed him posters at churches that suggested Christian alternatives to popular music groups. Caleb scoffed, shaking his head.

"Every single one recommended DC Talk."

His first concert was the Christian rapper Carman—known for his 1993 hit, "Satan, Bite the Dust!"—whom Caleb saw in Texas at age eleven.

"That'll ruin your chance at a music career," he said.

So maybe it was the '90s, maybe it was grunge, maybe it was music, maybe it was disconnection and anger and violence, but teenage Caleb was angry. He wanted out of the house as soon as possible, away from his younger sisters, especially two-years-younger Sarah, with whom he fought regularly. He hated his private Christian charter school, hated homeschooling, hated the stupid uniforms and dress codes that didn't allow for saggy pants or Kurt Cobain T-shirts or long cargo shorts. Eventually, Caleb got expelled from Chandler Christian School in eighth grade, the rare male victim of Christian school dress codes.

His parents, products of Midwestern and Christian conservatism, didn't quite know how to handle their angry son. Like most '90s American families, Caleb's didn't talk. They coexisted in a sort of silent rage, tensed at every moment for the trigger to be pulled with one another. All he wanted to do was to get out of that place. He hadn't believed in his family's god for a long time. During his senior year in high school he moved into the garage, and as soon as he graduated, he got an apartment with a group of friends. College, the middle-class American dream for so many '90s parents, couldn't have been further from his mind.

Like his sisters, Caleb's parents gave their son a biblical name, coming from the Hebrew Bible book of Numbers and denoting a spy sent ahead of Moses into the promised land of Canaan. The biblical Caleb bravely surveyed the land ahead, and, uniquely with Joshua, urged the Hebrew people and Moses onward with confidence that they would be able to take the land. In giving their son this name, Caleb's parents endowed him with a legacy of bravery, courage, truth, and witness. He would need all these traits in the immediate years and decades to come, though his parents couldn't have predicted it then.

By the time he moved out of the house, teenage Caleb had become his conservative Christian parents' worst nightmare, though they likely weren't aware of everything he'd been doing throughout his high school years. He remembers receiving a purity ring as a teenager and feeling embarrassed.

"I didn't have the heart to be like . . . too late," he said.

Caleb's conservative Christian parents taught him that to be a man of God was to be pure and pious, to pray, protect, and earn for his family. He recalls the ethos he was taught as being blended from a sort of blue-collar, working-class, white American ethic of hard work and honest pay. His upbringing was not the rigid, traditional complementarianism of the Southern Baptists who descended from plantations in the slaveholding South. Instead, Caleb represented a growing edge of white, male masculinity that would be popularized in American Evangelicalism in the early 2000s, a precursor of sorts to Pastor Mark Driscoll's young, restless, and reformed movement. It appealed to the Gen X and elder millennial boys who'd been reared on heavy metal and rejection of supposed "inauthenticity." It would end up as fertile fodder for a movement that championed strict gender roles and embraced an amoral approach to politics. But that all would come later. For now, Caleb was immersed in a toxic stew unique to the American West, more *Fight Club* than *Focus on the Family*.

Adrift and aloof from the would-be closeness of a nuclear family, teenage Caleb was still desperate for acceptance and belonging. He found it amidst a group of white supremacist, neo-Nazi skinheads who roamed the streets of Phoenix in the late '90s and early 2000s, around the same time as the release of *American History X*. He'd first fallen in with them earlier in high school, joining the group at age sixteen and crashing at their various trailers and grimy apartments before officially moving in with a few of them after high school.

While Caleb said his group wasn't a part of the skinhead drug smuggling gangs that famously ruled Phoenix in the late '90s and early 2000s, his group did know those guys, and they also liked street fighting, a lot. Violence was a part of the group bond, an assurance, likely born in prisons mostly populated by Black and Latinx men, that as a white guy on the street (or in prison) you had somebody looking out for you. Caleb said that's why girls were attracted to the group occasionally, too, for the sense of protection.

He described a scene alien from the plush and benign church office at Desert Springs where we were talking in January 2024. This Caleb wore dark jeans and stylish sneakers, the unofficial uniform of Evangelical nondenominational pastors. That Caleb wore what he called a "uniform," of "laces, braces, and boots." Even in sweltering Phoenix, they dressed this way: jeans cuffed at the bottom, black Doc Marten boots with red laces, matching suspenders, some kind of T-shirt, and a bomber jacket. They never wore hats.

"You wanted people to know you were a skinhead," Caleb said.

While skinhead groups have mostly fallen out of favor today among white supremacists in the United States, with young white recruits turning instead to alt-right groups who are more "image conscious" and politically connected, according to the SPLC,[7] white supremacist groups were still behind more than 80 percent of extremism-related US murders in 2022.[8] Also in April 2022, as many as twelve sets of human remains were found in Oklahoma buried on two sites, including property connected to one of the leaders of the Universal Aryan Brotherhood, in a state that's home to at least five major white supremacist prison gangs.[9] White supremacist prison gangs have also become heavily involved in drug trafficking, particularly of fentanyl and methamphetamine. In 2023, federal agents completed a major operation against a drug smuggling ring led by members of the Aryan Family, a white supremacist prison gang trafficking fentanyl, methamphetamine, and other drugs across much of the western United States, especially Washington state, Idaho, and Alaska.[10] The operation led to twenty-seven indictments and twenty-four arrests, with more than 1.9 million doses of fentanyl and 230 pounds of methamphetamine seized, in addition to 225 guns and firearm parts.[11]

Caleb said his skinhead gang didn't really do drugs, although they may have trafficked them, and there was a lot of drinking and frequent fighting, with guys riding around Phoenix late at night looking for trouble. One night, at a Burger King in Tempe, Caleb and his fellow skinheads got beat up by two Black men, whom the skinheads thought were Arizona State football players. The police ended up breaking up the fight, and, as Caleb remembered it, the police almost always took the skinheads' side, sometimes even driving Caleb and his friends around in their patrol cars looking for the supposed Black perpetrators. Caleb wasn't really a great fighter, but physical violence was part of the deal—part of belonging in the group.

"Phase one is you're in the group," he said. "Phases two to three you're wearing the costume. Phases four to five is you're doing violence."

As he had told me earlier, the belonging came first—and the activity and ideology went hand-in-hand. De-radicalization, then, is a process not primarily of the mind but of the heart.

It's tough to imagine for me now, as a parent of a young preteen boy, but Caleb said that prior to graduating high school, he was mostly able to hide his skinhead activities from his parents, who were both children of alcoholics. It seemed the whole family had entered into an unhappy stasis, unwilling to confront the monster in the room even after years of warning about the monsters of the outside world, who were supposedly threatening white Christians.

Absent familial intervention or conversation, it was up to Caleb to find his own way out of the white supremacist skinhead gang. He'd spent a few years at that point bouncing from trailer to dirty, dusty, rusting trailer, to rundown apartments filled with desperate, hollow young men, telling tales about the fights they'd won in prison and their dreams of world domination. A year or so after high school graduation,

Caleb's eyes started to widen as he looked around himself at his would-be skinhead role models. He didn't like what he saw.

"If we are the master race, and the skinheads are in charge, where are all the successful skinheads?" Caleb thought to himself. "What's being said and what's being done doesn't make sense to me anymore. Everyone is in a trailer. Every's getting shot at. Everyone's going to jail."

"I'm out."

In much the same way as he would later move out of the sphere of Mark Driscoll and White Jesus, rejecting the right-wing and narrow Christian faith of the young, restless, and reformed movement, Caleb was prone to make changes without hesitation once he made up his mind. Maybe it was his relative youth and his fierce independent streak that empowered him to make drastic changes without fearing the consequences. Much as he had found his initial identity as an angsty and angry '90s and early-2000s teen with the racist skinhead group, as Caleb realized that group no longer represented an identity he aspired to, he knew it was time to leave. He no longer felt a kinship or sense of belonging to most of the group members. Part of it was seeing their relative poverty and the way it made them powerless in a capitalistic world. Part of it was Caleb growing older and out of a group that was mostly teenagers or inmates, two groups he no longer fit into or wanted to fit into.

It is key to note here that some of the factors that drove Caleb away from the skinheads no longer apply to the major white supremacist groups who are recruiting white teenagers and young men today. Outside of the white supremacist prison gangs, the alt-right movement has attempted to clean up the image of neo-Nazis, with polo shirts, khakis,[12] and high-and-tight haircuts.[13] Many male white supremacist influencers also flaunt their affluence.[14]

But back then, when Caleb was leaving the skinhead group, it was the year 2000, and the grunge of the '90s was giving way to the cleaner hope of a new millennium, even for a teenager like Caleb with a chip on his shoulder. With Phoenix's skinhead groups under increased law enforcement scrutiny for drug dealing and violence, Caleb said it was relatively easy for him to just slip away. He doesn't know what has happened to most of the people he hung around with then. Quite a few had gone to prison. Many others drifted away, as he had. He told me then, as we talked in January 2024, that he hadn't thought about "all this stuff" for a long time. It embarrassed him now. He was such a different man. But there's no denying the hatred at the base of the group he'd been raised in as a teenager. They were unequivocally white supremacists, though Caleb does remember a few Latinx men with "darker complexions" making their way into the group.

"At that point there would always have to be a conversation about Spain, and the lineage of the conquistadors," Caleb said, noting the ways in which white supremacist movements or even conservative Christian movements that emphasize violent masculinity will appeal to the "machismo" of Latinx American men.

"As long as they behave according to the [white] cultural norms, they're in," Caleb said, noting that the Phoenix-area Trump rallies tended to be at least half Latinx men, similar to the draw of conservative Christian churches to Latinx immigrants, who were leaving the Catholic Church en masse.

But Caleb, now, was out. Still lacking belonging, he spent his days working for an internet-based company and doing freelance web development, while spending his nights as a drummer for a heavy metal band called Fracture Point. He was, at this point, spiritually curious. And his Christian upbringing had also instilled some sort of moral conscience.

"I knew I had done bad stuff," he said. "I had a God consciousness. But I didn't really want to go to church. I was really suspicious of Christians."

Still, he needed income and—maybe—purpose. So Caleb responded to a newspaper ad for a drummer at a nearby church, Desert Springs. He joined the worship band and started playing every week. Soon after that, Caleb's worship bandmate, Seth, saw that his friend was drifting and—maybe—open to a life change. As advised by so many Evangelicalism handbooks, Seth invited Caleb over for dinner and conversation, with his wife, Jamie. Remembering the hypocrisy he'd seen in people like his pastor and his parents growing up, Caleb was suspicious. He also felt resentful, knowing that Seth came from a relatively wealthy family. After years of hanging out with poor skinheads in trailers, who were in and out of prison, Caleb felt ill-at-ease. He had a lot of assumptions about what Seth and Jamie would be like, and he says he mostly accepted their invitation as an opportunity to prove himself right: that they were phonies just like the rest of that group.

Instead, that dinner was the beginning of a new phase of Caleb's life, marked by ever-increasing engagement with Christianity and with the church. Ironically, the thing that first brought Caleb's walls down was the fact that Seth offered him a beer.

"Christians didn't do that," Caleb remembered thinking, curious now about how his friend lived out his faith in such a different way than he'd been taught growing up.

Thus began a series of conversations and discoveries, leading Caleb out of white supremacist groups and into an exploratory Christian era that was rife with would-be guides to a new faith for a new American millennium. One of Caleb's first entrées into reconnection with his spiritual life at that time was a CD from a website and magazine called, "The Ooze," created by former Orange County, California, megachurch pastor Spencer Burke. The Ooze was at the vanguard of its time, a group of hipster-ish pastors from across the country who wanted to be open to a new version of Christianity, one that was not comprised of the organs and hymnals of a traditionalist past, but also one that did not echo the exclusionary social rhetoric and confining social roles of the predominately Southern Baptist Bible Belt. The movement, known now as the "emergent church," focused on intellectual inspiration and openness. No question was off-limits. Some of those featured in Ooze publications of the early 2000s have gone on to be progressive church leaders, affirming LGBTQ marriage and leadership in the church, and advocating for the social gospel: people like Doug Pagitt and Sarah Raymond Cunningham, both of whom I met, with Burke, around a decade after Caleb first listened to that CD, at a gathering for Christian writers and speakers on the East Coast.

Caleb was drawn to the emergent church for its intellectualism and its iconoclasm. Although later analyses of the movement rightly critique its lack of diverse voices and its reliance on privileged white male leaders, it was a time of unique openness and willingness to question the status quo in the American Church. For a brief moment in time, Christians had come together to ask the big questions without assuming that they already knew the right answers. But this period of openness and curiosity would be short-lived, for Caleb and for the emergent church. Two distinct roads led out of this Christian movement of the early 2000s. One road, the one less traveled, led toward an open, affirming, and liberating Christian experience popularized by authors like Rob Bell. The other road was paved by Pastor Mark Driscoll, who quickly captivated Caleb and countless other young, white Christian men and boys of the time.

Caleb was listening to the Ooze CD when suddenly he heard a loud, angry voice rise above the fray. Still fresh from the ethos of toughness and violence he experienced as part of the white supremacist skinhead group, Caleb found himself turned off by the gentle liberalism of some of the emergent church leaders.

"I'm listening to this CD," he said. "And I'm thinking . . . everyone is like pansies."

He got to the final track of the CD, which featured a message from Driscoll. Someone had asked him a question during a Q&A session, and, in characteristic form, Driscoll first responded by berating the questioner for his presuppositions and invocation of traditional conservative Christian dogma.

"What the hell do I care about C. S. Lewis?" Driscoll demanded angrily. "I care about what Jesus said!"

The apparent unvarnished authenticity of Driscoll's ministry appealed to Caleb's latent punk sensibilities.

"He's yelling at this guy, and he's cursing," Caleb remembered, thinking back to himself as a twenty-year-old ex-skinhead hearing Driscoll for the first time. "And I'm thinking, 'oh, I'm into this. If this is what we are talking about, I'm in.'"

Driscoll, at the time, appeared to reject the obvious consumerism and shallow theology of the church growth movement, popularized by genteel, almost teddy bear–like pastors such as Hybels and Warren. He was short, stocky, and from the Pacific Northwest. He didn't mince words.

Caleb dived in to all the Driscoll he could get his hands on. Driscoll had founded the Acts 29 church-planting organization just a few years earlier, in 1998, and there, and on the internet, Caleb could find a whole community of like-minded young men who were finding their identity and masculinity in this particular form of Christianity. Driscoll would publish his first book, *The Radical Reformation*, in 2004, and in 2006 would be at the foreground of the young, restless and reformed movement, with fellow pastors John Piper, Matt Chandler, John MacArthur, and CJ Mahaney, among others. It's critical to note that since then each of these pastors has faced his own well-publicized scandal over abuse, misconduct, and/or cover-up and corruption.

At the time, though, for Caleb and so many other young, white American Christian men, this seemed like a fresh and exciting place to establish your identity as a young man. Becoming a Christian didn't mean eschewing pleasure or strength or even violence and graphic sex. You could swear and drink and talk explicitly about women and try to make a lot of money. It was all OK because it was undergirded by a complex and intellectual theology that was rooted in the Bible.

"I'm freebasing all of this, like a drug," Caleb remembered, noting the intoxicating nature of Driscoll's movement and its appeal to young white men and boys. "I didn't even know who John Calvin was, but I was into Calvinism. It was cool. Aggressive. Certainty. Safety. Belonging. [It told me] that we are the strong ones. We are going to protect women. We are going to take care of our lives. And we can do it all and still have fun and be men."

Four years later, after leaving the skinheads and going to dinner at his Christian bandmate's house, Caleb's transformation to young Christian leader was complete. He was offered a staff position at Desert Springs and got married to Lori, a Sicilian Catholic originally from Brooklyn, who said nonetheless she somehow always knew she'd be married to a pastor. Lori had been in the youth group at Desert Springs, and the whole church was excited for this new young couple who was on fire for Jesus and for the church.

At this point Caleb, who didn't have an undergraduate degree, was nonetheless pursuing a degree from seminary. He audited classes at Phoenix Seminary for four years while continuing to work at Desert Springs and play for the worship band—and do web design on the side. All the while, he was still hard-core diving into Driscoll's brand of masculine, muscular Christianity. He found himself butting heads with lead pastor Efird over some of the new ideas.

"I was using Reformed words, but I didn't really know what it meant. I just kept pushing into it," Caleb said.

Alongside his devotion to Driscoll and other pastors of his ilk, like James MacDonald of Harvest Bible Chapel (who was removed in 2019 for "conduct harmful to the best interests of the church"), Caleb had also developed a fascination with mixed martial arts. He'd first started viewing the events with pirated copies on VHS during his time with the skinhead group, but now as a part of the young, restless, and reformed Christian movement, Caleb felt the same draw to male violence and displays of physical dominance.

After enrolling at Phoenix Seminary in 2010, Caleb heard about a program with Driscoll's then-church, Mars Hill, in Seattle, that would allow him to earn fifteen credit hours in a year for a reduced tuition rate. The program was so heavily subsidized by outside donors that it was cheaper for Caleb to attend that program *and* fly to Seattle at least once a month than it would have been to continue normally at Phoenix Seminary. Plus, for Caleb, going to Seattle was, in his words, "like going to Mecca."

But it was that year in close contact with people at Mars Hill (though Driscoll was mostly inaccessible to the program's seminary students) that led Caleb to question the theology he'd inhaled from the source of brutish masculinity. He called his time at Mars Hill a "Wizard-of-Oz experience," in which he saw the small and dangerous man behind the curtain, orchestrating an unreal and damaging fantasy.

"I was talking to people who had been fired," Caleb said. "I was seeing the 'bodies behind the bus,'" referring to Driscoll's later statement that the growth at Mars Hill necessitated leaving "bodies behind the bus" in order to continue dramatic church growth and influence.

He said the other young ministers in his group were troubled, too, by what they saw at Mars Hill, and by the destructive ways in which Driscoll's leadership had manifested itself. But no one really talked about it directly.

"We started making jokes. Like, yeah, it's 95 percent church and 5 percent Mafia. We came up with this gag called 'Strike Church.' And every time we saw or heard something absurd or hyperbolic at Mars Hill, we'd say, that's Chapter 32 in Strike Church."

They'd reference classic films of male identity, intrigue, violence, and ultimate inadequacy and defeat, like *The Godfather* and *Fight Club*, without realizing that the very cultural tropes they referenced contained within them warnings about imbibing extreme masculinity without space for compassion, love, and gentleness. Caleb said the young ministers, many like him, who came to Mars Hill without an extensive background in theology or biblical exegesis, didn't know enough to critique what was happening. But internally, they knew something wasn't right.

"[It was this feeling like] I think what I'm eating is bad food," he said, remembering his "scales-falling-from-his-eyes" moment at Mars Hill. "I don't think I like this."

To his credit, Caleb's propensity to be drawn into destructive masculine groups is matched by his own personal willpower to pull himself out when things are made apparently evil and wrong. Just like that, he moved away from Driscoll, Acts 29, and the young, restless, and reformed movement.

A few short years later, Mars Hill collapsed, and Driscoll was removed for various breaches and misconduct, including using church funds to purchase copies of his books, and a leadership style that was boorish and even abusive. He'd also been exposed as a damaging proponent of mistreatment of women, for advocating behaviors and attitudes in marriage conducive to abuse of women and children. By now a wealthy and powerful figure, but a Wizard without an Oz, Driscoll this time came to Caleb, who found himself sitting in a room of Phoenix-area pastors in 2015 listening to Driscoll pitch them on his plan to plant a new congregation in Scottsdale called "Trinity Church."

"This is weird," Caleb thought. "Look at him. He's shaken."

For all of his boisterous and boasting rhetoric about male strength and dominance, Driscoll had been exposed as a weak man in need of an audience and adoring crowds. Caleb couldn't help but see the contrast between his former hero and the man who had led Desert Springs for three decades. He found himself with a new respect for Efird's style of leadership: humble, patient, wise, listening. Caleb called it "consensus-building," a sharp contrast from the authoritarian commands that Driscoll barked out at Mars Hill, mostly to raise his own profile.

Also unlike Driscoll, Efird would leave pastoral ministry of his own accord, in September of 2015, having anointed Caleb as his likely successor as lead pastor. Caleb knew his leadership would have to be different than that of the pastors he'd once admired.

"By 2014 I was watching guys whose books I had on my shelves drop like flies," he said. "I had to think—what is this trash I've been giving myself to? There had to be more to ministry than organizational growth and personal celebrity. It wasn't working."

And so after years of thinking he should start his own church, in the mold of Mars Hill, instead Caleb became the latest lead pastor of Paradise Valley Village stalwart Desert Springs. Not flashy, not new, not hip, not necessarily popular—but a church that had so far stood the test of time. Of course, in 2015, the church's—and Caleb's—greatest tests were still to come.

A Former Skinhead Confronts Trumpism

Caleb began his new role as lead pastor excited about the possibilities for the future of Desert Springs. He knew that some people considered this part of Phoenix now to be a wasteland: not quite Scottsdale, not quite Paradise Valley, without much to make it stand out as a unique destination. But Caleb wanted to embrace the reality of this very neighborhood: situated an equal distance from poverty-stricken but culturally rich Palomino, home to people who represented more than twenty distinct nationalities as immigrants to America, including some of the Lost Boys of the Second Sudanese Civil War, who'd been resettled there twenty years ago after suffering terrible atrocities and, in some cases, being forced to serve as soldiers while still young boys—and the affluent Kierland Commons district of tony Scottsdale.

This was quite the full-circle moment for Caleb, who little more than a decade earlier could have been considered an American lost boy himself, drifting from white supremacist skinhead groups to the role of Mark-Driscoll-extreme-masculine-Jesus-MMA fanboy, to his position now as a father of four, leading a church, in the model of a former leader known for consensus and patience, hopeful to bring a community together.

Caleb set about immediately making quick changes, still with some of the brashness that had characterized his personality in his younger years. He felt compelled, called, to change Desert Springs from a traditional white Evangelical megachurch into a church that better represented growing, multicultural Phoenix. When I met Caleb at Desert

Springs in January 2024, he was proud to tell me about the Indian American engineers and visa holders who had moved in large numbers to Desert Springs' neighborhood. He talked about wanting to make Desert Springs, and its preschool, a welcoming place to all of its neighbors, including even the snowballing number of unhoused people, some of whom were setting up tents not far from the church's parking lot on busy Tatum Boulevard.

In 2024, Caleb still had hopeful plans and dreams for the church to serve as a sort of community center, and even a place that offered a home to a (secular) counseling center. But everything else had changed in the past nine years since he'd been serving as lead pastor. Caleb had barely been leading Desert Springs a year when Trump was elected in November 2016, with support from Arizona, specifically the white and Latinx Evangelicals of Maricopa County, who voted for him at high rates, helping to keep the state red, after Obama carried it in 2008 but not 2012. In his first year as lead pastor, Caleb and other staff leadership, as well as the church's board of directors, had led a movement to make the staff look more like Desert Springs' neighborhood.

"We went from an all-white, predominately male staff to hiring Latinos on the ministry team and adding a Black pastor, as well as lots of women in leadership," Caleb said. "We knew that staff was the easiest to change, but we were trying to make our church look more like our neighborhood. In Christ there is no [longer Jew or Greek, there is no longer slave or free, there is no longer male and female; for all of you are one in Christ Jesus, Galatians 3:28] . . . but our church is all Scottsdale white, wealthy people. I was disenchanted with the homogeneous growth model."

He kept reading his Bible and praying, feeling even more convinced that God was leading him and Desert Springs in a more inclusive direction, and speaking more explicitly about causes related to social justice and even racism.

But everything was about to get a lot more difficult.

"2016 [election day] happens," Caleb remembered. "I show up to church to see two of my Black teammates [staff members] in the parking lot, crying. I walk into the church office to see two staff members celebrating. I remember thinking, 'This is going to be harder than I thought.'"

But the church work continued. Every week had a Sunday. And even though Caleb felt inspired to bring change to Desert Springs, he also saw himself continuing on in a mission that had been begun by his predecessor. Efird had written op-eds in the *Arizona Republic* about compassion and care for immigrants from a Christian perspective. Caleb didn't think he was saying anything different than leaders had been saying at Desert Springs, and at Christian congregations across the country, for decades. But that was before congregation members spent their evenings glued to their screens, with news alerts popping up on their phones every few minutes, with the president, who'd won a larger proportion of white Evangelicals than anyone before, calling for a "total immigration ban," talking about "shithole countries," and signing executive orders banning travel to the United States from seven predominately Muslim countries—as well as suspending resettlement of Syrian refugees at a time when large parts of Syria had been overrun by the Islamic State.

"As the church, I was convinced it's never right to dehumanize people," Caleb said. "But I'd preach on this stuff, and I had people coming up to me in the lobby after the service, double barrel fingers in my chest."

"I was like . . . what's happening? I was so confused. I figured maybe 20 percent of the people in my congregation love Trump. But 80 percent, I understand their type of conservatism."

Caleb made a joke that Christmas season about King Herod, that he wanted to "make Jerusalem great again."

Now he was getting a steady stream of emails. Fingers pointed in his chest. People would approach him and say: "I heard you were a Democrat, and I wanted to make sure that was wrong," with their eyes narrowed.

Later he'd put the pieces together, that his congregation was desperate to know that he was on "their team." But at the time, the vitriol flew at him fast, and he could barely catch his breath. People were standing up in Sunday school class and saying they were leaving because Caleb was a Democrat. They told him they didn't trust him, because they knew Obama was "a Muslim," and Caleb said he didn't think so.

He recounted another time after worship when a passionate woman in her forties came up to him, on a mission to make sure he heard what she had to say. She told him that she was a huge Madonna fan, but she'd gotten rid of all her Madonna records. Caleb figured it had something to do with religion, that Madonna had insulted Jesus or Christianity in some way. But the woman shook her head. That wasn't it. It was something more decisive.

"[Madonna] said something negative about *our president*," she told Caleb, looking him directly in the eye. "I want you to know that I love our country, and I love our president."

Maybe as someone who'd worshipped his own flawed heroes only to watch them disappoint him, betray him, and be revealed as small and petty men, Caleb was well-positioned to pastor this white Evangelical flock in the midst of Trumpism. He certainly had the skills, language, and experience. He also had the courage. But he was unprepared for all that was to come.

Desert Springs kept continuing on its path. The leadership stood behind its lead pastor, even as attendance shrank and giving dropped. Caleb found other paying work in order to supplement his income when times were tight at church. They were making it, and the ministry at Desert Springs just kept going as it had for decades.

Then, COVID-19 struck America in March 2020. Following the medical guidelines and state restrictions around large gatherings, Desert Springs moved worship to an online-only format. Just a few weeks in, angry parishioners staged a protest service, live streamed from the lawn at Desert Springs, without permission from congregational leadership.

"This pastor has a Luciferian spirit," said Jeremy Wood, a former youth pastor in his fifties who would go on to help found Tipping Point Academy in Scottsdale, a private school that boasts it focuses on "teaching children through Bible-based Constitutional education," and conducts itself according to Christian nationalist ideology, including protesting the health restrictions and vaccine requirements instituted in many public schools during the pandemic.

The group that led the service outside Desert Springs was connected to the Phoenix-area Facebook group "Great 48!" which would go on to host more large-scale events during the pandemic as a protest against the health and safety guidelines implemented to protect Arizonans from early COVID-19 surges.

Like many American pastors, Caleb had begun the COVID-19 pandemic fearful and anxious that he would be inundated with parishioner funerals, haunted by scenes from his wife's family's native Sicily, where COVID-19 was raging through the population and causing scenes of mass death. That type of mass tragedy wouldn't come to Desert Springs, but instead COVID-19 wrought a different sort of trauma, intensified when the same Trump supporters who'd been angry at Caleb since early 2017 became even more enraged in light of COVID-19 restrictions and calls for racial justice after the murder of George Floyd at the hands of the Minneapolis police just two months into the pandemic.

The Sunday after Floyd's murder, Caleb remembered using many of the same phrases about racism in his sermon that he'd done five times before—in the case of other Black people who died in police-involved incidents, like Breonna Taylor and Ahmaud Arbery. Desert Springs then did a seven-week sermon series on race, called "The Way of the Reconciled," and Caleb brought in, via livestream, prominent Black pastors from around the country to preach to his congregation.

"I remember thinking, 'This is going to be so great,'" Caleb said.

Instead, he got "overwhelming" pushback. He was called "communist," and "Marxist," for, in his recollection, saying the same things about race he'd said to his congregation many times before.

"I was sitting with people who were so pissed," Caleb said. "They asked me, 'How could you do this? I never thought you were like this.'"

Conversely, Caleb was proud of his growth and evolution spiritually, mentally, and emotionally throughout his adult life. He was confident that God had led him to this place. He was grateful for the opportunities he'd had to change and evolve and listen and learn from others. He had this hope—this faith, really—that God could change hearts from hatred, anger, and violence into work for justice, peace, and love.

In the midst of the seven-week sermon series on race, Caleb himself contracted COVID-19. A month later, in July, he got shingles. That led to a complication called Ramsay Hunt syndrome, causing partial facial paralysis that Caleb dealt with all summer of 2020. One day he sat down and accounted for all that had happened in his Christian community since he'd become lead pastor, and specifically since Trump had been elected in 2016.

"In one day I counted 300 lost relationships," he said.

In September 2020, Caleb was a broken man. He went to the church's leadership board prepared to quit. Instead, he agreed to a three-month sabbatical. The board told Caleb they were behind him, whatever the cost.

"Put your foot on the gas," the lead financial person told Caleb. "If we don't follow our convictions in this moment, then who are we?"

They then paraphrased from the Hebrew Bible book of Esther: "Maybe we were made for such a time as this."

In his time away, Caleb took time to reflect. His anger faded into a deeper understanding of what had happened. He realized that in the years of 2013 to 2015, when people at his church applauded his ideas about diversity and multiculturalism, many of them merely "thought they'd be pegged a racist if they didn't applaud." An overattention to appearances popularized in those acquiescent, appeasing days of the church growth movement had covered over a sickening rot at the heart of white American Christianity. Caleb learned his church had maybe been OK with a multicolored church, but many of them didn't really want multiculturalism. Many of them did see Jesus the way Driscoll and others had depicted him: an angry white man with a penchant for violence and an appetite for sexual dominance and control.

Looking back clearly, Caleb began to see Trump as an apocalypse, and, in his words, "the best thing that happened to the Evangelical church in America."

"If you go to the doctor, you can't get well unless you know you're sick," Caleb added. "Once you know, you can start to apply healing. But it costs a lot. Eighty percent of the congregation that was here in 2016 is gone now."

The biblical prophet Isaiah spoke of a small but faithful remnant who would remain steadfast to God in the midst of national trauma, violence, and despair. And so with this remaining 20 percent, Caleb came back after his sabbatical with a renewed hope to continue to do the work he had been called to do.

He had been forever changed, though. That latent anger, once so at home among the skinheads and Driscoll fanboys, no longer found a refuge inside his soul. He couldn't get riled up like he used to. Instead, he found himself on a mission to combat Christian nationalism with faithfulness and love. He was still that Phoenix punk kid, still the outsider, seeking authenticity, truth, and a God who would not tolerate hypocrites. But he knew now that those who knew that God best weren't the angry, brash men of his youth. They were the gentle ones, the patient ones, the ones who led with love.

Today, Caleb still serves as lead pastor at Desert Springs. Dawn Farmer is the executive pastor, a rarity in a world of nondenominational Bible churches, most of whom do not allow women to lead men or preach to mixed groups. The staff and board represent many forms of diversity. The church's website is absent many of the standard lines from Evangelical megachurches that claim welcome but also allude to exclusionary stances for LGBTQ people or women's role in ministry. One of their core values says, "we are a bunch of misfits, bound together by the love and grace of God made known to us through Jesus."

When Caleb told me about how much the congregation had shrunk since COVID-19, I came to worship that Sunday morning in 2024 expecting to see lots of empty seats. But the service was well-attended, and there was a spirit of energy and commitment that I hadn't felt in some time since visiting similar Evangelical churches all over the country since 2016. The worship band that morning appeared to be led by a Black man and two Black women singing. I saw a few autistic people stimming during the service, people wearing hearing aids, people in wheelchairs—disabled people of all ages and backgrounds in attendance. Women were among those who helped serve communion and read aloud the words of Jesus to prepare the bread and wine for small groups to partake of the holy sacrament.

The congregation in attendance was not the airbrushed, apparently perfect, smiling, shiny families who so often populated the Evangelical megachurches I'd attended in the past, places where people were encouraged to hide their shame and shortcomings, to present as perfect even when they were struggling or suffering or addicted or abused. Instead, somehow, this group looked reminiscent of God's realistic kingdom: imperfect, a little messy, present, honest, worshipping.

Caleb was starting a sermon series focused on the Prophet Jeremiah's call to "pursue the flourishing of the city." He talked about what he loved about Phoenix, and all that ailed Phoenix. There was an awareness that the world was large and in need, and that white Christians were not placed by God at its central, special place. Instead, Caleb's posture was one of humble seeking, of hope against the odds.

I had asked him earlier about the other ministry work he was often called into, ministering in particular to troubled young men: military veterans suffering from PTSD and general trauma and challenges of life after deployment; first responders like police officers, firefighters, paramedics. Caleb said they all dealt with their pain in gallows humor, thinking they could fight it off or laugh it off or work it off, like so many young men do. Then they'd wake up at night covered in sweat, another nightmare, crying alone and afraid.

In contrast to the idea of manhood he had as a young white supremacist, and then as a young devotee of Driscoll and other pastors who championed an angry and extreme masculine Jesus, Caleb says now that he always tries to approach his ministry through the lens of the sword-cross metaphor. He says that he has spent a lot of time studying Jesus and what Jesus did when he and his followers were stressed and under threat.

"Every time they try to pick up a sword, he tells them to pick up their cross," Caleb said. "Swords don't actually change the world, but crosses do. If [young men] want to be powerful, pick the most powerful thing. Jesus shows the sword is weak. There's a bigger power that can actually transform lives."

I sat across from Caleb that January day for hours, listening to his whole story, of which I'd previously known bits and pieces but not the details, the extremes of the lows: the violence, the anger, the loss, and, ultimately, the hope. It struck me while we talked that the beginning of Caleb's story could have been the story of so many other angry, young, white Christian boys, some of whom end in up in the headlines for mass shootings or violent rampages, or maybe for a run for political office. I thought especially of how just a few months earlier I'd sat in the Columbia, South Carolina, office of the pastor of mass shooter and white supremacist Dylann Roof, and I'd heard him tell me about Dylann as a teenager, lost and angry, drifting from one friend's trailer to the next.

It's unpleasant to consider that your friend and pastoral colleague could have something so deeply in common with a white supremacist mass shooter. It's even worse to consider the paths that my sons—or your sons—or the young white Christian men and boys you love—could be led down in similar ways. Those paths are at this point well-worn, trod and entrenched by political and Christian leaders who have learned there's a lot of money in preaching violent masculinity to lonely white teen boys longing for belonging and clear identities.

The path out at first appears not so well-worn, not quite as clear. Who is the man who rejects what appears to be simple strength and power in order to recant what he has once believed, leave his friends and community, and subject himself to a more honest and vulnerable existence? A man like this once died on a cross. But it's not just that man, though he once led the way. We all know these men, too. Maybe you are one of these men. Confident enough to turn around. To look with open eyes at those who've led you astray and say: "This is all bullshit." To reject the message that says openness and love might make you weak, and instead turn toward the world, wounds and all, bending forward, offering up another cheek.

Caleb's story reminds us that just as many roads lead in, toward radicalization and violence and despair for boys and young white men in America, many roads also lead out. Many men also have rejected this path as one that leads only to ruin and pain.

I want to end with one more story of one more young white man. His story demonstrates the same truths that Caleb's does, though it does so by showing that the very thing so many white Christian men and boys—and those of us who love them—fear most, may be the very thing that saves them.

Becoming Antonio

Antonio[15] wasn't sure he'd be able to talk with me on that blustery January day we'd originally scheduled for an interview. He was working on boats, as he often did, during a break from seminary. The East Coast had been rattled with blizzards, heavy snowfall, and roaring winds for the past few days. Antonio wasn't sure he'd have a reliable cell phone connection, much less a quiet place for us to talk and for him to tell me the depths of his winding story, for me to understand the journey that had brought him here after years of confusion, tragedy, pain, trauma, forgiveness, grace, searching, rejecting, finding God.

A writer friend of mine had taught Antonio in a few courses, and she told me a curious story about how he, a trans man, had found himself in almost ad hoc counseling and care conversations at right-wing Christian rallies with mostly white, middle-aged Christian men. He'd written a paper on the subject for his master of divinity degree, with a concentration on chaplaincy. The paper was titled, in part: "The Jihad of Liberation." After growing up the child of a former Evangelical pastor, homeschooled in conservative Christian traditionalism, Antonio said he now practiced both Muslim and Christian traditions, while holding onto faith in Jesus as a central figure of devotion, but not necessarily of divinity. All this likely would have sounded heretical to young Antonio, and he likely never would have believed he could find himself at a Christian seminary studying such things, potentially pursuing a career as a chaplain. But then, as I'd already seen in Caleb's story, and in the story of so many young, white Christian men I'd been studying, and in my own life—God moves through our lives in mysterious and even meandering ways, if only to finally arrive at a place of greater love, understanding, acceptance, and grace.

That word—grace. I kept returning to it as I heard Antonio unfold his story.

He was brought up in the Presbyterian Church in America (PCA), a conservative branch of American Presbyterianism founded in 1973 in Birmingham, Alabama. Its predecessor body was the Presbyterian Church in the United States (PCUS), originally the Presbyterian Church in the Confederate States in America. The PCA split off from the PCUS rather than submit to a merger to become the PCUSA. The PCA is loath to admit the role of racial disunity—during the civil rights movement, in the South, in its formation. But the denomination has again and again taken positions against progress and inclusion for all sorts of marginalized groups, beginning in the South during the segregation of Black Americans, and continuing on with a refusal to ordain women or LGBTQ people, or to allow gay marriage. New York City pastor and *Reason for God* author Tim Keller is probably the most well-known PCA leader, though the denomination was also home to former Republican vice president Dan Quayle and former senators Jim DeMint (R-SC) and Ben Sasse (R-NE). The PCA, like its leading champion, Keller, had a penchant for making its exclusionary beliefs seem somehow anodyne and even aligned with pop culture and a forward-looking church, even as its leaders fought vociferously against social movements like gay rights, abortion rights, or feminism more broadly. Antonio's dad had been a church pastor, but he lost his job when Antonio was a baby, and instead became what Antonio remembers as "leadership-adjacent" in their new church, almost so that Antonio and his younger brother still felt like "PKs" (pastor's kids).

While Caleb's family emphasized a sort of blue-collar, hardworking, freethinking, western version of conservative Christianity, Antonio's family was even more rooted in the academic discipline of raising their children according to conservative Christian principles. Antonio remembers homeschooling until middle school—and his brother until high school—with his mom as their only teacher, using fundamentalist Christian curriculum. Meanwhile, his dad got a PhD in economics, writing a dissertation wondering if God was an economist. He was perhaps perfectly situated, then, to grow in prominence in an American conservative church culture that had come to emphasize economics and recruit "businessmen" under the church growth model popularized by pastors Warren and Hybels. Still, Antonio's dad never quite settled professionally. He worked low-paying TA jobs and did other side jobs to try and pay the bills, supplemented by Antonio's mom's inheritance after her mother's death. The family was surely not well-off, but they lived in economically depressed areas, and they were relatively affluent compared to their impoverished neighbors, so Antonio didn't notice the financial worry much. He had other demons to battle.

For years, hidden and concealed from the rest of the family, Antonio's father had been sexually abusing his child. Antonio tried to tell his mom, but he said she didn't believe him.

"She thought it was anti-Christian rebellion," Antonio said, because at the very same time, Antonio was starting to question the misogyny and patriarchal structures of their church. He had begun to question things as he left the family home more often, beginning at a Christian charter school with other homeschoolers for the first two years of middle school, and then starting an early college program at the community college at age fourteen.

Around that time, Antonio (who was born biologically female) started to realize that he was queer, though he didn't quite have the language for what he felt inside.

"I knew there was something different about me," he said. "At the time, I would have said I was experiencing same-sex attraction. I wasn't sure if God made people gay. I knew God didn't want me to act on my same-sex attraction."

Instead of hearing her child's cries for protection, Antonio's mother instead cracked down on her teenage daughter. She was practicing what Antonio now calls "punitive parenting." Life at home had become unbearable. But outside the home, Antonio was meeting new people and feeling more confident in his queer identity. He got a full-time job and moved out the day he turned eighteen. Nine months later, then still living as a woman, he was married to a community college classmate, a man a decade older.

"It was definitely some purity culture stuff," Antonio says, looking back at the quick marriage. "I wanted the stability of marriage. I was thinking that was the only option."

At the same time, Antonio was wrestling with his faith.

"I knew that the Calvinist God would be evil for condemning us to hell, as people with original sin. I just kept thinking that if all this is true, then God is either evil or God doesn't exist."

Antonio says his husband at the time was gentle and patient, giving him the reassurance he'd never had before that "I was gonna be OK." He desperately needed that reassurance, because in sharing about his queerness publicly, Antonio had been "pushed out" by his church.

"A lot of the community just stopped talking to me," he said. "I really experienced the loss of support and community through that experience. [My husband] was really a rock in that time."

Antonio also connected with his then-father-in-law, and the two of them would go clamming, or out on the boat, or do construction work together. These were simple but deeply meaningful experiences for Antonio, who never got time like that with his own father.

"He was in many ways the father that mine was not," Antonio said.

As Antonio leaned more and more into this new supportive community surrounding him, he felt his understanding of his own identity continue to shift. He realized that he was not just queer but transgender and started to begin the transition process from female to male, and to use he/they pronouns. His gender identity is still evolving today, and Antonio says he is "tired of all the gender wars."

"Basically what I tell people is I feel much more comfortable in a masculine expression. I feel like my spiritual work is to exist as a man in the world."

He and his husband were divorced after four years of marriage, in July 2020, though Antonio says they still have positive regard for one another and did not end on bad terms.

"We were on a similar journey of self-discovery," Antonio said. "We were both just going in different directions."

His ex-husband wanted to remain in the Pacific Northwest town where they'd met, but Antonio was on the move. He spent the next few years before seminary working for environmental nonprofits, continuing to do the work with his hands he'd always loved to do, as well as working with mutual aid groups to address homelessness and overdose prevention. The work was active and meaningful, but Antonio missed the rites of faith and religion he'd grown up with, divorced from the baggage of his abusive and angry parents. Eventually, during a sweep of a houseless camp where Antonio and his fellow workers were attempting to assist people, he met a Mennonite pastor who was "yelling about Jesus." Antonio and the pastor ended up meeting every week to talk about theology. He started reading voraciously, finding liberation theology and ideas about communalism, libertarian socialism, and anarcho-communism. True to his western roots, Antonio says "I'm big on autonomy, but I don't want to be individualistic about it."

As I watched Antonio's deep-set eyes bore into mine, and he shared passionately about his calling to Christian anarchism, I saw within his face and heard within his words so many of the other young, white Christian boys and men who have been a part of my research journey, and a part of my life in general. I think back to the restless isolation and uncertainty turned to racist hatred in the case of mass shooter and white supremacist Dylann Roof. I think back to Connor, lining up for drill at the Citadel, and still finding a place for his tears to flow after the overdose death of his friend. I think of the confirmation students in the rural Midwest who dreamt up an idyllic paradise with only white boys and naked girls; of the rural teenage boys learning at the feet of an ex-military couple of pastors, in a garage on an autumn night in Minnesota, down the road from the white supremacist *Hof*, and how they told me that to be a man was to be kind, and that Jesus wasn't white after all. I think of small, angry, screaming Pastor Mark Driscoll, desperate to reclaim his manhood by the repression of women and anyone who might reveal his own thinly veiled inadequacy. I think of my blond-and-red-haired sons, running blithely down the city sidewalk, telling me they liked to hear me preach, getting in trouble at school for playing too rough, brave, kind, nervous, afraid, hugging me, ignoring me, loving the world and the people they meet, growing up and into men, with fits and starts and imperfections.

Antonio told me that what made him go to seminary was in part a calling back to some of the same "themes in the spaces I was raised in," even though those same places and themes he also now saw as at least partially Christian nationalist.

"There's a libertarian bent," he told me, of his conservative Christian upbringing. "An emphasis on freedom and community-building. A deep community and relationship to land, even if sometimes in an extractive way. There's a relationship to place."

"It's been a long road, and it will continue to be a long road for me."

Antonio said he's been through years of therapy and is "as healed as someone can be" with a history of sexual abuse. Through that process, he found a way to forgive his dad.

"I realized that if I had been socialized as a boy, and gone through some of the experiences my father experienced, who's to say I wouldn't end up like him? Seeing my dad's dysfunction, my compassion has increased."

Antonio's process of forgiveness and grace is not prescriptive or even necessarily recommended for other survivors, each of whom have their own paths to follow. I include his story here not to recommend others do the same, but instead to lift up his uniqueness, and the inescapable power of *grace* in everything Antonio had explained to me. This was especially moving because I understood that I had not often expressed that same sense of grace toward trans people in my own Christian past. In my own growing-up faith development, tangential to '90s Evangelical purity culture, I learned not only to repress and be ashamed of my own femininity and sexuality, but I also learned fear and shame related to LGBTQ people, something that has taken me a long time to undo, even as I have socially and theologically supported full affirmation of LGBTQ people in the church for more than a decade now.

The miraculous and hopeful part of this story for young, white Christian men in America can find its culmination here, because here we have Antonio, who spent his childhood abused and victimized by a father who'd been shaped by a harsh masculine mold and a Christian culture that did not leave space for men to be vulnerable and seek love. Here we have Antonio, who in his own transgender masculinity has found a deep well of compassion and understanding for the very men who propagate the culture of Christian masculinity that terrorized his childhood years.

Here we have Antonio, at the right-wing rallies, off to the side talking to men about construction and "bro-ing" out, wearing coveralls, but then also talking about fathers and grandfathers and pain and longing and God. At a Proud Boys rally in Oregon during Trump's presidency, Antonio and nine of his "comrades," including community organizers, social workers, biker moms in recovery, public defenders, and other friends, formed an impromptu "de-escalation cooperative."[16] This group of ten dispersed themselves, standing between protesters and counter-protesters, something Antonio described as "creating space for activated people to reconsider their actions."[17] Antonio talked to militiamen, "using humor to diffuse tension," and "asked questions about their lives."[18] He wrote later of the experience, "My goal was to humanize myself as a queer person and to help the agitators feel heard in their distress."[19] Later on that day, a rally attendee and Iraq war veteran named Mike, wearing a baton and a loaded .45 on his hip, shared with Antonio about his "key formative experiences, all of which had been traumatic."[20]

Writing later of the experience, Antonio wrote: "When I consider Mike's childhood, I am overcome with empathy for his search for safety."[21]

Antonio felt not only compassion but deep connection to Mike's story, adding, "While I cannot deny that I hold contempt for Mike's Christian nationalist and fundamentalist Evangelical beliefs, I remember how well they served me as a teenager. These doctrines were a fortress of cosmic security in the face of political unrest, financial instability, and familial abuse. However, it was also through my experiences of suffering that I was able to grasp the existence of systemic oppression. Had I not been raised as a girl under patriarchy, were I not bisexual and transgender, I may have found myself standing by Mike's side as his comrade."[22]

Antonio said he first entered into Christian nationalist and right-wing spaces because in some way they represented where he had come from—people he had formerly known and even loved—and he wanted to cling to a sense of common humanity. Even despite the challenges and pain his life has wrought, Antonio still has a desperate and deeply rooted hope for the future. He sees the spirit of God working change in his own life, in powerful ways, and he can't help but believe that the spirit of God could also be at work in changing these Christian nationalist men.

"They're just men," Antonio says. "I don't always like the phrase 'Christian nationalist,' even though I use it. They're shaped by culture and experiences just like me. With my own healing journey, it has really blurred the line between oppressor and oppressed . . . it shifted things for me. We are all harmed. I noticed cycles of harm. None of us are innocent."

Antonio said his father's dad had four affairs and was "married to his work." His mother once told him that his father had "eaten his dad's cigarettes in order to feel close to him."

The pain and sorrow and shame of generations can run deep, like a river, through our lives, twisting and turning and shaping us and our paths in ways we don't always understand. But here we have Antonio: the transgender seminary student reading his Bible next to his Qur'an. He's still young. He's still figuring it out. His manhood is in process, revealing itself—like how all boys become men, like how God reveals Godself, as the Apostle Paul writes, "as in a mirror, dimly, but then we will see face-to-face."[23]

Conclusion

When writing about a threatening cultural phenomenon, especially one that concerns members of our own families and communities, there's an intense pressure to provide some sort of clear solution to the problem. I think many of us, if given the option, would love to walk into our neighborhood pharmacy and hand in a prescription for how to heal the troubled young men in our lives and protect the rest of us from their occasional dangerous rage and violence.

Listicles have become a popular form of modern-day journalism. I know, because I click on them all the time. And I think I could have written a really popular, maybe even viral, listicle, with a title like: "Ten Ways to Keep Your Son from Becoming an Angry Misogynist," or, "Fifteen Ways to Help the Men in Your Life Embrace Their Emotions and Vulnerabilities." The thing is, like I said: I've read a lot of these articles. I've also read the studies where they use statistical analysis to put groups of people into categories with catchy names, in order to form some kind of shorthand for understanding (typically threatening) human behavior. I know that kind of research and analysis has its place. I cite some of those studies in the chapters of this book, in fact. But ultimately, if you have read this book hoping to be handed a simple prescription, you are going to end up disappointed.

I do not believe general prescriptions work when it comes to human social behavior and relationships. As medical caregivers know, prescriptions must be individualized. Different people require different dosages, different drug combinations, different frequencies. I could give you a few steps to follow, but those steps would be much more well-advised were they suggested by someone who knows you and your loved ones well. Again, as prescribers know, the best care is forged in relationship. The best cures are administered with an ample dose of love.

If I told you that boys and young men who've fallen victim to the seductive song of violent misogyny rooted in right-wing Christian rhetoric simply need generic love to pull them out, you would rightly tell me that care and compassion alone do not stop the bullets directed at the world from angry young men, and at angry young men and boys themselves.

On the other hand, if I told you that the solution to the problems and threat of young boys and men in America lies only in the pursuit of telling hard truths and seeking justice and pursuing punishment, you'd rightly tell me of the wisdom of recovery, which reminds us that change begins in love and trusting relationship, and that the truth spoken without love is rarely heard by those who need it most. You'd tell me that punishment, on its own, only leads to more anger and violence.

I believe that prescriptions and lists of cures might make us feel better for a brief moment, and statistical analysis that categorizes troubled people into a variety of numerical groups might make a catchy headline. But have you ever told a loved one that they fit neatly into a statistical group of dangerous and troubled people? Have you ever found yourself in one of those groups? Did it lead to lasting personal or societal change, absent trusting and loving relationships in community?

And so I turn, instead, again, to the most powerful form of truth that exists in this world.

It is a form of truth that lodges itself in the most visceral part of your memory, the part that returns to you again and again when you can't sleep at night and you're thinking about that thing or that person who worries you the most. This is a form of truth that teaches us about God, as in the stories of the ancient Hebrews, who cared most that we knew God was gracious and merciful, abounding in steadfast love—and who cared little that we might understand the exact date of the creation of the world, or the (lack of) scientific evidence for humans being created alongside dinosaurs.

Only the stories can save us.

And so instead of telling you ten ways to stop worrying about the young men in your life, or ten ways to prevent another school shooting (a task that our legislators really ought to be taking on), I told you about John and Ryan and Travis and Eric and the rarefied air of King Street in Charleston, South Carolina, and how they knew the right things to say, and they were trying, but it was still so hard to reckon with the massacre that happened just down the road from their high, white steeple, in the earnest, privileged, and progressive church that had to account for its slaveholding past. I told you about Dylann, and his family, and his pastor, Tony, who made ashes with the Reverend Clementa Pinckney at Tony's church in Columbia, where Dylann worshiped, too, weeks before Dylann would kill nine Black people at a Bible study led by Pastor Pinckney at his church in Charleston. I told you that Dylann killed out of a ferocious racist hatred that scared and shamed his church of conservative white Christians. I told you about how badly so many of us white Christians want to separate ourselves from stories like Dylann's, to put him into a box where we don't fit. But Dylann's and Tony's and Clementa's lives intertwined inextricably, and we have to question our role in why it all ended in the death of Clementa and eight of his parishioners. Dylann and Tony's story can't just be their story. It's a story of white American Christian masculine rage, and the violent, destructive paths down which it can lead.

Then I told you about Connor, about the slow pace of change in places of vaunted white male American tradition and power, and about coming to terms with the sins of the past. I told you about his friend's death to a drug overdose, and the way he cried, and how he realized he'd been taught to stuff his emotions inside for a very long time, and how that hadn't made him stronger but only more brittle and prone to breaking.

I told you about Bishop Yehiel Curry, and his work with young Black men on the South Side of Chicago, and how he encouraged us to smash the box of the violent demands of hierarchical masculinity. You read about the Reverend Heather Roth Johnson, a former Southern debutante who teaches children in her Minnesota congregation and around the country through the storytelling style she first learned in Madagascar, and the lesson she tries to teach most: an image of a gentler God.

You came along with me to Phoenix, where we visited Kara and Noah and their three little boys, who were allowed to buy dolls even after their parents' misgivings and nervousness rooted in being raised in patriarchal, traditional conservative Christian families. Kara told us about growing up in a family where women were raised to follow and submit to men, about losing friendships to cultish complementarian

Christian communities, about their church shrinking by 80 percent after their pastor spoke with compassion for the murdered George Floyd and called for a commitment to racial justice. They talked about the pain of watching the descent of the once-proud Arizona GOP into Christian conspiracy, anger, and violence. But amidst their sadness and fear, Kara and Noah remained steadfast, committed together to raising their boys in kindness, love, acceptance, and inclusion.

You met Joe, and Linda, and Amy, all public educators who carry their own fear and trepidation into the classroom to meet the boys and young men they teach each day, and who nonetheless keep teaching and caring anyway, because they love their students, and they believe what they're doing in school every day matters for the future of the world.

You read about small-town pastors and military veterans Dan and Janine, who hold confirmation classes for teenagers in their garage, up the hill from the chicken coop, and you listened as Dan, who has seen with his own eyes the scarring of battles and war and violence and terror in the Middle East, told his students that while Jesus was not white, Jesus was kind and loving and forgiving and listened to women. Just a few miles down the road from the church building purchased by a white supremacist group, you met Jake and Aaron and Levi, who watch The Millennial Farmer on YouTube, who told me they want to grow up to be like their dads and grandfathers, who said that to be a man means being kind, respectful, and standing up—not for yourself—but for the needs and concerns of others.

And finally, you read the stories of Caleb and Antonio, about paths of pain and isolation and anger and rejection, and how they were led out of dangerous places and into love by a God who was somehow constant, whether God was preaching on an Evangelical stage in Phoenix or whistling in the sea air on a boat deck next to a transgender seminary student who was called to be a chaplain to Christian nationalist men and boys at Trump rallies.

You heard more stories than these—too many to list here—and I know as you read them all, you are thinking also of yourself and the stories written on your heart, the sons and husbands and fathers and uncles and friends and students and even the ones you've read and heard about, the sermons that made the inside of your stomach curl into itself, feeling the bile rise in your throat. The videos that made you oddly interested and also afraid. The ones you read about in terrifying news stories, wearing black masks, carrying AR-15s. The social media accounts that say men must be this way, that sell protein powder and exercise routines next to heavily made-up women in dresses cinched at the waist, holding fat-cheeked baby boys, who are never crying.

The only thing I know how to do, as a journalist and a pastor and a wife and a parent, is to follow the stories where they lead. To heed the warnings and danger within them, and hold on fast, as tightly as I can, to the hope. It's the stories that make us see ourselves in one another, that help us see God where we'd least expect God, and show us an unlikely path away from the madness and pain and death that is all violent masculinity has to offer. It's not that I believe we're beyond saving, beyond hope, resigned to a life of guarding ourselves at all times against those in the world whom we hate or who hate us. Instead, what I believe is that only the stories can save us. Only stories can make us reach for a common humanity far beyond the insecure, desperate, greedy, grasping hands of a fake White Jesus. These stories encourage us to extend our hands out to one another at a time when, especially for boys and young men, the more popular thing to do seems to be balling your hands into a tight fist. We can't hold that fist forever. Aren't your muscles tense and tired? What if we taught this instead to boys and young men? Maybe you recognize the song of a bygone era in America.

Shake another hand, shake a hand next to ya,
Shake another hand and sing along!
Shake another hand, shake a hand next to ya
Shake another hand and sing . . . sing this song.
Ah la la la la la le lu ya, Ah la la la la la le lu ya!
Ah la la la la la le lu ya, Ah la la la la la le alleluia.

Acknowledgments

Disciples of White Jesus began over hastily prepared cheese, crackers, and carrots at my kitchen table. Dawn Rundman, an editor for 1517 Media and a neighbor of mine, had told me she had an idea for me. A mom of two teenagers, Dawn was working on a series of books aimed at practical use inside churches, and she was interested in having me write one about the rise in right-wing radicalization among white boys and young men. That wasn't the book I'd planned on writing next, after my first book, *Red State Christians*. I had wanted to write something less "political," more personal, and maybe more palatable in casual conversation, one that would lead to fewer deep sighs and awkward silences, only followed by people pulling me into corners at social gatherings and telling me about the trauma happening inside their families and communities. I knew this book would be just like *Red State Christians* in that sense, and I wasn't sure I was ready for something like that again.

Still, as a mom of two white boys myself—Dawn's idea quickly took root. I found myself sharing about it to other parents, pastors, and fellow writers. My agent, Sarah Smith, told me that the topic was of great interest in New York City publishing circles. Around that same time, while I was still working on another book proposal, I was invited onto a podcast with Pastor Caleb Campbell, whose story is one of the most important in this book. When Caleb told me about his journey from racist skinhead groups to the world of young, restless, and reformed violent Christian masculinity, to his present role as vocal resistor of Christian nationalism and outspoken prophet against the leadership of pastors like Mark Driscoll, my brain really started whirring about Dawn's idea. I started a Gmail folder filled with almost-daily news stories about troubled young white men and boys, some of whom became violent, got into trouble, or tumbled into depths of despair. I also dived deep into my own sons' YouTube algorithms, and I noticed that names like that of misogynist sex offender Andrew Tate had become well-known among their fellow elementary school boys at their relatively progressive, public urban elementary school. Meanwhile, Donald Trump was running for president again, and *Roe v. Wade* had been overturned.

As we talked around my kitchen table, I told Dawn that I was all-in with her idea. But I knew myself: I wouldn't be able to constrain myself to the more narrowly conceived, shorter book that she'd originally envisioned. I wondered if we might move the idea to 1517's trade publisher, Broadleaf Books, and sell it to a wider, secular audience, with a lengthier word count and room for some research travel.

As is true of all great editors, Dawn creatively and enthusiastically agreed to follow the idea where it led. At Broadleaf Books, Lisa Kloskin and Andrew DeYoung embraced the book immediately and gave it the legs it needed to become the book I ended up writing. Also integral to making this all work together was the great negotiating work of my agent, Sarah, and literary assistant Anna Zinchuk at the David Black Agency, who helped to finalize the contract. I got the final contract offer at a Montana brewpub with my family after spending the day whitewater rafting in Glacier National Park. Four long years after publication of *Red State Christians*, I couldn't have been more thrilled to move forward on book number two. And it never would have happened without Dawn's vision and trust in me.

So many deserve huge gratitude in the creation of this project. Again, my agent, Sarah, who worked with me and didn't lose hope after those years of searching for the right next project—and who always gives me the push I need to try something new, like Substack! And again Lisa, my editor, who was kind and patient and enthusiastic, and knew just what to change to make the story even more powerful.

I'm grateful to all those who agreed to be interviewed for this project, and those who helped me make much-needed connections for those interviews: Lee Bennett, again, Caleb Campbell, Eric Childers, Christa Forsythe, Bryant Kaden, Tony Metze, Eileen Campbell-Reed, Darryl and Jennifer Thul, Layton Williams Berkes, and the vast community of pastors, teachers, community members, church members, and honest, hardworking people spread across America who were willing to share their stories with me.

I'm hugely indebted to the work of courageous women writers in the space of Christian nationalism and violent masculinity: Beth Allison Barr, Kristin Du Mez, Kaitlyn Schiess, Sarah Stankorb, and so many more. Their work emboldened me and made space for this book to be published.

I'm also grateful to the men who write in this space, the ways they've pushed back against narrow and violent visions of masculinity and fatherhood and what it means to be a man who follows Jesus: Brad Onishi, Sam Perry, Jared Yates Sexton, Jemar Tisby, Andrew Whitehead, and again: so many more.

To all the parents, pastors, teachers, coaches, community leaders who told me your own stories about the boys and young men in your life, your concerns for them, your dreams for them—and your promise to me that this book was important and that the work mattered deeply to you.

To the teenage boys and young men who opened your hearts to me and shared emotionally and vulnerably, in many cases, with a woman you'd only just met. Thank you for helping me to see your hearts and listen and learn.

To my brother, Kevin, who read the first books I ever made with markers and a stapler as a big sister in Maple Grove, Minnesota, and who still reads and gives me feedback today, as an educator and a husband and father of a son himself.

To my dear friend, Lyz, who has known me since we were both just teenagers in the '90s and early 2000s, surrounded by Christian purity culture and limiting gender roles, and trying to find our own creative voices. I'm so grateful we both claimed our stories and our truths, and now we get to share that truth in word and in art. I know a part of our conversations is in this book, and you helped give me the courage to write it.

And of course, to Ben, my first reader and first love, always and forever.

Notes

Chapter 1: The Violence of White Christian Masculinity

1. Minors' names have been changed to protect their identities.
2. Luke 4:18.
3. Jeremy Borden, Sari Horwitz, and Jerry Markon, "From Victims' Families, Forgiveness for Accused Charleston Gunman Dylann Roof," *Washington Post*, June 19, 2015, https://www.washingtonpost.com/politics/south-carolina-governor-urges-death-penalty-charges-in-church-slayings/2015/06/19/3c039722-1678-11e5-9ddc-e3353542100c_story.html.
4. Borden, Horwitz, and Markon, "From Victims' Families."
5. William Faulkner, *Requiem for a Nun* (New York: Random House, 1951).
6. Rachel Kaadzi Ghansah, "A Most American Terrorist: The Making of Dylann Roof," *GQ*, August 21, 2017, https://www.gq.com/story/dylann-roof-making-of-an-american-terrorist.
7. "Overview of Recent US Mass Shootings Motivated by Hate," *Reuters*, August 28, 2023, https://www.reuters.com/world/us/us-mass-shootings-motivated-by-hate-2023-08-28/.
8. "Council of Conservative Citizens," *Wikipedia*, https://en.wikipedia.org/wiki/Council_of_Conservative_Citizens.
9. "Dylann Roof," *Wikipedia*, https://en.wikipedia.org/wiki/Dylann_Roof.

Chapter 2: White Christian Men

1. Caitlin Byrd, "'It's Been a Long Time Coming.' The Citadel Honors First Black Cadets with Portrait," *The State*, November 22, 2021, https://www.thestate.com/news/charleston/article255967682.html.
2. Byrd, "'It's Been a Long Time.'"
3. Byrd, "'It's Been a Long Time.'"
4. "Shannon Faulkner," *Wikipedia*, https://en.wikipedia.org/wiki/Shannon_Faulkner.
5. "Shannon Faulkner," *Wikipedia*.
6. "Shannon Faulkner," *Wikipedia*.

NOTES

7. "Shannon Faulkner," *Wikipedia*.
8. "The Citadel Student Population," *College Factual*, 2023, https://www.collegefactual.com/colleges/citadel-military-college-of-south-carolina/student-life/diversity/#google_vignette.
9. "Charleston, SC: Census Place," *Data USA*, https://datausa.io/profile/geo/charleston-sc/#:~:text=The 5 largest ethnic groups,-Hispanic) (1.77%).
10. "QuickFacts, South Carolina," *United States Census Bureau*, https://www.census.gov/quickfacts/fact/table/SC/PST045222.
11. "The Citadel," *Wikipedia*, https://en.wikipedia.org/wiki/The_Citadel.
12. Name changed to protect the cadet's privacy.
13. Connor referred to his diagnosis as ADD; most current statistical data uses the terminology of attention-deficit/hyperactivity disorder.
14. "Data and Statistics about ADHD," *Centers for Disease Control and Prevention*, https://www.cdc.gov/ncbddd/adhd/data.html#:~:text=Boys (13%) are more,ADHD than girls (6%).&text=Black, non-Hispanic children and,-Hispanic children (3%).
15. Hillary Flynn, "Citadel Cadets, Faculty Say There's Pervasive Racism at the School," *Post and Courier*. January 11, 2023, https://www.postandcourier.com/education-lab/citadel-cadets-faculty-say-there-s-pervasive-racism-at-the-school/article_0d90b2f6-8099-11ed-b7c1-53723174cf63.html#.
16. Flynn, "There's Pervasive Racism at the School."
17. Peter Jamison, "The Revolt of the Christian Homeschoolers," *Washington Post*, May 30, 2023, https://www.washingtonpost.com/education/interactive/2023/christian-home-schoolers-revolt/.
18. Manu Raju, "Graham Foe: Women Cause Divorces," *Politico*, April 25, 2014, https://www.politico.com/story/2014/04/lindsey-graham-det-bowers-south-carolina-senate-2014-elections-106007.
19. Raju, "Graham Foe."
20. Raju, "Graham Foe."
21. Raju, "Graham Foe."
22. Matthew 18:6–7.
23. While Connor was homeschooled his final two years of high school, he was still able to play football for the high school team.
24. Michel Martin and Emma Bowman, "Why Nearly All Mass Shooters are Men," *All Things Considered*, podcast audio, March 27, 2021, https://www.npr.org/2021/03/27/981803154/why-nearly-all-mass-shooters-are-men.
25. "Number of Mass Shootings in the United States between 1982 and December 2023, by Shooter's Race or Ethnicity," *Statista*, January 8, 2024, https://www.statista.com/statistics/476456/mass-shootings-in-the-us-by-shooter-s-race/.
26. "KSHB: Suicide Rates High in Middle-Aged White Men," *Saint Luke's Kansas City*, September 21, 2022, https://www.saintlukeskc.org/about/news/kshb-suicide-rates-high-middle-aged-white-men.
27. Lisa Geller, "Study: Two-Thirds of Mass Shootings Linked to Domestic Violence," *The Educational Fund to Stop Gun Violence*, 2021, https://efsgv.org/press/study-two-thirds-of-mass-shootings-linked-to-domestic-violence/.
28. John 11:35.

Chapter 3: Created in ~~His~~ God's Image?

1 John 1:18.
2 Kaitlyn Schiess, "The Bible through Slave-Holding Spectacles," *The Ballot and the Bible: How Scripture Has Been Used and Abused in American Politics and Where We Go from Here* (Grand Rapids, MI: Brazos Press, a Division of Baker Publishing Group, 2023), 41.
3 John Piper, "Marriage: A Matrix for Christian Hedonism," *Desiring God: Meditations of a Christian Hedonist* (Colorado Springs, CO: Multnomah Books, 1986), 210.
4 Piper, "Marriage: A Matrix," 211.
5 Piper, "Marriage: A Matrix," 212.
6 Mark Driscoll and Grace Driscoll, "Men and Marriage," *Real Marriage: The Truth about Sex, Friendship and Life Together* (Nashville, TN: Thomas Nelson, 2012), 55.
7 See Genesis 32:22–32.
8 Rachael Fugardi, "Nine Years after Deadly 'Incel' Attack, Threat of Male Supremacism is Growing," *Southern Poverty Law Center*, May 23, 2023, https://www.splcenter.org/news/2023/05/23/after-incel-attack-male-supremacism-growing.
9 Fugardi, "Threat of Male Supremacism."
10 Fugardi, "Threat of Male Supremacism."
11 Kristin Kobes Du Mez, *Jesus and John Wayne: How White Evangelicals Corrupted a Faith and Fractured a Nation* (New York: Liveright, a Division of W.W. Norton & Company, 2020), 65.
12 Jonathan Merritt, "The Book That Revolutionized 'Christian Manhood': 15 Years after 'Wild at Heart,'" *Religion News Service*, April 22, 2016, https://religionnews.com/2016/04/22/the-book-that-revolutionized-christian-manhood-15-years-after-wild-at-heart/.
13 John Eldredge, *Wild at Heart: Discovering the Secret of a Man's Soul* (Nashville: Nelson Books, an imprint of Thomas Nelson, 2001), 9–10.
14 Eldredge, *Wild at Heart*, 28.
15 Eldredge, *Wild at Heart*, 36.
16 Mark Driscoll, *Who Do You Think You Are? Finding Your True Identity in Christ* (Nashville: Thomas Nelson, 2016), 2.
17 Grace Ji-Sun Kim and Susan M. Shaw, *Surviving God: A New Vision of God through the Eyes of Sexual Abuse Survivors* (Minneapolis, MN: Broadleaf, 2024), 133.
18 Kim and Shaw, *Surviving God*, 133.
19 John 17.
20 Revelation 21.
21 Beth Allison Barr, *The Making of Biblical Womanhood* (Grand Rapids, MI: Brazos, 2021).
22 Jared Yates Sexton, *The Man They Wanted Me to Be: Toxic Masculinity and a Crisis of Our Own Making* (Berkeley, CA: Counterpoint, 2019), 196.
23 See John 11:1–44.

Chapter 4: WWJB

1. P. J. Grisar, "Absolutely Every Anti-Semitic Thing Mel Gibson Has Ever Said," *Forward*, June 24, 2020, https://forward.com/culture/449521/mel-gibson-anti-semitism-timeline-winona-ryder/.
2. Athanasius, Saint, Patriarch of Alexandria, *St. Athanasius on the Incarnation: The Treatise De Incarnatione Verbi Dei* (London: A. R. Mowbray & Co., 1970), 93.
3. Du Mez, *Jesus and John Wayne*, 99.
4. Matthew 26:52.
5. "'It's a Bible': Trump outside Church,'" YouTube video, 1:10, posted by *The Independent*, June 1, 2020, https://www.youtube.com/watch?v=LWEuY_15iVc.
6. Matthew 21:10–11.
7. Matthew 21:13b.
8. William Shakespeare, *Macbeth* (Ware, England: Wordsworth Editions, 1992), 5.5.30-31. Reference is to act, scene, and line.
9. Matthew 21:14–16.
10. Mark Driscoll and Grace Driscoll, *Real Marriage: The Truth about Sex, Friendship, and Life Together* (Nashville: Thomas Nelson, 2012), 27.
11. John 15:15.
12. Driscoll and Driscoll, *Real Marriage*, 47.
13. Rosecrans Baldwin, "Do You Need a Visit to the Confident Man Ranch?" *GQ*, September 28, 2023, https://www.gq.com/story/confident-man-ranch-profile.
14. Driscoll and Driscoll, *Real Marriage*, 54.
15. See also "The Rise and Fall of Mars Hill" podcast from *Christianity Today*, 2021–22, https://www.christianitytoday.com/ct/podcasts/rise-and-fall-of-mars-hill/.
16. Names changed for privacy purposes.
17. Josh Shepherd, "Deacon at Doug Wilson's Church Indicted on Possession of Child Pornography," *The Roys Report*, May 4, 2022, https://julieroys.com/deacon-doug-wilson-church-indicted-possession-child-pornography/.
18. Mary DeMuth, "I'm Sick of Hearing about Your Smoking Hot Wife," *Christianity Today*, April 19, 2013, https://www.christianitytoday.com/ct/2013/april-web-only/im-sick-of-hearing-about-your-smoking-hot-wife.html.
19. Driscoll and Driscoll, *Real Marriage*.
20. Driscoll and Driscoll, *Real Marriage*, 157.
21. Driscoll and Driscoll, *Real Marriage*, 156.
22. "The Rise and Fall of Mars Hill" podcast from *Christianity Today*, 2021–22, https://www.christianitytoday.com/ct/podcasts/rise-and-fall-of-mars-hill/.
23. Sarah Stankorb, *Disobedient Women: How a Small Group of Faithful Women Exposed Abuse, Brought Down Powerful Pastors, and Ignited an Evangelical Reckoning* (Nashville: Worthy Books, 2023).
24. Eldredge, *Wild at Heart*, 24.
25. Eldredge, *Wild at Heart*, 26–27.
26. Sarah D Wire, "At Far-Right Roadshow, Trump is God's 'Anointed One,' QAnon Is King, and 'Everything You Believe Is Right,'" *Los Angeles Times*, October 12,

2023, https://www.latimes.com/politics/story/2023-10-12/reawaken-america-trump-maga-qanon-christian-nationalism.
27 Eldredge, *Wild at Heart*, 31.
28 Du Mez, *Jesus and John Wayne*, 298.
29 Luke 2:41–52.
30 Diana Butler Bass, "All the Marys," a sermon preached on July 22, 2022, *Wild Goose Festival*, https://dianabutlerbass.substack.com/p/mary-the-tower.
31 John 11:27
32 Bass, "All the Marys."

Chapter 5: Oppressors and Victims

1 Heather Cox Richardson, "May 15, 2023." *Letters from an American* (newsletter), May 15, 2023, https://heathercoxrichardson.substack.com/p/may-15-2023.
2 Richardson, "May 15, 2023."
3 Richardson, "May 15, 2023."
4 Angela Denker, "Why 'Trads' Seek to Root the Church's Future in the Past," *U.S. Catholic*, July 19, 2022, https://uscatholic.org/articles/202207/why-trads-seek-to-root-the-churchs-future-in-the-past/.
5 Mark Wingfield, "'Operation Reconquista' Aims to Return Mainline Churches to 'Orthodoxy,'" *Baptist News Global*, November 13, 2023, https://baptistnews.com/article/operation-reconquista-aims-to-return-mainline-churches-to-orthodoxy/.
6 "95 Theses to the United Methodist Church," *Operation Reconquista*, September 24, 2023, https://www.operationreconquista.com/copy-of-95-theses-to-the-episcopal-ch.
7 Matthew 26:52.
8 Richardson, "May 15, 2023."
9 Richardson, "May 15, 2023."
10 Richardson, "May 15, 2023."
11 Noah Goldberg, "A Pride Flag, an Argument, and Gunfire: The Senseless Killing of Laura Ann Carleton," *Los Angeles Times*, August 22, 2023, https://www.latimes.com/california/story/2023-08-21/a-pride-flag-an-argument-and-gunfire-the-senseless-killing-of-laura-ann-carleton.
12 Goldberg, "A Pride Flag."
13 Brian Slodysko, "How Trump's MAGA Movement Helped a 29-Year-Old Activist Become a Millionaire," *Associated Press*, October 10, 2023, https://apnews.com/article/election-2024-trump-turning-point-maga-d08a98e-439fa4e902cb756d7e35153db#.
14 Slodysko, "How Trump's MAGA Movement."
15 Slodysko, "How Trump's MAGA Movement."
16 Slodysko, "How Trump's MAGA Movement."
17 Slodysko, "How Trump's MAGA Movement."
18 Nikki McCann Ramirez, "Man Boobs and Raw Eggs: The Most Absurd Moments from Tucker Carlson's Ball-Tanning Special," *Rolling Stone*,

October 5, 2022, https://www.rollingstone.com/politics/politics-news/tucker-carlson-end-of-men-most-absurd-moments-1234606090/.
19 Ramirez, "Man Boobs and Raw Eggs."
20 Mary McNamara, "Column: Spain's Soccer Chief Kissed a World Cup Winner. What He's Done Since Might Be Worse," *Los Angeles Times*, August 28, 2023, https://www.latimes.com/entertainment-arts/story/2023-08-28/jenni-hermoso-luis-rubiales-spain-womens-world-cup-kiss-aftermath.
21 McNamara, "Spain's Soccer Chief."
22 McNamara, "Spain's Soccer Chief."
23 McNamara, "Spain's Soccer Chief."
24 McNamara, "Spain's Soccer Chief."
25 Sofia Resnick, "A Men's Movement Takes Reins in a Nationwide Quest to End Abortion," *Minnesota Reformer*, September 13, 2023, https://minnesotareformer.com/2023/09/13/a-mens-movement-takes-reins-in-a-nationwide-quest-to-end-abortion/.
26 Resnick, "A Men's Movement."
27 Resnick, "A Men's Movement."
28 Resnick, "A Men's Movement."
29 Resnick, "A Men's Movement."
30 Brian Fraga, "US Bishops Again Declare Abortion 'Preeminent Priority' for Catholic Voters," *National Catholic Reporter*, November 15, 2023, https://www.ncronline.org/news/us-bishops-again-declare-abortion-preeminent-priority-catholic-voters#:~:text=At their November 2019 plenary,was inconsistent with Francis' teachings.
31 Elizabeth Spiers, "Beware the Men Who Double Down," *New York Times*, September 9, 2023, https://www.nytimes.com/2023/09/09/opinion/trump-rubiales-misogyny.html#:~:text=There are many men who,for their pleasure and use.
32 Lyz Lenz, "Get Involved, Because the Nazis Certainly Are: Talking with Amanda Moore about Her Time with the Alt-right," *Men Yell at Me*. September 20, 2023, https://lyz.substack.com/p/get-involved-because-the-nazis-certainly.
33 Danny Gallagher, "Conservative Host Steven Crowder Caught on Video Berating His Wife," *Dallas Observer*, April 28, 2023, https://www.dallasobserver.com/arts/steven-crowder-caught-on-camera-emotionally-abusing-his-pregnant-wife-16453793.
34 Meryl Kornfield, "The Scorched-Earth Activist Trying to Take Down Hunter Biden," *Washington Post*, September 17, 2023, https://www.washingtonpost.com/politics/2023/09/17/garrett-ziegler-pursuit-hunter-biden/.
35 Kornfield, "The Scorched-Earth Activist."
36 Kornfield, "The Scorched-Earth Activist."
37 Kornfield, "The Scorched-Earth Activist."
38 Leo Sands, "How Often Do Men Think about Ancient Rome? Quite frequently, It Seems," *Washington Post*, September 14, 2023, https://www.washingtonpost.com/lifestyle/2023/09/14/roman-empire-trend-men-tiktok/.
39 David Kelly, "Getting Medieval: This Sport Is a Brutal Human Demolition Derby with Armor, Axes, and Swords," *Los Angeles Times*, July 10, 2023,

NOTES

https://www.latimes.com/world-nation/story/2023-07-10/medieval-combat-sport-buhurt-is-a-human-demolition-derby-with-full-armor-swords-axes.
40 Kelly, "Getting Medieval."
41 "KSHB: Suicide Rates High in Middle-Aged White Men," *Saint Luke's Kansas City*, September 21, 2022, https://www.saintlukeskc.org/about/news/kshb-suicide-rates-high-middle-aged-white-men.
42 Lyz Lenz, "Male Loneliness is Killing Us," *Men Yell at Me*, August 30, 2023, https://lyz.substack.com/p/male-loneliness-is-killing-us.
43 Lenz, "Male Loneliness."
44 Lenz, "Male Loneliness."
45 Magdalene J. Taylor, "Have More Sex, Please!" February 13, 2023, *New York Times*, https://www.nytimes.com/2023/02/13/opinion/have-more-sex-please.html.
46 Taylor, "Have More Sex."
47 bell hooks, *The Will to Change: Men, Masculinity, and Love* (New York: Washington Square Press, 2005), 65.
48 Matthew Loftus, "Young Men Need a Model Not an 'Ubermensch,'" *Christianity Today*, August 29, 2023, https://www.christianitytoday.com/ct/2023/august-web-only/masculinity-manhood-manosphere-crisis-model-not-ubermensch.html.
49 Sexton, *The Man They Wanted Me to Be*.
50 Sexton, *The Man They Wanted Me to Be*, 249.
51 Caitlin Gilbert and Tara Parker-Pope, "A Silent Crisis in Men's Health Gets Worse," *Washington Post*, April 17, 2023, https://www.washingtonpost.com/wellness/2023/04/17/mens-health-longevity-gap/.
52 Gilbert and Parker-Pope, "A Silent Crisis."
53 Gilbert and Parker-Pope, "A Silent Crisis."
54 Gilbert and Parker-Pope, "A Silent Crisis."
55 Christine Emba, "Men are Lost. Here's a Path Out of the Wilderness," *Washington Post*, July 10, 2023, https://www.washingtonpost.com/opinions/2023/07/10/christine-emba-masculinity-new-model/.
56 Christine Emba, "Men are Lost. Here's a Path Out of the Wilderness."
57 Jo Piazza and Peggy Orenstein, "Protecting Boys from Toxic Social Media with Peggy Orenstein," *Under the Influence Podcast*, podcast audio, November 5, 2023, https://podcasts.apple.com/au/podcast/under-the-influence-with-jo-piazza/id1544171101.

Chapter 6: Schoolboys

1 Heather Jones, "ADHD in Boys vs. Girls: Differences in Symptoms and Prevalence," *Verywell Health*, February 9, 2024, https://www.verywellhealth.com/do-adhd-symptoms-differ-in-boys-and-girls-5207995#:~:text=Boys are diagnosed with ADHD, being more prevalent in boys.
2 Jones, "ADHD in Boys vs. Girls."
3 For more reading on these topics, I recommend *Savage Inequalities* by Jonathan Kozol (Crown Publishing: July 24, 2012), *Ghosts in the Schoolyard* by Eve

L. Ewing (University of Chicago Press: April 10, 2020), *Stringing Rosaries* by Denise K. Lajimodiere (North Dakota State University Press: June 20, 2019), and *Boarding School Seasons* by Brenda J. Child (University of Nebraska Press: Feb. 1, 2000).

4 Meg Jacobs, "Trump Is Appointing People Who Hate the Agencies They Will Lead," *CNN*, December 12, 2016, https://www.cnn.com/2016/12/10/opinions/government-is-the-problem-jacobs/index.html.

5 "Betsy DeVos," *Wikipedia*, https://en.wikipedia.org/wiki/Betsy_DeVos.

6 Mario Koran, "'No More Skewed history': Why Black Families Homeschooling Grew Fivefold," *The Guardian,* February 9, 2023, https://www.theguardian.com/education/2023/feb/09/homeschooling-black-families-parents-us.

7 Hannah Natanson, "Youngkin Takes Office with Immediate Focus on Education, Thrilling Some and Terrifying Others," *Washington Post*, January 16, 2022, https://www.washingtonpost.com/education/2022/01/16/virginia-glenn-youngkin-education/.

8 Name changed for privacy.

9 "Lake Harriet Upper Elementary," *U.S. News & World Report*, https://www.usnews.com/education/k12/minnesota/lake-harriet-upper-elementary-412182#:~:text=Overview of Lake Harriet Upper Elementary&text=The school's minority student enrollment,enrolls 4% economically disadvantaged students.

10 "Lexington-Hamline Neighborhood in Saint Paul, Minnesota (MN), 55104 Detailed Profile." *City-Data*, 2023, https://www.city-data.com/neighborhood/Lexington-Hamline-Saint-Paul-MN.html.

11 Name changed for privacy.

12 "The US-Dakota War of 1862," *Minnesota Historical Society*, https://www.usdakotawar.org/history/aftermath/trials-hanging#:~:text=On December 26, 1862, 38,of Mankato and surrounding land.

13 "Dakota War of 1862," *Wikipedia*, https://en.wikipedia.org/wiki/Dakota_War_of_1862.

14 A helpful resource on this topic is *Reclaiming Two-Spirits* by Gregory Smithers (Beacon Press: April 26, 2022).

15 Name changed for privacy.

16 "Glencoe-Silver Lake School District," *U.S. News & World Report,* https://www.usnews.com/education/k12/minnesota/districts/glencoe-silver-lake-school-district-101040.

17 "Adverse Childhood Experiences (ACEs)," *Centers for Disease Control and Prevention*, https://www.cdc.gov/violenceprevention/aces/index.html.

Chapter 7: To Fear and Love God So That?

1 Name changed for privacy.

2 Name changed for privacy.

3 Thomas W. Hilgers, "The Work We Do Is Because of You!" *Saint Paul VI Institute*, https://popepaulvi.com/the-work-we-do-is-because-of-you/.

4 Hilgers, "The Work We Do."

5 "Suicide Statistics," *The American Foundation for Suicide Prevention*, Centers for Disease Control and Prevention Data, 2021, https://afsp.org/suicide-statistics/.
6 Name changed for privacy.
7 Name changed for privacy.

Chapter 8: Innocuous White Supremacists and Midwestern Small Towns

1 Kim Bellware, "Facing a First Amendment Fight, a Small Minnesota Town Allows a White Supremacist Church," *Washington Post*, December 14, 2020, https://www.washingtonpost.com/religion/2020/12/14/murdock-white-church/.
2 Maria Cramer, "Fear Spreads in Minnesota Town as 'Extremist Group' Moves to Open Church," *New York Times*, January 9, 2021, https://www.nytimes.com/2021/01/09/us/minnesota-asatru-folk-assembly.html.
3 Bellware, "Facing a First Amendment Fight."
4 Bellware, "Facing a First Amendment Fight."
5 "Asatru Folk Assembly," *Southern Poverty Law Center*, https://www.splcenter.org/fighting-hate/extremist-files/group/asatru-folk-assembly.
6 "Asatru Folk Assembly."
7 John Reinan, "Big Crowd in Murdock, Minn., Grills Representative of Controversial Nordic Heritage Church," *Star Tribune*, October 15, 2020, http://www.startribune.com/big-crowd-in-western-minnesota-town-grills-controversial-nordic-heritage-churhc/572739031.
8 Reinan, "Big Crowd in Murdock."
9 Reinan, "Big Crowd in Murdock."
10 Kati Perry, Tim Meko, and Kevin Uhrmacher, "Small Towns Don't Vote Like Other Rural Areas," *Washington Post*, August 9, 2023, http://www.washingtonpost.com/politics/2023/08/09/small-town-voting-trump/.
11 "Swift County, Minnesota," *Election Results*, https://countyvotes.us/27151/.
12 "Swift County, Minnesota."
13 Libby Nelson, "'Why We Voted for Donald Trump': David Duke Explains the White Supremacist Charlottesville Protests," *Vox*, August 12, 2017, https://www.vox.com/2017/8/12/16138358/charlottesville-protests-david-duke-kkk.
14 "Are White Supremacists Coming for Your Teens?" *Anti-Defamation League*, November 25, 2019, https://www.adl.org/resources/blog/are-white-supremacists-coming-your-teens.
15 "Are White Supremacists Coming."
16 "Are White Supremacists Coming."
17 Tonya Mosley, "Former White Supremacist Explains Why Young White Men Join Extremist Groups," *WBUR Boston*, August 9, 2019, https://www.wbur.org/hereandnow/2019/08/09/why-young-men-join-white-supremacist-groups.
18 Mosley, "Former White Supremacist Explains Why Young White Men Join Extremist Groups."

19　Mosley, "Former White Supremacist Explains Why Young White Men Join Extremist Groups."
20　Mosley, "Former White Supremacist Explains Why Young White Men Join Extremist Groups."
21　Amanda Seitz, "White Supremacists Are Riling Up Thousands on Social Media," *Associated Press/PBS News Hour*, June 10, 2022, https://www.pbs.org/newshour/politics/white-supremacists-are-riling-up-thousands-on-social-media.
22　TJ L'Heureux et al., "A Right-Wing Sheriffs Group That Challenges Federal Law Is Gaining Acceptance around the Country," *Associated Press*, August 21, 2023, https://apnews.com/article/constitutional-sheriffs-5568cd0b6b27680a28de8a098ed14210.
23　Mosley, "Former White Supremacist Explains."
24　Name has been changed for privacy.
25　Name has been changed for privacy.

Chapter 9: Wild West, Wild Men, and De-radicalization

1　"Neo-Nazism," *Wikipedia*, https://en.wikipedia.org/wiki/Neo-Nazism.
2　"Skinhead," *Wikipedia*, https://en.wikipedia.org/wiki/Skinhead.
3　"Hooliganism," *Wikipedia*, https://en.wikipedia.org/wiki/Hooliganism.
4　"White power skinhead," *Wikipedia*, https://en.wikipedia.org/wiki/White_power_skinhead.
5　"Aryan Brotherhood," *Southern Poverty Law Center*, https://www.splcenter.org/fighting-hate/extremist-files/group/aryan-brotherhood.
6　"Aryan Brotherhood."
7　"White power skinhead," *Wikipedia*, https://en.wikipedia.org/wiki/White_power_skinhead.
8　Kanishka Singh, "White Supremacists behind Over 80% of Extremism-Related U.S. Murders in 2022," *Reuters*, February 23, 2023, https://www.reuters.com/world/us/white-supremacists-behind-over-80-extremism-related-us-murders-2022-2023-02-23/.
9　Josh Marcus, "Police Investigating Whether White-Supremacist Prison Gang behind Bodies Found in Oklahoma," *The Independent*, September 16, 2022, https://www.the-independent.com/news/world/americas/crime/oklahoma-aryan-brotherhood-bodies-police-b2169115.html.
10　"Drug Ring Tied to Aryan Prison Gang Indicted with 24 Federal Arrests," *U.S. Department of Justice*, U.S. Attorney's Office, Western District of Washington, March 27, 2023, https://www.justice.gov/usao-wdwa/pr/drug-ring-tied-aryan-prison-gang-indicted-24-federal-arrests.
11　"Drug Ring Tied."
12　Robin Givhan, "Neo-Nazis Are Using Fashion in an Attempt to Normalize. The Fashion Industry Needs to Speak Up," *Washington Post*, August 22, 2017, https://www.washingtonpost.com/news/arts-and-entertainment/wp/2017/08/22/neo-nazis-are-using-fashion-in-an-attempt-to-normalize-the-fashion-industry-needs-to-speak-up/.

13 Scott Christian, "This Wildly Popular Haircut Has a Serious Neo-Nazi Problem," *Esquire*, August 15, 2017, https://www.esquire.com/style/news/a51116/high-and-tight-fascism-neo-nazis-white-supremacists/.
14 Lance Williams, "White Nationalist Richard Spencer Gets His Money From Louisiana Cotton Fields—and the US Government," *Mother Jones*, March 17, 2017, https://www.motherjones.com/politics/2017/03/richard-spencer-cotton-farms-louisiana-subsidies/.
15 Name has been changed for privacy.
16 From a graduate school paper written by Antonio.
17 From a graduate school paper written by Antonio.
18 From a graduate school paper written by Antonio.
19 From a graduate school paper written by Antonio.
20 From a graduate school paper written by Antonio.
21 From a graduate school paper written by Antonio.
22 From a graduate school paper written by Antonio.
23 1 Corinthians 13:12.